Child Trafficking in China

Ling Han

Child Trafficking in China

A Human Rights-Based Perspective

Springer

Ling Han
Law School (Lawyers College)
Guangzhou University
Guangzhou, China

ISBN 978-981-97-3716-1 ISBN 978-981-97-3717-8 (eBook)
https://doi.org/10.1007/978-981-97-3717-8

This Springer imprint is published by the registered company Springer Nature Singapore Pte Ltd.
The registered company address is: 152 Beach Road, #21-01/04 Gateway East, Singapore 189721, Singapore

Preface

In the crisp autumn of 2005, my mother and I embarked on a train journey across half of China, spanning 2565 km, to my university. It was a first for me—being so far from home and spending two full days on a train. As we entered Fujian Province, our train slowed, meandering for hours through hills lush with banana trees. Sitting by the window, the endless greenery unfolded before me, but soon, monotony set in. Breaking the silence, my mother remarked, "No wonder those girls sold to rural Fujian couldn't escape. Look at this endless expanse". Her gaze turned to me, filled with concern, "Be careful at university. Don't trust strangers, and never wander off campus alone. In a place like this, one could disappear without a trace. If you were sold here, you would never escape". Growing up in the late 80s and early 90s China, such cautionary tales were not uncommon, echoing the protective instincts of many families.

In October 2022, Sun Yue, the sister of a child who was trafficked, published a book titled "Reunion". This poignant work details her family's agonising 14-year search for their son, who was abducted at the tender age of four. Sun Haiyang, the father of the abducted child, became a well-known figure in China following the 2014 release of the highly acclaimed film "Dearest (亲爱的)", which drew attention to his plight. His story captured the nation's heart once more when his son, Sun Zhuo, was discovered after a relentless 14-year search. Sun Zhuo had been sold to a family over 1700 km away from his home in Shenzhen and was living under a false name. The Sun family's ordeal is emblematic of the harrowing experiences faced by countless Chinese parents who have lost their children to traffickers and have dedicated years to searching for them. Despite the overwhelming odds, the Suns were among the fortunate few who experienced the joy of being reunited with their missing child.

Thanks to the "Skynet Project" launched in 2001, incidents of child trafficking akin to the case of Sun Zhuo are now reported with less frequency compared to past years. However, instances of successful or attempted child abductions continue to be documented, with evidence often captured on video by both private and public surveillance systems. In addition, the sale of children for illegal adoption is not far from our life. During the second year of my doctoral research, I engaged in a brief discussion about my project with a new Ph.D. candidate from China, whom I had met at a social gathering. Her reaction underscored the gravity of the issue: "This is a serious problem. Do you know? One of my cousins, a boy, was acquired by my uncle". This anecdote was not unique in my experience. In my childhood, in the neighbourhood of my grandparents' residence, there was a girl with dwarfism named Maomao, approximately ten years my senior. Our childish games often involved comparing the sizes of our hands with hers, her tiny hands reminding us of a doll's. Following her marriage to a young man afflicted with polio, they had adopted a daughter from an impoverished family the subsequent year. These stories, among others, vividly illustrate the persistent undercurrents of societal challenges we face.

While acknowledging the potential biases inherent in personal narratives, I am compelled to delve deeper into this issue using scientific research methods and more reliable data sources. Given the clandestine nature of child trafficking, it is clear that determining the full scale of this issue within the entire country is an impractical goal. Rather, my research aims to unearth more nuanced insights: identifying those at greatest risk of becoming victims of child trafficking and understanding the reasons behind their vulnerability. Furthermore, it seeks to pinpoint the gaps in current protective measures for children against such crimes

Guangzhou, China Ling Han

Acknowledgements

This book's existence owes much to the support and encouragement of numerous individuals, whose contributions have been invaluable. I am particularly indebted to the University of Padova, the Human Rights Centre, and the Fondazione Cassa di Risparmio di Padova e Rovigo for their financial support throughout my university studies, three years of research, and the early phases of my career during the pandemic.

Special thanks are extended to my supervisors, Prof. Yang Songcai and Prof. Paolo De Stefani. Their guidance transcended the academic realm, offering friendship alongside professional mentorship. From them, I learnt the importance of diligence, meticulous attention to detail in teaching, a commitment to thoroughness and precision in research, and the maintenance of integrity in challenging circumstances.

I am also grateful to Prof. Adam Possamai for his supervision during my visiting study at Western Sydney University. His advice on article writing was instrumental in my initial foray into academic publishing.

My appreciation also goes to the Human Rights Centre of the University of Padua, along with all the professors and colleagues associated with the Centre. I am particularly thankful to Prof. Marco Mascia, my mentor in human rights studies since 2008, and Prof. Pietro de Perini, who offered early "warnings" about the challenges of the research journey. The generous assistance provided by my colleagues Benedetta, Donatella, and Luca at the Centre has been indispensable.

The completion of this book would not have been as seamless without the contributions from Yang Shanglin, Dang Zhenmin, He Shuya, Lin Minzhi, Lin Ziqi, and Luo Zhimin at Guangzhou University, who assisted in updating the data. My affiliation with Guangzhou University has afforded me a sanctuary for continuing my research and sharing my knowledge with the next generation.

My journey has also been supported by a network of friends who provided emotional sustenance. Claudia and her parents offered me a home in Italy. In Sydney, my friends Geoff, Lin, Keat, and Amy extended warm care. The joy brought to me by Da Zhang Wei and my friends from DM48 during stressful times, along with the valuable advice and encouragement from Desirée, has been a source of strength.

Lastly, but most importantly, the unwavering support of my family—especially my mother, father, and dear grandmother—has been the cornerstone of my achievements. Their belief in my choices has been a constant source of encouragement.

Contents

Abbreviations

AI	Artificial Intelligence
ASEAN	Association of Southeast Asian Nations
BBHJ	Bao Bei Hui Jia (Baby Coming Home)
CCCPC	Central Propaganda Department of the Central Committee of the Communist Party of China
CEDAW	Convention on the Elimination of All Forms of Discrimination against Women
COMMIT	Coordinated Mekong Ministerial Initiative against Trafficking
CRC	Convention on the Rights of the Child
CRC-OPSC	Optional Protocol to the Convention on the Rights of the Child on the Sale of Children, Child Prostitution and Child Pornography
CRPD	Convention on the Rights of Persons with Disabilities
ECOSOC	United Nations Economic and Social Council
GMS	Greater Mekong Sub-region
GRP	Gross Regional Product
ICAT	Inter-Agency Coordination Group against Trafficking in Persons
ICCPR	International Covenant on Civil and Political Rights
ICERD	International Convention on the Elimination of All Forms of Racial Discrimination
ICESCR	International Covenant on Economic, Social and Cultural Rights
ICMW	International Convention on the Protection of the Rights of All Migrant Workers and Members of Their Families
ILC	International Law Commission
ILO	International Labour Organization
IMCS	Inter-ministerial Joint Conference System for Anti-Trafficking in Women and Children
IOM	International Organization for Migration
MPS	Ministry of Public Security
NPA	National Plan of Action
OHCHR	United Nations Office of the High Commissioner for Human Rights
OSCE	Organization for Security and Co-operation in Europe

PRC	People's Republic of China
SAAR	South Asian Association for Regional Cooperation
SPA	Subregional Plan of Action
UNAIDS	United Nations Joint Programme on HIV/AIDS
UNDP	United Nations Development Programme
UNESCO	United Nations Educational, Scientific, and Cultural Organisation
UNICEF	United Nations Children's Fund
UNODC	United Nations Office on Drugs and Crimes
WHO	World Health Organization

List of Figures

Chapter 5

Chapter 1
The Crime of Human Trafficking: An Introduction

As is well known, human trafficking—including the trafficking of children—represents a serious crime and a violation of human rights that affects every country. Like the illicit trafficking of drugs and firearms, human trafficking is often carried out by transnational organised criminal groups at a low cost. Due to its clandestine nature, estimating the number of victims is enormously challenging. The United Nations Office on Drugs and Crime (UNODC) reported that approximately 25,000 cases of human trafficking were detected globally in 2016, with 30% of the victims being children (UNODC 2018); however, these figures are believed to be only the tip of the iceberg (Kragten-Heerdink et al. 2018; Liu 2010; Rafferty 2007; Savona and Stefanizzi 2007; UNODC 2006; Laczko and Gozdziak 2005).

China, as one of the most populous countries globally, is not immune to human trafficking. The country has participated actively in numerous international, regional, and bilateral agreements aimed at combatting trafficking in women and children. It is often recognised as both an origin and destination for cross-border trafficking in persons (UNODC 2006, 2016, 2018). Chinese women and girls are frequently trafficked from China to wealthy countries, seeking better lives but instead finding themselves in debt bondage to traffickers. In some cases, they are forced into the sex industry or sweatshops to pay off their debts. China is also known as a destination country for human trafficking, with women and children from Southeast Asian countries being trafficked into China for exploitation in arranged or forced marriages, prostitution, labour, illegal adoption, and other forms of exploitation.

There is extensive literature on transnational trafficking in persons, investigating it from a variety of disciplinary perspectives, such as studies conducted by Burke (2022), Villa (2019), Lee (2013), Shelley (2010, 2013), Winterdy et al. (2011), Cameron and Newman (2008), Ebbe and Das (2007), Obotaka (2006), and many others. Moreover, there are also numerous studies focused on specific regions or countries, including Europe (Antonopoulos et al. 2019; Wylie and McRedmond 2010; Surtees 2008; Englund et al. 2008), Africa (Hoffman and Abidde 2021; Iroanya 2018; Cohen 2003), Asia (Yea 2019; UN-ACT 2016; Mendoza et al. 2016; Spires

L. Han, *Child Trafficking in China*, https://doi.org/10.1007/978-981-97-3717-8_1

2015; Gu 2007; Rosenberg 2003), and America (Chisolm-Straker and Stoklosa 2017; Marcus et al. 2016; Palmiotto 2014). However, the academic investigation into child trafficking in China remains relatively limited. Research by Chinese scholars has predominantly centred on the legal and sociological dimensions, including legislative frameworks (Liu 2003, 2010; Yang 2008; Zhao and Meng 2014). Other inquiries have delved into the criminological aspects of child trafficking, exploring its characteristics, underlying causes (Gao 2010; Li et al. 2013; Liu 2000; Shen 2016; Xing 2017), as well as its criminal investigation (Huang 2009). In many of these studies, children are only a subgroup of a broader topic, such as the trafficking of women or human trafficking.

Considering the differences between victims across various gender and age groups, it is reasonable to assert that child trafficking and the trafficking of women differ in their underlying causes, patterns of criminal activity, and consequences. Therefore, this necessitates divergent strategies for their eradication. However, the empirical investigation into child trafficking within China remains notably sparse, with the majority of studies being confined to a limited geographical area or a small number of cases (Zhou et al. 2023; Shen 2016; Yuan and Yang 2001; Yang 2000; Li 2000). Notably, in recent years, there has been a noticeable shift towards the adoption of quantitative analysis methods in this field of research. Among such endeavours, Li Gang and colleagues have undertaken pivotal studies examining the geographic and spatiotemporal characteristics of child trafficking, utilising data sourced from the NGO "Bao Bei Hui Jia (BBHJ)". These studies have delved into the geographical nuances of child trafficking in China, encompassing victim demographics, temporal and spatial variations of the crime, and victim trafficking flows (Li et al. 2017a; b). Wang et al. (2018) expanded upon this research to analyse the child trafficking network at both the provincial and city levels, employing the same data source.

Further contributions to this field have been made by scholars analysing national data on court judgements, accessible via "China Judgements Online",[1] the sole official national online database of court judgements. This dataset underpinned two interconnected studies analysing 447 court verdicts issued between 2013 and 2015 concerning child trafficking. The first study offered a comprehensive overview of the crime's characteristics (Xing et al. 2017), while the second scrutinised incidents of child sale perpetrated by parents (Xing 2017). Additionally, Xin and Cai (2018) utilised this judicial database to investigate the characteristics, patterns, and contributory factors of child trafficking in China. Common findings across these studies highlight that most victims of child trafficking are younger than 3 years; boys are more frequently trafficked than girls; and the predominant motive behind trafficking is illegal adoption.

A significant majority of Chinese scholars addressing human trafficking have proposed strategies to prevent and counteract this crime (See, e.g., Wang et al. 2018; Lin 2015; Yuan and Yang 2001; Li 2000; Yang 2000). Among these recommendations are the imposition of stringent penalties and intensified crackdowns, poverty alleviation, heightened awareness among those most vulnerable, bolstered law enforcement

[1] See http://wenshu.court.gov.cn.

capabilities, and increased inter-sectoral collaboration. Nevertheless, only a minimal number of studies have undertaken a thorough examination of the victims' vulnerabilities both prior to and subsequent to their trafficking, an analysis critical for the formulation of effective policies aimed at both crime prevention and victim protection (UNICEF Innocenti Research Centre 2009; UNODC 2009a). Furthermore, merely a select few investigations have approached the issue from a human rights perspective (Shen et al. 2013; Yuan and Yang 2001) akin to international studies. A couple of global inquiries offer a comprehensive approach, tackling prevention, protection, and prosecution in a unified manner (Rijken 2009; Obokata 2006).

This study illuminates a form of trafficking that, despite its prevalence in China, has remained largely overlooked in wider discourse. The focus here is on intra-state child trafficking, a phenomenon not sufficiently addressed by previous international research. Child trafficking within China exhibits distinct characteristics and complexities that set it apart from the transnational trafficking of women and children. These distinctive features have their origins in ancient Chinese history. In this chapter, both the historical and factual contexts of child trafficking in China will be scrutinised, alongside key concepts fundamental to understanding this research.

1 A Brief History of Child Trafficking in China

The issue of child trafficking, a subset of human trafficking, emerged as a concern in international politics at the outset of the twentieth century (Gallagher 2010, p. 13). Initially, the primary focus was on the trafficking of women and children for prostitution, commonly referred to as "White Slave Traffic." This term described slavery-like practices involving the recruitment and trade of women and young girls for prostitution (Gallagher 2010; Obokata 2006). The International Agreement for the Suppression of the White Slave Traffic of 1904, the first Convention against White Slavery, aimed to protect women and girls from being procured abroad for "immoral purposes." The subsequent International Convention for the Suppression of the White Slave Traffic of 1910 also addressed the trafficking of women and girls, with an emphasis on the process of procurement and transportation.

While "White Slave Traffic" serves as a direct predecessor to current international trafficking concerns, the roots of child trafficking in China can be traced back to the abduction of children into slavery and illegal adoption. Compared to contemporary transnational human trafficking, trafficking in China has a much longer history. The such crime has afflicted the Chinese populace since ancient times. Traditionally, efforts to prohibit child trafficking in China have centred on domestic cases. The earliest Chinese penal law against human trafficking dates back to the Tang Dynasty (618–907 AD), with similar prohibitions found as early as the Eastern Han Dynasty (25–220 AD). Despite the existence of slavery alongside bans on human trafficking until the twentieth century, it was only after the fall of the Qing government that slavery was formally abolished. Nonetheless, the phenomenon of child trafficking persisted beyond the collapse of the feudal system. Following a period of war and political instability from 1912 to 1979, child trafficking has re-emerged as a significant concern in China since the 1980s. In its modern guise, the presence of slavery is no longer a requisite for the crime to be constituted. However, certain features, such as the "abduction" and "sale" of children, have been inherited, with children being forcibly abducted and sold, or sold by their own parents.

Despite the Chinese government's concerted efforts to address the crime of child trafficking, including police crackdowns on criminal networks and the imposition of increasingly severe penalties, the tragedies have continued to affect Chinese families and society at large. Civil society organisations also play an active role in combating the crime and supporting victims. Nevertheless, the question of how to effectively prevent and counteract child trafficking remains a topic of ongoing, vibrant discussion in China.

A. **Slavery, the sale of people and trafficking bans in ascent China**

The phenomenon of child trafficking in China, and the legal frameworks established to criminalise the practice, are deeply entrenched in the nation's history, exhibiting unique characteristics. Contemporary research identifies human trafficking in China as a legacy of the feudal slavery system (see Ge 2019; Yao and Guo 2008; Song 2004; Yu 2000; Ma 1997). Within the feudal caste system, individuals outside the ruling echelons were categorised into two principal groups: "commoners (良民 liang min)" encompassing gentries, peasants, labourers, and merchants; and "outcastes (贱民 jian min)" comprising slave servants, maid concubines, prostitutes, courtesans, and others deprived of full personal freedom (Huang 2013; Ma 1997). The elite, including monarchs, nobility, and affluent commoners, were permitted to employ servants, maids, and concubines.

As elucidated in Ma's (1997) examination of human trade in ancient China, the elite have been significant patrons of human trafficking since the Han Dynasty. The demand for enslaved servants by the upper classes went hand in hand with the extreme poverty of their subjects, fuelling a vast black market in the trade of human beings. The early Han period, marked by extensive warfare and catastrophes, saw individuals resorting to selling their children and spouses for sustenance. Emperor Gaozu of Han (202–195 BC) notably issued an edict permitting those in desperate straits to sell their offspring (Wang 2014; Ma 1997). Some unscrupulous people took the opportunity to make money from human trafficking by abducting women and children or buying them from desperately poor people at low prices and selling them to wealthy homes. These people were called "*ren fan zi*"—literally "human dealers", commonly translated as "human traffickers"—and they often colluded with the gentry and bandits (Ma 1997).

The trafficked people were mainly women and children (Ma 1997; Yu 2000; Yao and Guo 2008). They are primarily trafficked within China, but there are some records of them being sold to neighbouring countries and overseas (Yu 2000). The trafficked persons might be sold by their husbands, parents, traffickers, or even themselves to become slaves to their buyers, including enslaved servants (奴婢), enslaved maids or concubines (侍女、侍歌), courtesans or prostitutes (家女), slaves performing dance and singing (歌舞家), and servants who work for the owner in business (家奴).

Although tenants (佃客) were free commoners, they or their family members might also become slaves of the landlord due to debt bondage. Boys were also sold as heirs (嗣子) to eunuchs or rich men who had no sons. Except for the heirs, trafficked persons lost their personal freedom and dignity. The owner usually gave slaves a new name and could trade, abuse or even kill them with impunity (Ma 1997). Usually, an indenture for the sale of the person was signed by the seller and the buyer, while sometimes, it also had signatures of referrers, witnesses, and official managers on it (Huang 2013; Ma 1997). These found deeds are evidence of official involvement in the sale of human beings.

According to current research, the first written records of the human trafficking ban date to the Tang or even the Eastern Han period of the Han Dynasty. Illegal activities of human traffickers and the flourishing black markets in human beings not only harmed the people and the local security, but also undermined the feudal order. Therefore, Emperor Guangwu of Han (25–57 AD) issued several edicts concerning the prohibition of the sale of enslaved servants and maids, the release of slaves, and the prohibition of human trafficking (Ge 2019; Ma 1997). In the "Book of Later Han—Annals of Emperor Guangwu" (范 2007), it was recorded several times that Emperor Guangwu ruled that the trafficked persons should be released without hindrance if they wished to return to their original families, and obstructors should be punished in accordance with the "Human Trafficking Law (略人法)".[2] Records of penalties for human trafficking can be found in the "Book of Wei": the death penalty was applied to those who have committed the abduction of persons, the abduction and sale of persons, and the sale of persons as slaves; 1-year penalty to who sell their own child; the death penalty also applied to who sell elders relatives in five generations; and who sell women, children and slaves should be sent into exile (Wei, pp. 2880–2881).

Based on the rules of the previous dynasties, the Tang Code—the penal code of the Tang Dynasty—provided a clear definition of the crime of "human trafficking (*lueren luemairen*略人略卖人)", including both the "abduction of persons (*lueren*)" and the "abduction and sale of persons (*luemairen*)". It explained the acts and means elements of the offence, namely "abduction", "fraudulence", and "sale". More specifically, the act of "abduction (*lue* 略)" could be accomplished by both violent and non-violent means, that is, fraudulence. All the "unpeaceful" means were considered violent; fraud committed against children under 10 years of age amounted to violent abduction. The article provided different levels of penalties applicable in various circumstances, taking into account whether violence was used, whether the victim consented, the class and age of the victim, whether the sale was completed, and the final situation of the victim, i.e., sold as an enslaved servant (outcastes), family soldier (部曲, a class between commoners and outcastes), wife or maid-concubine, heir, or sibling (commoners). For instance, the death penalty by hanging should be applied to those who committed violent abduction and sale of a commoner and any form

[2] Book of Later Han—Annals of Emperor Guangw Volume II: 甲寅，诏吏人遭饥乱及为青、徐贼所略为奴婢下妻，欲去留者，者听之。敢拘制不还，以卖人法从事。[...] 冬十二月甲寅，诏益州民自八年以来被略为奴婢者，皆一切免为庶(民)〔人〕;或依托为人下妻,欲去者,者听之;敢拘留者,比青、徐二州以略人法从事。

of abduction and sale of a commoner under ten years old as a slave, while violent abduction and sale of a commoner as a family soldier was punished with a 1500 kms exile. In the case of the non-violent sale of a commoner into slavery with the consent of the trafficked person, both offender and the victim should be exiled for 1000 kms. When the trafficked person came from a lower class, the penalise became one level lower. For instance, the violent abduction and sale of other person's family soldiers as enslaved people was punished with exile for 1500 kms instead of death by hanging, as in the case of trafficking a commoner.[3] It is noteworthy that certain forms of slave trafficking and the sale of children or grandchildren by parents or grandparents were not considered "human trafficking", although they were prohibited by subsequent provisions of the same penal code.[4] Persons who harbour the trafficked person and buy the trafficked persons with knowledge of the offence committed by the trafficker were also punishable.

These provisions in the Tang Code regarding the "abduction and sale" of people set the groundwork for China's subsequent laws against human trafficking. The penal code of China's last feudal government (Qing Dynasty: 1636–1912 AD), the Great Qing Code, retained the name of the crime of human trafficking as set forth in the Tang Code, but contained more detailed provisions and penalties (Guo 2017). The abduction and sale of slaves, the sale of one's own children and wife, as well as many other conditions, were included in the crime of "human trafficking".[5]

From 1912 to 1949, China went through a humiliating and turbulent period, characterised by colonisation, invasion, and constant war. Human trafficking was no longer a major concern for those in power. The penal codes drawn up in the late Qing and by the government of the Republic of China (1912–1949) respectively, which were modelled on the penal law of Japan and Germany, removed the crime of human trafficking (Huang 2013). However, despite the abolition of slavery by the Republican government in the first decade of the eighteenth century, the phenomenon of human trafficking did not end therewith.

B. **The recurrence of child trafficking after the establishment of New China**

After the founding of the People's Republic of China (PRC) in 1949, for almost three decades, the crime of child trafficking disappeared in the country. It might be due to the central government's strict control over food, household registration, and labour (Yang 2006), as well as the severe penalties for criminals (Chu 1996). However, it would be imprudent to simply assume that ancient forms of child trafficking were once eradicated in the new China. The lack of records may also be due to the absence of laws prohibiting human trafficking, or the lack of concern about trafficking as people were struggling amid conflict, poverty and political unrest at the time.

Literature about human trafficking in contemporary China always takes the period of the 1980s as a watershed, when the crime once again became a widespread public concern (See, e.g., Li et al. 2017b; Xing 2017; Shen et al. 2013; Huang 2009; Yang

[3]《唐律疏议 卷第二十》292.

[4]《唐律疏议 卷第二十》293, 294.

[5]《大清律例·刑律·贼盗中之三》.

2006; Liu 2000; Wang 1992; Xie and Jia 1989). Following the reform and opening-up policy, child trafficking in China resurged at the end of the 1970s and became widespread in the 1980s–1990s (Li 2000; Yuan and Yang 2001; Zhang 2006). Since the 1980s, hundreds of thousands of cases of child trafficking have been reported in China every year. The flourishing of the abduction and sale of children coincided with the political reform, the marketisation of the Chinese economy and the enforcement of the one-child policy. The trafficking patterns are very similar to those of the past: child victims were abducted by traffickers by means of abduction and fraudulence (Wang 1992) and sold to buyers.

In 1979, the PRC welcomed its first Criminal Law adopted by the National People's Congress after three decades of turbulence following the establishment of the new government. The crime of human trafficking was again criminalised, being enshrined in Article 141 of the Criminal Law of the People's Republic of China (hereinafter Criminal Law). The name of the crime was slightly changed from "*lueren luemairen* (略人略卖人)" to "*guaimai renkou* (拐卖人口)". Rather than having changed the name, it is better to say that the name was translated into modern Chinese. Although the name became slightly different in Chinese due to the evolution of the language, the core elements of the crime—"abduction" and "sale"—remained unchanged. The definition of human trafficking will be better developed in the next section.

In the late 1970s, the central government realised the need to take action to curb the criminal activities of trafficking of women and children (Wang 1992, pp. 139–142). In 1983, the then President of China issued an order to crack down on crimes that endangered public security. The order imposed harsh punishment, up to the death penalty, on those who committed the crime of child trafficking.[6] The crackdown actions continued in the 1990s with the establishment of temporary coordination offices in many provinces with the mandate to combat the trafficking of women and children (Wang 1992, p. 141). This trend of running special police operations continued until recent years.

Although the Chinese government has adopted numerous measures to tackle child trafficking, the tragedy has never ceased to plague Chinese families and society. In modern child trafficking, children are sold to buyers for a series of purposes, including illegal adoption, forced begging, forced marriage, sexual exploitation, and conducting criminal activities (Chen 2000; Lin 2015; Liu 2010). In many cases, children were abducted violently and sold afterwards, while there were also countless cases of children being sold by their parents (Xing 2017; Li et al. 2013; Wang 1992). Child trafficking became a trending subject of literature and cinematographic works, newspaper reports, TV coverage, social media discussions, and academic research. From 1994 to 2015, at least six Chinese films have featured the stories of trafficked

---

[6] Standing Committee of the National People's Congress, (1983) 关于严厉打击刑事犯罪活动的决定[Decision of the Standing Committee of the National People's Congress Regarding the Severe Punishment of Criminals Who Seriously Endanger Public Security (Expired)], Issued on 9 February 1983, invalidated by: Criminal Law of the People's Republic of China.

children and their parents.[7] Heart-breaking stories on the silver screen mirrored the mainstreaming understanding of Chinese society to child trafficking: children were abducted and sold to someone for illegal adoption, forced street begging, or committing criminal activities, and the parents of the victim spent years and decades desperately searching for their beloved child across the country. Parents pulled out all the stops, distributing photos of their children and making enquiries on their own or in groups, while their chances of success are like looking for a needle in a haystack.

As time passes, more and more people have become involved in anti-trafficking activities. In 2007, Zhang Baoyan and her husband created the first Chinese family tracing website named *Bao Bei Hui Jia* ("Baby Coming Home" in Chinese, hereinafter BBHJ), followed by a non-governmental organisation (NGO), "BBHJ Volunteer Association", to run the website, helping trafficked, abandoned and street children return home. Since the 2010s, social media have been one of the main battlegrounds in the fight against child trafficking. In 2011, a Chinese scholar launched a campaign "#Take a Photo, Save a Child# (#随手拍照解救乞讨儿童#)"[8] on Weibo, one of the largest social media in China. It invited people to post photos of street begging children, hoping to rescue potential victims of child trafficking. The initiative was welcomed and followed by tens of thousands of users, and it became a trend worth remembering for Chinese civil society and social media. Since then, street begging children or beggars with children have virtually disappeared. The participation of civil society in combating child trafficking in China will be further developed in the last Chapter.

In recent years, new technologies have been developed to assist the police in the fight against child trafficking. For instance, in 2016, when this research was conceptualised, the Ministry of Public Security of China launched the first Chinese Child Abduction Emergency Alert Platform, "Tuanyuan (Reunion) 1.0".[9] This was followed by the launch of an anti-trafficking DNA system in the same year and a special project called "Reunion Operation" in 2020. Thanks to new technologies, including DNA testing, AI facial recognition, and video surveillance system, in June 2020, police found homes for 11,198 missing and abducted children over the years.[10]

---

[7] The films are the followings: Wang Jin (1994) 广州来了新疆娃 [Xinjiang Kids in Guangzhou], Pearl River Film Studio; Guo Kaimin (1994) 天伦 [Tian Lun], Youth Film Studio of Beijing Film Academy; Huang Jun (1996) 陌生人 [Strangers], Children's Film Studio; Yan Gaoshan (2014) 爱在旅途 [Journey of Love], The Commission of Politics and Legislative Affairs of CPC Xinjiang Uyghur Autonomous Region Committee, Shanghai Xiangsheng Film and TV Production and Distribution Co., Ltd, and Tianshan Film Studio; Peter Chan (2014) 亲爱的 [Dearest], Dongyang Enlight Pictures Co., Ltd; and Peng Sanyuan (2015) 失孤 [Lost and Love], China Film Group Corporation.

[8] "Take a Photo, Save a Child", *Human Rights in China*, 12 January 2012, retrieved from https://www.hrichina.org/en/crf/article/6457 [accessed on 16 June 2019].

[9] Xinhua News Agency (2016) "运用'互联网+反拐'公安部儿童失踪信息紧急发布平台上线[Using 'Internet + to combat trafficking': the Chinese Child Abduction Emergency Alert Platform of the Ministry of Public Security went live]", retrieved from http://www.cac.gov.cn/2016-05/15/m_1118868850.htm [accessed on 21/06/2019].

[10] Esnc.cn (2022) "公安部:重拳打击侵犯未成年人违法犯罪行为 [MPS: Heavy-Handed Crackdown on Offences and Crimes against Minors]", retrieved from https://www.chinanews.com.cn/gn/2022/06-01/9768820.shtml [accessed on 17/11/2022].

Despite all the efforts made by multi-level stakeholders to crack down on the crime, how to effectively prevent and combat child trafficking in China remains an unsolved question. Recently, there have been increasing calls for imposing more severe punishment for traffickers. Ms. Zhang Baoyan, the co-founder of BBHJ and deputy of the National People's Congress, suggested that penalties for the offence related to child trafficking should be increased to no less than ten years, up to the death penalty. Her legislative proposal has been widely supported on *Weibo*.[11] However, the effectiveness of the death penalty and its challenge to the principle of proportionality leave Ms. Zhang's proposal open to question—the anti-trafficking measures should not come at the expense of human rights. Whether evaluating existing measures or developing new policies, much more research on child trafficking in China is needed, such as its causes, routes and patterns.

2 The Issue of Definition and Translation

Since this work focused on child trafficking in China, the first issue that needs to be clarified is the definition of this crime in Chinese. The English legal term "trafficking" has a Chinese version, which is linked to Chinese history and culture and is different from the international definition. Therefore, before explaining child trafficking within the Chinese legal framework, it is necessary to explain the use of terms in Chinese and the problem of translation between English and Chinese. The international definition of "trafficking in persons" is a basic line for this study; thus, this section first explains how this crime is defined in international law. Then it explains the differences in terminology between Chinese and English linguistic contexts. Finally, it introduces how the crime of trafficking is criminalised within the Chinese legal framework.

A. **Child trafficking in international law**

The international community's engagement with the issue of child trafficking originates from its broader efforts to eliminate the buying and trafficking of women and girls for prostitution and other forms of sexual exploitation. With the adoption of the International Convention for the Suppression of the Traffic in Women and Children in 1921, it became acknowledged that children of both genders and any ethnicity could be victims of trafficking. However, the International Convention for the Suppression of the Traffic in Women of Full Age, established in 1933, failed to deliver any significant advancements in combating child trafficking. Conversely, the Convention for the Suppression of the Traffic in Persons and of the Exploitation of the Prostitution of Others, ratified in 1949, expanded its concern to include domestic trafficking.

Child trafficking is considered a sub-category of human trafficking or trafficking in persons, a concept that was not formally defined in international law until the year

[11] China Youth Daily, (2019) "一条微博超20万赞 [Over 200 thousand likes for one Weibo message]", retrieved from http://m.ce.cn/zt/2019/2019lh/ygs/201903/06/t20190306_31625997.shtml [accessed on 02/07/2019].

2000. This occurred when the Protocol to Prevent, Suppress and Punish Trafficking in Persons, Especially Women and Children, supplementing the United Nations Convention against Transnational Organized Crime (hereafter referred to as the Palermo Protocol), was adopted on 15 November 2000.[12] The Palermo Protocol provided the first internationally agreed-upon definition of what constitutes "trafficking in persons". According to Article 3, trafficking in persons, which covers both adults and children, is:

> [T]he recruitment, transportation, transfer, harbouring or receipt of persons, by means of the threat or use of force or other forms of coercion, of abduction, of fraud, of deception, of the abuse of power or of a position of vulnerability or of the giving or receiving of payments or benefits to achieve the consent of a person having control over another person, for the purpose of exploitation. Exploitation shall include, at a minimum, the exploitation of the prostitution of others or other forms of sexual exploitation, forced labour or services, slavery or practices similar to slavery, servitude or the removal of organs.

In the context of child trafficking, as delineated in Paragraph (c) of Article 3, the mechanisms by which the prohibited deeds are carried out are deemed inconsequential (Gallagher 2010). Regarding the age criteria for children, Paragraph (d) clarifies that the term "child" refers to "any individual below the age of eighteen years".

From this, it is inferred that the Palermo Protocol's definition of child trafficking encompasses "the recruitment, transportation, transfer, harbouring or receipt of persons under eighteen years of age, for the purpose of exploitation. Exploitation shall include, at a minimum, the exploitation of the prostitution of others or other forms of sexual exploitation, forced labour or services, slavery or practices similar to slavery, servitude or the removal of organs".

This definition is structured around two pivotal elements: action and purpose. The "action element" is satisfied through a variety of activities, such as "recruitment, transportation, transfer, harbouring, or receipt of persons". This broad spectrum of actions indicates that the definition not only encompasses the procedural aspects of trafficking, like recruitment, transportation, and transfer, but also the resultant condition of trafficking, including harbouring and receipt (Gallagher 2010, pp. 29–30). Thus, the concept of trafficking extends beyond the literal notion of movement or transport; it also encompasses acts like purchasing or acquiring control, so long as these actions are undertaken with the intent of exploitation. This reflects the drafters' objective to hold accountable all individuals involved in the trafficking chain, from the initial recruiter through to the trafficker and the ultimate purchaser.

The "purpose element" introduces the requirement of *mens rea*, or criminal intent, into the trafficking definition. The expression "for the purpose of" necessitates that the perpetrator had the intention to execute certain acts with the goal of exploiting the victims. Crucially, to satisfy the purpose element, it is not necessary for the intended exploitation to be realised. It suffices that exploitation was the intended outcome when the perpetrator engaged in any of the proscribed acts, namely recruitment,

[12] UN General Assembly, (2001) Resolution adopted by the General Assembly [without reference to a Main Committee (A/55/383)], 55/25. United Nations Convention against Transnational Organized Crime, 8 January 2001, A/RES/55/25.

transportation, transfer, harbouring, or receipt (Gallagher 2010, p. 34). Nonetheless, discerning the intentions of the initial recruiter or broker can be significantly more challenging than with the direct exploiter. Defining "exploitation" as a specific intent might limit the scope of the law to those actors directly involved in exploitation, given the greater difficulty in proving *mens rea* for those such as transporters, recruiters, or brokers, who may claim ignorance of the exploitation's ultimate aim. This is particularly pertinent in cases involving loosely connected criminal organisations or networks.

The Palermo Protocol refrained from offering a precise definition of "exploitation". Instead, it presented a non-exhaustive list that encompasses, "at a minimum, the exploitation of the prostitution of others, or other forms of sexual exploitation, forced labour or services, slavery or practices akin to slavery, servitude, or the removal of organs" (Gallagher 2010; OHCHR 2010). The expressions "exploitation of the prostitution of others" and "other forms of sexual exploitation" were intentionally not defined within this framework.[13] However, the characterisation of these types of exploitation can be derived from earlier international agreements, including the Forced Labour Convention of 1930, the UN Convention for the Suppression of the Traffic in Persons and of the Exploitation of the Prostitution of Others of 1949, and the 1956 Supplementary Convention on the Abolition of Slavery, the Slave Trade, and Institutions and Practices Similar to Slavery.

While a strict interpretation of international law may exclude illegal adoption from the trafficking definition on the grounds that illegal adoption per se is not inherently exploitative (Gallagher 2010), a broader legal consensus emerging globally suggests otherwise. Illegal adoption is increasingly recognised as a form of exploitation encompassed by trafficking statutes. Notably, the legislative bodies of the European Union have resolved to modify its anti-trafficking directive to explicitly categorise illegal adoption as a type of exploitation within the trafficking definition (Council of the EU 2024). Furthermore, numerous countries have classified illegal adoption and the sale of children as constitutive elements of human trafficking offences (UN CTOC 2013 para. 58; Harvey-Blankenship et al. 2010; Gjermeni et al. 2008; Leifsen 2008; Meier and Zhang 2008; Liu 2000). Many scholars and experts contend that the commodification of children through illegal adoption often entails coercion, thereby qualifying it as a form of child trafficking (de Boer-Buquicchio 2017; UN-ACT 2012; Gallagher 2010; UNICEF Innocenti Research Centre 2009; Leifsen 2008; Meier and Zhang 2008; Rafferty 2007; Smolin 2007; Inter-Parliamentary Union and UNICEF 2005; Smolin 2004; UNDP 2004). Additionally, UNICEF experts assert that in cases of child trafficking, if the recruitment or transportation is achieved through any means outlined in Article 3 of the Palermo Protocol, such as threats, violence, abduction, or deception, the act should be deemed trafficking, irrespective of the ultimate intention (UNICEF Regional Office for CEE/CIS 2006).

---

[13] The *travaux préparatoires* of the negotiations for the elaboration of the United Nations Convention against Transnational Organized Crime and the Protocols thereto specify: "The terms 'exploitation of the prostitution of others' or 'other forms of sexual exploitation' are not defined in the Protocol, which is therefore without prejudice to how States Parties address prostitution in their respective domestic laws".

An additional international accord pivotal to this discourse is the Optional Protocol to the Convention on the Rights of the Child on the Sale of Children, Child Prostitution, and Child Pornography (CRC-OPSC), ratified on 25 May 2000. Article 2 of the CRC-OPSC delineates that the "*sale of children denotes any act or transaction through which a child is transferred by any individual or collective to another in exchange for remuneration or any other compensation." It's imperative to distinguish between* "trafficking in children" and the "sale of children" as they represent two related yet discrete phenomena. Trafficking may transpire without the exchange of remuneration at any stage of the process, whereas the sale of children does not inherently entail exploitation for its definition to apply (UNICEF Innocenti Research Centre 2009).

Notwithstanding these differences, these two concepts are linked in many ways. The preamble of the CRC-OPSC provides that the sale of children, child prostitution and child pornography belong to purposes of trafficking in children.[14] Subsequently, any action as set out in Article 3 of the Palermo Protocol taken against a child, for the purpose of the sale of the child, is a form of trafficking. Also, the UNODC (2009b, pp. 17–18) affirmed that the sale of children is on the list of human rights violations that shall be considered a form of modern-day slavery. International criminal law has recognised that the sale of a human being is a primary indicator that a course of conduct constitutes enslavement, which enables the prosecution of the offence of the sale of children under the umbrella of trafficking crimes (Harvey-Blankenship et al. 2010, p. 12).

Child trafficking is not necessarily transnational. Although the Palermo Protocol is aimed at preventing and suppressing international trafficking in persons and organised crimes, the definition set forth in Article 3 does not require that the crime be cross-border. Similarly, Article 3 (1) of the CRC-OPSC requires State Parties to criminalise the prohibited offences committed either domestically or internationally.[15] The Special Rapporteur on violence against women, Ms Radhika Coomaraswamy, also suggested replacing the widely accepted distinction between internal and cross-border traffic with the focus on the separation of the victim from his or her community.[16] In short, the definition and standards compiled in the international agreements mentioned in this section are valid also for the intra-State child trafficking.

B. **The issue of translation**

Before exploring the nuances of child trafficking within the Chinese legal context, it's crucial to clarify the terminology used in Chinese and the challenges encountered

---

[14] The preamble of the CRC-OPSC expresses concern at "the significant and increasing international traffic of children for the purpose of the sale of children, child prostitution and child pornography".

[15] Article 3 of the CRC-OPSC: 1. Each State Party shall ensure that, as a minimum, the following acts and activities are fully covered under its criminal or penal law, whether these offences are committed domestically or transnationally or on an individual or organised basis [...].

[16] UN Commission on Human Rights, (2000), "Integration of the human rights of women and the gender perspective—violence against women", *Report of the Special Rapporteur, Ms Radhika Coomaraswamy, on violence against women, its causes and consequences, on trafficking in women, women's migration and violence against women*, 29 February 2000, E/CN.4/2000/68, para. 13.

when translating these terms into English, particularly the term "trafficking" as it is used in this research. The term "trafficking (in persons)", as delineated in the Palermo Protocol, is officially translated into Chinese as "*fanyun* (贩运)", which is similarly applied in the contexts of arms or drug trafficking. However, "*fanyun*" does not feature in Chinese legal, regulatory, or policy discourse and is not a term widely recognised or utilised by the general populace. Instead, the term "*guaimai* (拐卖)", which literally means "abduction and sale" and is often interpreted as "trafficking," has been in use for centuries in China. This term is a modern rendition of the older term "*luemai*". It's important to note the distinct differences between the definition of "*guaimai*" in Chinese legislation and that of "trafficking" as outlined in the Palermo Protocol.

To avoid potential confusion stemming from these translation discrepancies, this work adopts different terminologies as follows:

- **"Child trafficking", "human trafficking", or "trafficking of women and children":** These phrases are employed to describe the criminal act of "*guaimai*" as defined in Article 240 of the Criminal Law of China, translating directly to "abduction and sale". They are also used to refer to the general phenomenon of trafficking, without making explicit distinctions based on regional definitions.
- **"Trafficking in persons", "trafficking in women", or "trafficking in children":** These terms are exclusively used to describe the offence as defined in Article 3 of the Palermo Protocol.
- **"Children" in Case Studies:** Within case studies, the term "children" is used to denote any individual under the age of 18.

C. **Child trafficking in Chinese legal framework**

The approach to combating child trafficking in China exhibits distinct characteristics, shaped significantly by the nation's traditional culture and extensive historical evolution, resulting in unique features of child trafficking. As explained in the previous section, this divergence from international norms is notably influenced by a legal heritage that traces back to the Tang Dynasty, if not earlier. This historical legacy is a key factor in why contemporary Chinese legal definitions and provisions pertaining to child trafficking do not entirely align with international law standards.

Despite this, in 2000, China ratified two pivotal international treaties aimed at addressing child trafficking: the Palermo Protocol and the Optional Protocol to the Convention on the Rights of the Child on the Sale of Children, Child Prostitution and Child Pornography (CRC-OPSC). As a State Party to these treaties, China is obligated to enact legislative and other measures that criminalise the behaviours outlined in both documents.

However, the integration of these international frameworks into China's Criminal Law has been relatively limited. The current law predominantly reflects the doctrines of ancient Chinese penal codes. This historical influence suggests a nuanced intersection between traditional legal principles and contemporary international human rights obligations, highlighting the complexities inherent in harmonising domestic and international law within the unique context of Chinese legal culture.

In 1979, marking a significant legal milestone, the PRC promulgated its first Criminal Law since the establishment of the new government there decades earlier. This law, adopted by the National People's Congress and hereinafter referred to as the 1979 Criminal Law, was instrumental in introducing formal legal measures against human trafficking or "abduction and sale of persons" (*guaimai*). Article 141 of this law criminalised such acts, imposing a maximum sentence of five years' imprisonment for those found guilty of human trafficking.[17] However, this early legislation lacked a detailed definition of what constituted "abduction and sale", leaving room for ambiguity in its enforcement and interpretation.

It took nearly two decades for a more explicit definition of this offense to emerge. The 1979 Criminal Law underwent a substantial amendment and was replaced by a new version adopted in 1997, hereinafter referred to as the Criminal Law. This revised law, in its Article 240, explicitly defines the crime of "abduction and sale of women and children" as follows:

> Abducting and trafficking women or children refers to any act of abducting, kidnapping, buying, selling, transporting, or transferring a woman or a child for the purpose of selling the victim".[18]

A notable shift in this revision was the narrowing of the scope of recognised victims of trafficking from "persons" to specifically "women and children". This change signifies a strategic emphasis on the groups most vulnerable to human trafficking. This selective focus in the law can be seen as both a response to the most prevalent forms of trafficking in China and an implementation of the recommendations of UN human rights bodies, more specifically the Committee on the Elimination of Discrimination against Women (CEDAW).

Particularly relevant is the input from the CEDAW. During its eleventh session, the Committee underscored the critical issue of violence against women, including the trafficking of women and girls, in its General Recommendation No. 19. This recommendation emphasises the importance of national legal frameworks specifically addressing the unique vulnerabilities faced by women and girls in the context of trafficking.[19] Chinese delegates, while presenting China's second periodic report at the same session, articulated the government's commitment to intensifying the legal battle against the trafficking of women and girls. They pledged to impose "severe punishment of criminals who abduct and traffic in or kidnap women or children",[20] reflecting a direct response to the Committee's advocacy and guidance.

The definition of child trafficking in Chinese law, akin to the framework established in Article 3 of the Palermo Protocol, incorporates two fundamental elements:

---

[17] If the circumstance is serious, the sentence shall be above 5 years.

[18] This research involves translation of law and legal instruments. If not specified otherwise, the source of Chinese-English translation is the Peking University Institute of Legal Translation Studies (http://en.pkulaw.cn/).

[19] CEDAW, (1992) CEDAW General Recommendations No. 19: Violence against Women, 1 February1992, A/47/38, pp. 3–5.

[20] Ibid. p. 41.

action and *purpose*. The "action" element encompasses a three-stage process: recruitment (which includes abduction by force or fraud, kidnapping, and purchasing), transfer (encompassing transport and harbouring), and the act of selling. The "purpose" element is succinctly defined as "selling the victim", diverging from the notion of "exploitation" as delineated in the Palermo Protocol. Significantly, the offence culminates once the offender has the intention to sell the victims, rendering the purpose of the ultimate buyer—whether exploitative or not—irrelevant for the conviction of those involved in earlier stages. This critical aspect of the law relieves prosecutors of the burden of proving that individuals engaged in abduction, recruitment, transfer, or sale were cognisant of the buyer's intended exploitation of the victim. This facet of the law aims to enhance the prosecution of child trafficking, especially in modern scenarios characterised by the involvement of multiple individuals or criminal networks.

Despite these strengths, there are two significant shortcomings in this definition. Firstly, under the current legal provisions, buyers of trafficked children face less severe penalties compared to traffickers, though they are no longer granted immunity. Secondly, and crucially, if the prohibited acts are committed solely for exploitation purposes, without involving the sale of the victims—as in cases where children are recruited or abducted for labour or sexual exploitation only—these acts do not fall under Article 240's purview. Consequently, children subjected to such exploitation are not recognised as trafficking victims under this section, revealing a gap in the legal protection afforded to all potential victims of child trafficking.

As the last buyer in the trafficking process does not fulfil this purpose element, the offence terminates when the victim is sold to the last buyer. The purpose of the buyers, which may or may not be exploitative, is irrelevant for the determination of the offence either for traffickers or for themselves. Prosecutors do not need to prove that the offender, who abducts, recruits, transfers and sells a victim, is aware of the buyer's purpose. This purpose element allows each person responsible for any prohibited conduct at each node of the entire criminal network to be held liable, as long as the selling purpose is proved. The final purpose of the trafficking chain, exploitative or not, is irrelevant to convicting perpetrators involved in previous parts of the trafficking process. This provision would maximise the likelihood that all those involved in child trafficking would be charged, particularly in modern forms of child trafficking, which frequently involve multiple persons or criminal organisations. However, it has two non-negligible flaws. First, buyers of trafficked children are charged differently from traffickers, with much lighter penalties according to current provisions, although they are not immune. In addition, if the prohibited acts are merely for exploitation and not the sale of the child, the offender cannot be punished under Article 240. Consequently, children recruited or abducted, for example, only for labour or sexual exploitation rather than for sale, are not considered victims of trafficking.

By ratifying the Palermo Protocol, China has the obligation to implement these treaties by taking legislative, policy, and other appropriate measures, such as establishing as a criminal offence the conduct set forth in Article 3 of the Palermo Protocol.

Table 1 A comparison of the key elements of the definition of child trafficking in the international and national legal framework

	Palermo protocol	Chinese legal framework
Age	Under 18 years old	Under 14 years old
Action	Recruitment, transportation, transfer, harbouring or receipt	Abducting, kidnapping, buying, selling, transporting, or transferring
Purpose	Exploitation	Selling

However, the current legal definition of child trafficking is not in line with international standards (see Table 1). The most critical difference lies in the age limits of child victims and the purpose element. According to the most recent judicial interpretation issued by the Supreme People's Court in 2016, "child" under Article 240 refers to any person under *fourteen years of age* (emphasis added).[21] This setting of the maximum age of children is in stark contrast to the standards established by the Palermo Protocol[22] and CRC,[23] i.e., 18 years old. Since Article 240 only applies to children and women, male minors between 14 and 18 years old are not protected by this article or any other national policy related to child trafficking. By the same token, adult men in China cannot be considered and thus protected as victims of human trafficking.

In a more complicated case, parents selling their own children, one or both parents can be prosecuted for child trafficking, but the purpose element determining the offence is slightly different. Unlike traffickers, parents don't abduct, recruit or buy a child to sell; instead, only one act fits in their action element—selling. In this case, it is inappropriate to hold that the purpose element remains the sale of the child. However, the purpose of selling the child might be various. In China, it is not uncommon to hear stories of children being adopted by their parents from very poor families. Then what are the differences between civil adoption and child trafficking committed by parents, and what makes the actions of these parents accountable under child trafficking? In 2010, before the ratification of the Palermo Protocol, the Supreme People's Court issued the *Opinions on Legally Punishing the Crimes of Abducting and Trafficking in Women and Children*, providing a detailed explanation to the applicability of Article

---

[21] Supreme People's Court of PRC, (2016) 最高人民法院关于审理拐卖妇女儿童犯罪案件具体应用法律若干问题的解释 [Interpretation of the Supreme People's Court on Several Issues concerning the Application of Law in the Trial of Cases regarding Crimes of Trafficking in Women and Children], Interpretation No. 28 [2016] of the Supreme People's Court, issued on 21 December 2016, entered in force on 1 January 2017, at Article 9, retrieved from http://www.court.gov.cn/zixun-xiangqing-33641.html.

[22] Article 3 paragraph (d) specifies that for the purpose of this protocol, "child" means "any person under 18 years of age".

[23] UN Convention on the Rights of the Child, at Article 1.

240 of Criminal Law in the case of parental sale of children.[24] The sale of one's own child, in the following four conditions, is considered a crime of child trafficking:

(1) using fertility as a means of profit and selling one's own children immediately after parturition;

(2) selling one's own child for the purpose of profit, knowing that the buyer has no intention of raising the child or not taking into consideration the intention of the buyer;

(3) "sending" one's own children for obtaining a disproportionately large amount of money in the form of refund or compensation;

(4) other actions, the purpose of which can be proved as illegal economic gain.

In short, when parents sell their children for "*illegal economic gain*" or "illicit profit" instead of merely giving them into adoption, they are in breach of Article 240 of the Criminal Law. This illicit profit may be the price of the child itself, or the remuneration for the mother's maternal fertility. In any case, human beings are degraded, commodified, and made a tool for profit. At the same time, this legal opinion did leave some space for those who have a genuine need to place a child for adoption. It specified that when parents give their child to others, not for the purpose of making illegal profits, but because of the hardship of life or because of the influence of patriarchal culture (preference of male child and discrimination against female child), and if they only receive a small amount of compensation for "nutrition" or "gratitude", it is not considered a case of child trafficking but "civil adoption". However, legislators failed to give a directly applicable and precise explanation for the term "a small amount of compensation", which distinguishes "civil adoption" from trafficking.

Although "exploitation" is not the key element to determining child trafficking, it may lead to aggravating circumstances. Subparagraphs (3) and (4) of Article 240 provide that offenders are not only punishable, but the penalty is aggravated if they rape or sexually exploit the trafficked women (and children) or sell them into a condition of potential sexual exploitation. However, only sexual exploitations are listed in this article; all other forms of exploitation are not considered aggravating circumstances.

The complete list of aggravating circumstances is: [the offender].

(1) being a ringleader of a gang engaged in the trafficking of women and children;

(2) trafficking three or more women and/or children;

(3) raping the woman who is a victim of trafficking;

[24] The Supreme People's Court, the Supreme People's Procuratorate, the Ministry of Public Security, and the Ministry of Justice, (2010) 最高人民法院、最高人民检察院、公安部、司法部印发《关于依法惩治拐卖妇女儿童犯罪的意见》的通知 [Notice of the Supreme People's Court, the Supreme People's Procuratorate, the Ministry of Public Security and the Ministry of Justice on Issuing the Opinions on Legally Punishing the Crimes of Abducting and Trafficking in Women and Children], Documents of Judicial Interpretation Nature, No. 7 [2010] of the Supreme People's Court, issued and entered in force on 15 March 2010, at para. 17, retrieved from http://en.pkulaw.cn/display.aspx?cgid=095d828db4ce796bbdfb&lib=law.

(4) enticing or forcing the trafficked woman to engage in prostitution, or selling such woman to any other person who would force her to engage in prostitution;

(5) kidnapping a woman or child by means of violence, coercion or anaesthesia for the purpose of selling the victim;

(6) stealing a baby or an infant for the purpose of selling the victim;

(7) causing serious injury or death to the trafficked woman or child or to her or his relatives or any other serious consequences; or

(8) selling a woman or a child out of the territory of China.

According to Article 240, offenders of trafficking of women and children shall be sentenced to fixed-term imprisonment of not less than five years but not more than ten years and shall also be fined. When aggravating circumstances exist, the penalty becomes fixed-term imprisonment of not less than 10 years or life imprisonment and a fine or confiscation of property. If the circumstances are especially serious, the offender shall be sentenced to death and to confiscation of property. Although the text only mentions trafficked women as victims of sexual abuse and exploitation, it can be deduced that these provisions also apply when the victim is a trafficked female child.

Since Article 240 only covers traffickers, buyers who buy trafficked persons for purposes other than selling are not criminalised as traffickers, although they are not left unpunished either. According to Article 241—the "crime of buying trafficked women or children"—"*whoever buys a trafficked woman or child shall be sentenced to fixed-term imprisonment of not more than 3 years, detention or public surveillance*". Therefore, the criminal offence set forth in Article 240 is the precondition of the crime of buying a trafficked woman or child (Article 241). It has partially filled the blank left by Article 240, criminalising those who buy a trafficked woman or child, whether for the purpose of exploitation or not. However, penalties for traffickers and buyers are very different. The buyer who did not abuse the child victim nor obstruct the trafficked woman from returning to her original place of residence according to her would enjoy impunity until 2015 when Article 241 was amended as:

> Where in buying a trafficked woman or child, the child is not abused, and their rescue is not obstructed, a mitigated punishment may be convicted; where it is in accordance with the woman's wishes, and her return to her original residence is not obstructed, it may be given a mitigated punishment, or punishment may be commuted.[25]

In the case of the buyer abusing or exploiting the trafficked person, Article 241 shall be applied in combination with other criminal offences. As set forth in 241, when the buyer forcibly has sexual relations with the trafficked woman, he shall be convicted and punished in accordance with the provisions of Article 236 under the crime of rape. If the buyer illegally deprives or restricts the personal freedom of the victim or commits any criminal acts, such as harming and humiliating the

[25] Standing Committee of the National People's Congress, (2015) 中华人民共和国刑法修正案(九) [Amendment (IX) to the Criminal Law of the People's Republic of China], Order No. 30 of the President, at Article 15.

victim, the buyer shall be convicted and punished in accordance with the relevant provisions of Criminal Law. Combined punishment may be applied if the buyer has committed multiple crimes against the trafficked person. If the buyer sells the trafficked person afterwards, he or she shall be convicted and punished in accordance with Article 240 without further proof of the buyer's purpose.

There are some other crimes related to the international definition of trafficking in persons; the crime of selling human organs (Article 234A), the crime of forced labour (Article 244), the crime of abducting children, and organising people with disabilities and children for begging or engaging in criminal activities (Article 262), the crime of organising and forcing others into prostitution (Article 358), and crime of luring others into prostitution (Article 359). However, these crimes and the crime of child trafficking are not directly connected in law. The shortcomings of this decentralised legislation are apparent (Pan 2012; Liu 2010). Victims of forced labour or forced prostitution, for instance, are not considered victims of trafficking if they were abducted but not sold into exploitative condition. Consequently, they cannot enjoy the protection and assistance services offered to victims of trafficking, and the offenders are not convicted and punished as traffickers. In addition, this inconsistency between the Chinese definition of child trafficking and the international definition of trafficking in children increases the difficulty of collecting data on the crime, thus affecting the study of the problem worldwide (Laczko and Gozdziak 2005).

References

Antonopoulos, Georgios A., Andrea Di Nicola, Atanas Rusev, and Fiamma Terenghi. 2019. *Human Trafficking Finances: Evidence from Three European Countries*. 1st ed. SpringerBriefs in Criminology. Springer International Publishing. http://gen.lib.rus.ec/book/index.php?md5=e0003a75dcb0e8eb4636c35672e72400.

de Boer-Buquicchio, Maud. 2017. 'Before the Inter-American Court of Human Rights Expert Opinion by the United Nations Special Rapporteur on the Sale and Sexual Exploitation of Children: RAMÍREZ BROTHERS AND FAMILY VS. GUATEMALA'. https://www.ohchr.org/sites/default/files/Documents/Issues/Children/Submission/Opinions28April2017.PDF.

Burke, Mary C., ed. 2022. *Human Trafficking: Interdisciplinary Perspectives*. 3rd ed. Criminology and Justice Studies. Routledge. http://gen.lib.rus.ec/book/index.php?md5=F94AB617F0172CD65DD41704C5DE3830.

Cameron, Sally, and Edward Newman. 2008. *Trafficking in Humans: Social, Cultural and Political Dimensions*. Tokyo: United Nations University Press.

Chen, Shiqu. 2000. '打击拐卖妇女儿童犯罪的形势与对策'. *Public Serurity Studies (公安研究)* 72 (4): 37–40.

Chisolm-Straker, Makini, and Hanni Stoklosa. 2017. *Human Trafficking Is a Public Health Issue: A Paradigm Expansion in the United States*. 1st ed. Springer International Publishing. http://gen.lib.rus.ec/book/index.php?md5=bac28aadc00a067cefcb0f93b2330071.

Chu, Huaizhi. 1996. *Theory of combating "six evils"*. 中国检察出版社.

Cohen, Jonathan. 2003. *Togo, Borderline Slavery: Child Trafficking in Togo*. Vol. 15. 8. Human Rights Watch.

Council of the EU. 2024. 'Fight against Human Trafficking: Council and European Parliament Strike Deal to Strengthen Rules'. https://www.consilium.europa.eu/en/press/press-releases/

2024/01/23/fight-against-human-trafficking-council-and-european-parliament-strike-deal-to-strengthen-rules/.
Ebbe, Obi NI, and Dilip K. Das. 2007. *Global Trafficking in Women and Children*. Boca Raton, FL: CRC Press.
Englund, Cecilia, Minna Viuhko, Anniina Jokinen, Kauko Aromaa, Aigi Resetnikova, Anna Markina, Ulf Söderström, and Marie Nilsen. 2008. *The Organisation of Human Trafficking: A Study of Criminal Involvement in Sexual Exploitation in Sweden, Finland and Estonia*. Swedish National Council for Crime Prevention.
Gallagher, Anne T. 2010. *The International Law of Human Trafficking*. Cambridge: Cambridge University Press.
Gao, Xiaoying. 2010. 'Criminological probe into the crime of abducting and trafficking children [拐卖儿童罪之犯罪学探析]'. *Journal of China Youth University for Political Sciences [中国青年政治学院学报]* 2010 (6): 90–94.
Ge, Xiangyu. 2019. '中国古代略人略卖人罪研究 [Study on the Crime of Trafficking in Ancient China]'. 西南政法大学.
Gjermeni, Eglantina, Mary P. Van Hook, Saemira Gjipali, Lindita Xhillari, Fatjon Lungu, and Anila Hazizi. 2008. 'Trafficking of Children in Albania: Patterns of Recruitment and Reintegration'. *Child Abuse & Neglect* 32 (10): 941–948.
Gu, Minkang. 2007. 'Trafficking in Women and Children in China'. In *Global Trafficking in Women and Children*, edited by Obi NI Ebbe and Dilip K. Das, 67–77. Boca Raton: CRC Press.
Guo, Mengyuan. 2017. '清代"略人略卖人"行为的法律规制'. *法制博览[Legality Vision]* 9: 241. CNKI:SUN:FBZX.0.2017–09–136.
Harvey-Blankenship, Michele, Phuong N. Pham, and Rachel Shigekane. 2010. *Genetic Tracing, Disappeared Children and Justice*. 10. Innocenti Working Papers. UNICEF. https://www.unicef-irc.org/publications/609-genetic-tracing-disappeared-children-and-justice.html.
Hoffman, Alecia Dionne, and Sabella Ogbobode Abidde. 2021. *Human Trafficking in Africa: New Paradigms, New Perspectives*. Springer. http://gen.lib.rus.ec/book/index.php?md5=FF974513793BFBCD9F1C60E52DDF30B7.
Huang, HuaLun. 2009. 'Where Are Our Daughters, Mothers, Sisters, and Wives? A Typological Analysis of Missing Women and Girls in Greater China, 1900–2000s'. *Asian Journal of Criminology* 4(2): 8–106. https://doi.org/10.1007/s11417-008-9058-z.
Huang, Yuan-Sheng. 2013. '晚清民國禁革奴婢買賣的理念與實踐 [The Context of Prohibition against Human Trafficking in Late Qing and the Republic of China]'. 政大法學評論, no. 134. 國立政治大學: 47–114.
Inter-Parliamentary Union, and UNICEF. 2005. *Combating Child Trafficking: Handbook for Parliamentarians*. Handbook for Parliamentarians 9.
Iroanya, Richard Obinna. 2018. *Human Trafficking and Security in Southern Africa: The South African and Mozambican Experience*. 1st ed. African Histories and Modernities. Palgrave Macmillan. http://gen.lib.rus.ec/book/index.php?md5=abaee5f8af0fd3a0f7ea763760191943.
Kragten-Heerdink, Suzanne L. J., Corinne E. Dettmeijer-Vermeulen, and Dirk J. Korf. 2018. 'More Than Just "Pushing and Pulling": Conceptualizing Identified Human Trafficking in the Netherlands'. *Crime and Delinquency* 64(13): 1765–1789. https://doi.org/10.1177/0011128717728503.
Laczko, Frank, and Elzbieta Gozdziak. 2005. *Data and Research on Human Trafficking: A Global Survey*. Geneva, Switzerland: International Organization for Migration.
Lee, Maggy, ed. 2013. *Human Trafficking*. Willan Publishing.
Leifsen, Esben. 2008. 'Child Trafficking and Formalisation: The Case of International Adoption from Ecuador'. *Children & Society* 22 (3): 212–222. https://doi.org/10.1111/j.1099-0860.2008.00152.x.
Li, Chunlei, Ren Ren, and Xiaoxu Zhang. 2013. 'Research on the status quo and countermeasures for the rescue and protection of trafficked children in China: Analysis based on 133 reported cases in recent years [我国被拐卖儿童救助保护现状及完善对策研究——基于对近年 133 个公

开报道案例的分析]'. *Journal of People's Public Security University of China (Social Sciences Edition) [中国人民公安大学学报: 社会科学版]* 2013 (6): 16–25.

Li, Gang, Huijuan Wang, Ran Tan, and Ying Fu. 2017a. 'Spatiotemporal Characteristics and Formation Mechanism of Child Trafficking in China Based on "successful Cases" [中国拐卖儿童犯罪的时空特征与形成机制 ——基于"成功案例"的管基]'. *Geographical Research [地理研究]* 36 (12): 2505–2520. https://doi.org/10.11821/dlyj201712019.

Li, Gang, Ran Tan, Huijuan Wang, Xiang Yan, and Yan Shao. 2017b. 'Geographic Characteristics of Child Trafficking Crime in China [中国拐卖儿童犯罪的地理特征研究]'. *Scientia Geographica Sinica [地理科学]* 37 (7): 1049–1058. https://doi.org/10.13249/j.cnki.sgs.2017.07.010.

Li, Jie. 2000. 'Analysis on the Present Situation, Causes, Harm and Countermeasures of the Crime of Human Trafficking in the Zhenxiong Country [浅析镇雄县拐卖人口犯罪的现状, 原因, 危害及对策]'. *Journal of Yunnan Police College [云南警官学院学报]*, no. 2: 36–39.

Lin, Jiezhen. 2015. 'Child Trafficking Crime Analysis from a Penal Perspective [刑事视野下的拐卖儿童犯罪分析]'. *Legality Vision [法制博览]* 3: 99–100.

Liu, Heping. 2000. '拐卖妇女儿童犯罪的特点, 原因及对策 [Feature and causes of the crime of abduction and sale of women and children and strategy against it]'. *公安研究 [Policing Studies]* 2000 (4): 41–44.

Liu, Xianquan. 2003. 'Improving Chinese criminal law in respect of punishing crime of abducting and trafficking in persons [论我国惩治拐卖人口犯罪的刑法完善]'. *Law Science [法学]* 2003 (5): 93–100.

Liu, Guofu. 2010. 'Review and development thinking on Chinese laws on anti-trafficking in persons: An international law perspective [中国反贩运人口法律的理性回顾和发展思考: 以国际法为视角]'. *Journal of Gansu Political Science and Law Institute [甘肃政法学院学报]* 2010(5): 74–85.

Ma, Yushan. 1997. 中国古代的人口买卖. Beijing: The Commercial Press International Co., Ltd.

Marcus, Anthony, Jo Sanson, Amber Horning, Efram Thompson, and Ric Curtis. 2016. 'Pimping and Profitability:Testing the Economics of Trafficking in Street Sex Markets in Atlantic City, New Jersey'. *Sociological Perspectives* 59 (1): 46–65. https://doi.org/10.1177/0731121416628552.

Meier, Patricia J., and Xiaole Zhang. 2008. 'Sold into Adoption: The Hunan Baby Trafficking Scandal Exposes Vulnerabilities in Chinese Adoptions to the United States'. *Cumberland Law Review* 39 (1): 87–130.

Mendoza, Martha, Robin McDowell, Margie Mason, and Esther Htusan and the Associated Press. 2016. *Fishermen Slaves: Human Trafficking and the Seafood We Eat*. AP Editions. http://gen.lib.rus.ec/book/index.php?md5=2F49026A997AFFEBFFCD62C5C9566A6A.

Obokata, Tom. 2006. Trafficking of Human Beings from a Human Rights Perspective: Towards a Holistic Approach. Vol. 89. Leiden and Boston: Martinus Nijhoff Publishers.

OHCHR. 2010. Commentary on the Recommended Principles and Guidelines on Human Rights and Human Trafficking. New York and Geneva: United Nations Publication.

Palmiotto, Michael J. 2014. 'Forced Labor in the United States'. In *Combating Human Trafficking: A Multidisciplinary Approach*, edited by Michael J. Palmiotto, 157–174. Boca Raton, FL: CRC Press.

Pan, Xingcheng. 2012. 'Trafficking in Human Beings: Conceptual Interpretation and Legislative Appraisal - Focusing on the UN Supplementary Protocol [贩运人口: 概念诠释与立法评析——以联合国《补充议定书》为中心]'. *Tan Qiu [探求]* 2012 (2): 105–113.

Yvonne Rafferty. 2007. 'Children for Sale: Child Trafficking in Southeast Asia'. *Child Abuse Review* 16(6): 401–422. https://doi.org/10.1002/car.1009.

Rijken, Conny. 2009. 'A Human Rights Based Approach to Trafficking in Human Beings'. *Security and Human Rights* 20 (3): 212–222. https://doi.org/10.1163/187502309789192513.

Rosenberg, Ruth. 2003. *Trafficking of Women and Children in Indonesia*. Jakarta: International Catholic Migration Commission and American Center for International Labor Solidarity.

Savona, Ernesto U., and Sonia Stefanizzi. 2007. *Measuring Human Trafficking: Complexities and Pitfalls*. New York, NY: Springer.
Shelley, Louise. 2010. *Human Trafficking: A Global Perspective*. Cambridge: University Press.
Shelley, Louise. 2013. 'Human Trafficking as a Form of Transnational Crime'. In *Human Trafficking*, edited by Maggy Lee, 116–137. Willan Publishing.
Shen, Anqi, Georgios A. Antonopoulos, and Georgios Papanicolaou. 2013. 'China's Stolen Children: Internal Child Trafficking in the People's Republic of China'. *Trends in Organized Crime* 16 (1): 31–48. https://doi.org/10.1007/s12117-012-9167-z.
Shen, Anqi. 2016. 'Female Perpetrators in Internal Child Trafficking in China: An Empirical Study'. *Journal of Human Trafficking* 2 (1): 63–77. https://doi.org/10.1080/23322705.2016.1136537.
Smolin, David M. 2004. 'Intercountry Adoption as Child Trafficking'. *Valparaiso University Law Review* 39 (2): 281–235.
Smolin, David M. 2007. 'Child Laundering as Exploitation: Applying Anti-Trafficking Norms to Intercountry Adoption under the Coming Hague Regime'. *Vermont Law Review* 32 (1): 1–56.
Song, Qian. 2004. '试论宋代略卖人口的几个问题 [Experimental Discussion on Several Issues of the Slight Sale of Population in the Song Dynasty]'. *乐山师范学院学报 [Journal of Leshan Teachers College]* 19 (9): 80–84.
Spires, Robert Weber. 2015. *Preventing Human Trafficking: Education and NGOs in Thailand*. New edition. Solving Social Problems. Ashgate Pub Co. http://gen.lib.rus.ec/book/index.php?md5=949aa58e692d912c4c78d849a1faa9d5.
Surtees, Rebecca. 2008. 'Traffickers and Trafficking in Southern and Eastern Europe: Considering the Other Side of Human Trafficking'. *European Journal of Criminology* 5(1): 39–68. https://doi.org/10.1177/1477370807084224.
UN CTOC. 2013. *Report on the Meeting of the Working Group on Trafficking in Persons Held in Vienna from 6 to 8 November 2013*. CTOC/COP/WG.4/2013/5.
UN-ACT. 2016. Human Trafficking Vulnerabilities in Asia: A Study on Forced Marriage between Cambodia and China. Bangkok: UNDP.
UN-ACT. 2012. 'China: National Trafficking Trends'.
UNDP, Europe and the CIS. 2004. *Trafficking in Human Beings: A Guidance Note*. UNDP.
UNICEF Innocenti Research Centre. 2009. Handbook on the Optional Protocol on the Sale of Children, Child Prostitution and Child Pornography. New York: The United Nations Children's Fund.
UNICEF Regional Office for CEE/CIS. 2006. Reference Guide on Protecting the Rights of Child Victims of Trafficking in Europe. Geneva: UNICEF.
UNODC. 2006. *Trafficking in Persons: Global Patterns*.
UNODC. 2009a. *International Framework for Action To Implement the Trafficking in Persons Protocol*. Vienna.
UNODC. 2009b. *Anti-Trafficking Practitioners' Manual*.
UNODC. 2016. *Global Report on Trafficking in Persons 2016*. Global Report on Trafficking in Persons. Vienna, Austria.
UNODC. 2018. *Global Report on Trafficking In Persons 2018*. Global Report on Trafficking in Persons. Vienna, Austria.
Villa, Monique. 2019. *Slaves Among Us: The Hidden World of Human Trafficking*. Rowman & Littlefield Publishers. http://gen.lib.rus.ec/book/index.php?md5=17ebcfcf680962efad7a0013 41423300.
Wang, Zhen, Liyuan Wei, Sha Peng, Liangchun Deng, and Beibei Niu. 2018. 'Child-Trafficking Networks of Illegal Adoption in China'. *Nature Sustainability* 1 (5): 254–260. https://doi.org/10.1038/s41893-018-0065-5.
Wang, Lingshu. 1992. 失落的小太阳: 拐卖儿童纪实. Beijing: China Writers Publishing House.
Wang, Zijin. 2014. '汉代"卖子""鬻子孙"现象与"卖人法"'. 中国古代法律文献研究 VIII: 89–104.
Winterdyk, John, Benjamin Perrin, and Philip Reichel. 2011. *Human Trafficking: Exploring the International Nature, Concerns, and Complexities*. Boca Raton, FL: CRC Press.

Wylie, Gillian, and Penelope McRedmond. 2010. *Human Trafficking in Europe: Character, Causes and Consequences*. New York: Palgrave Macmillan.

Xie Zhihong, and Jia Lusheng. 1989. 古老的罪恶: 拐卖妇女纪实. 浙江文艺出版社.

Xin, Yanyu, and Tianji Cai. 2018. 'Child Trafficking in China: Evidence from Sentencing Documents'. *International Journal of Population Studies* 4 (2): 1–11. https://doi.org/10.18063/ijps.v4i2.817.

Xing, Hongmei, Ran Chen, and Fang Xu. 2017. 'The Developmental Characteristics of the Crime of Child Trafficking: An Analysis of 447 Verdict [拐卖儿童犯罪的发展特点——对 447 份判决书的分析]'. *Juvenile Delinquency Prevention Research [预防青少年犯罪研究]* 2017 (1): 38–43.

Xing, Hongmei. 2017. 'Study on Rime of Selling of Children by Parents [出卖亲生子女犯罪研究]'. *Journal of People's Public Security University of China (Social Sciences Edition) [中国人民公安大学学报: 社会科学版]* 33 (4): 17–24.

Yang, Suizhang. 2000. 'Investigation on the crime of trafficking in women and children in Yuncheng area of Shanxi Province in recent years [山西省运城地区近年来拐卖妇女儿童犯罪的调查]'. *Journal of Shanxi Police Officer College [山西警官高等专科学校学报]* 30 (3): 36–38.

Yang, Huili. 2006. '拐卖妇女、儿童罪探析'. China University of Political Science and Law.

Yang, Wenlong. 2008. 'On the Restoration of the Crime of "Trafficking in Persons [论"拐卖人口罪"的恢复]'. *Hubei Social Sciences [湖北社会科学]*, no. 3: 150–152.

Yao, Jiaru, and Liping Guo. 2008. '中国古代拐卖人口犯罪及治理对策'. *Journal of Railway Police College (铁道警官高等专科学校学报)* 18 (5): 17–22.

Yea, Sallie. 2019. *Paved with Good Intentions?: Human Trafficking and the Anti-Trafficking Movement in Singapore*. Palgrave Macmillan. http://gen.lib.rus.ec/book/index.php?md5=1D157D1CF02F100BF608FE9CD2563A7C.

Yu, Guilin. 2000. '宋代买卖妇女现象初探'. *Journal of Chinese Historical Studies (中国史研究)* 2000 (3): 102–112.

Yuan, E., and Zhenyu Yang. 2001. 'An Analysis of the Crime of Abducting and Selling Women in Frontier Ethnic Areas in China: A Case Study of Wenshan Zhuang and Miao Autonomous Prefecture in Yunnan Province [当前我国边疆民族地区拐卖妇女犯罪活动分析研究——以云南省文山壮族苗族自治州为例]'. *Collection of Women's Studies [妇女研究论丛]* 2001 (2): 17–22.

Zhang, Bin. 2006 '中国如何冲破打拐迷局 [How can China break the puzzle of crackdown human trafficking]', People's Police [人民公安] 2006 (2): 18–21.

Zhao, Junfu, and Qingtian Meng. 2014. 'Reflections on Revising the Provisions of the Criminal Law Relevant to the Crime of Buying Women and Children Victims of Trafficking [关于修改《刑法》收买被拐卖妇女儿童犯罪相关条款的思考]'. *Public Security Studies [公安研究]*, no. 2: 43–46.

Zhou, Junjun, Gang Li, Jiaobei Wang, Tingting Xu, Qifan Nie, Xing Gao, and Annan Jin. 2023. 'Exploring Variations and Influencing Factors of Illegal Adoption: A Comparison between Child Trafficking and Informal Adoption'. *Child Abuse & Neglect* 140 (June): 106124. https://doi.org/10.1016/j.chiabu.2023.106124.

范晔. 2007. *后汉书 [The Book of Later Han]*. Beijing: 中华书局.

Chapter 2
Addressing Child Trafficking Adopting a Human Rights-Based Approach

Child trafficking represents a multifaceted issue that cannot be entirely grasped or addressed effectively from a singular perspective. It is often closely related to various social issues, including gender-based discrimination, poverty, social security problems, child abuse, migration, and (transnational) organised criminal activities, amongst others. Whilst these perspectives offer insightful understandings, confining our study to a single discipline may impede a full comprehension of the matter. A more holistic understanding of child trafficking is achievable through a human rights lens. By prioritising the rights of both victims and potential victims while also emphasising the responsibility of duty bearers, this approach takes into account all dimensions of the problem. It explores the underlying causes, the far-reaching consequences, and pursues appropriate resolutions. In short, by embracing a human rights-based framework, we are better positioned to unravel the complexities of child trafficking and develop efficacious strategies to thwart and eradicate this abominable crime.

The human rights-bases approach is defined as "a conceptual framework for dealing with a phenomenon; normatively based on international human rights standards; operationally directed to promoting and protecting human rights." (OHCHR 2014, p. 8). It was initially conceived in 2002 by the United Nations (UN) agencies involved the sector of development cooperation and poverty reduction (UNDP 2003). This approach is highly regarded for its appropriacy in addressing complex issues of multi-disciplinary and human-centred nature, and quickly gained acceptance as a guiding principle by many UN agencies working in other sectors such as human trafficking (OHCHR 2002), education (UNICEF and UNESCO 2007), climate change (OHCHR 2008), disabilitics (UN 2022), just to namc a fcw. It didn't takc vcry long for this UN working approach to be adopted by scholars to guide their research. The three essential attributes concerning the objective, activities and guiding principles for a policy, programme, or research adopting a human rights-based approach are (McConnell and Smith 2018; OHCHR 2006):

L. Han, *Child Trafficking in China*, https://doi.org/10.1007/978-981-97-3717-8_2

- As policies and programmes are formulated, their main objective should be to promote and protect human rights;
- A human rights-based approach identifies rights holders, duty bearers (usually States) and respective entitlements and obligations. This approach works towards strengthening the capacities of rights holders to secure their rights and of duty bearers, to meet their obligations; and:
- Core principles and standards derived from international human rights law should guide all aspects of the response at all stages.

Therefore, adopting a human rights-based approach to combat child trafficking necessitates addressing the following pivotal inquiries:

- Whose rights are infringed upon, and what specific rights are compromised?
- Who holds responsibility, and what obligations do they bear?
- What strategies ought to be deployed to mitigate and avert the crime of child trafficking, consistent with international human rights legislation?

The experts of the Office of the United Nations High Commissioner for Human Rights (OHCHR) posited that the human rights approach obliges governments and others entities to acknowledge two critical aspects when addressing trafficking in persons: Firstly, it necessitates an understanding of "the ways in which human rights violation arise through the trafficking cycle". Secondly, it involves recognising "the ways in which States' obligations under international human rights law are engaged" (OHCHR 2014). Consequently, this approach establishes fundamental evaluative criteria for national policies and programmes. In assessing the effectiveness of anti-trafficking strategies, it is vital to consider whether initiatives aimed at preventing child trafficking address the vulnerabilities of the victims and whether efforts to combat child trafficking align with international human rights standards. Moreover, responses to child trafficking, including policies and programme outcomes, must adhere to core human rights principles such as non-discrimination.

1 The Legal Framework Addressing Child Trafficking

Child trafficking constitutes a multifaceted and multidimensional challenge that requires a multi-pronged response. It demands not just reactive crime control, but proactive international police cooperation to dismantle trafficking networks. Moreover, this issue goes beyond mere law enforcement: it necessitates comprehensive crime prevention strategies and robust victim protection protocols. At its core, it challenges the efficacy of international laws and principles, demanding their rigorous enforcement and integration with national legislative and administrative efforts. This complex issue requires a harmonised global response, leveraging both legal frameworks and human rights principles to effectively combat this heinous crime. This cooperative approach is essential at the national level as well. Law enforcement agencies alone are inadequate to resolve the problem. Other sectors must be involved to address the root causes of child trafficking, including identifying the most vulnerable groups, addressing the demand, and protecting victims from secondary victimisation.

A. International instruments pertaining to child trafficking

International legal and non-legal frameworks addressing child trafficking fall into two main categories. The first encompasses instruments specifically tailored to combat human trafficking within the realm of crime control. The second includes human rights treaties in which issues of child trafficking are addressed in conjunction with other concerns. Moreover, various international conventions that address related issues, such as child labour and international adoption, are also pertinent. Notably, the tenets of human rights are fundamental across these instruments. These principles of human rights are also consistently incorporated within international crime control treaties. Spanning international, regional, and bilateral levels, these frameworks are geographically extensive. Despite international law's intrinsic "soft" nature, these instruments provide States with essential principles and guidelines, alongside platforms for cooperation. Box 1 below presents a comprehensive list of pertinent international and regional treaties associated with child trafficking.

(1) *International specialised instruments*

The Palermo Protocol, adopted by the United Nations in 2000, stands as the cornerstone in the international community's effort to combat human trafficking. It not only presents the first widely accepted definition of "trafficking in persons" but also establishes a framework for transnational and multidisciplinary cooperation. The Protocol introduces the "Prevention—Prosecution—Protection—Partnership" (4Ps) mechanism, designed to facilitate the prevention and combatting of trafficking, provide protection and assistance to victims, and promote cooperation among State Parties towards these goals. Ratifying countries are obligated under the Palermo Protocol to establish domestic criminal offences to counteract trafficking, adopt measures for victim protection and assistance, and formulate comprehensive anti-trafficking policies. It is under the auspices of the UNODC, which is responsible for offering technical assistance, supporting the implementation of anti-trafficking strategies, and acting as the custodian of the Protocol, thereby ensuring its principles are upheld globally.

Box 1 List of relevant international and regional treaties associated with child trafficking

Specialist trafficking treaties and crime control treaties:

- 2000 UN Convention against Transnational Organized Crime
- 2000 Protocol to Prevent, Suppress and Punish Trafficking in Persons Especially Women and Children, supplementing the United Nations Convention against Transnational Organized Crime

Human rights treaties:

- 1966 International Covenant on Civil and Political Rights
- 1966 International Covenant on Economic, Social and Cultural Rights
- 1965 Convention on the Elimination of All Forms of Racial Discrimination
- 1979 Convention on the Elimination of All Forms of Discrimination against Women
- 1984 Convention against Torture and Other Cruel Inhuman or Degrading Treatment or Punishment
- 1989 Convention on the Rights of the Child
- 2000 Optional Protocol to the Convention on the Rights of the Child on the sale of children, child prostitution and child pornography
- 1990 Convention on the Protection of the Rights of All Migrant Workers and Members of Their Families
- 2006 Convention on the Rights of Persons with Disabilities

Other international treaties:

- 1926 Convention on Slavery
- 1956 Supplementary Convention on the Abolition of Slavery, the Slave Trade and Institutions and Practices Similar to Slavery
- 1930 ILO Forced Labour Convention (C29)
- 1957 ILO Abolition of Forced Labour Convention (C105)
- 1973 ILO Minimum Age Convention (C138)
- 1999 ILO Worst Forms of Child Labour Convention (C182)
- 1980 Hague Convention on the Civil Aspects of International Child Abduction
- 1993 Hague Convention on Protection of Children and Co-operation in Respect of Intercountry Adoption

Regional treaties:

- 2002 SAARC Convention on Preventing and Combating Trafficking in Women and Children for Prostitution
- 2002 SAARC Convention on Regional Arrangements for the Promotion of Child Welfare in South Asia
- 1981 African Charter on Human and Peoples' Rights
- 1990 African Charter on the Rights and Welfare of the Child
- 1994 Inter-American Convention on International Traffic in Minors
- 1994 Inter-American Convention on the Prevention, Punishment and Eradication of Violence against Women
- 2000 Charter of Fundamental Rights in the European Union
- 2005 Council of Europe, Convention on Action against Trafficking in Human Beings

Based on the Palermo Protocol, various non-binding instruments were created by the UNODC, aiming at providing practical guidance and frameworks for implementation. The most important ones are:

- Toolkit to Combat Trafficking in Persons (2006 and 2008): These toolkits provide practical help for drafting legislation, creating comprehensive national anti-trafficking strategies, and assisting in the implementation of the Palermo Protocol.
- Model Law against Trafficking in Persons (2009) and Model Legislative Provisions against Trafficking in Persons (2020): These documents offer comprehensive guidance for tailoring legislation to national legal systems, thus facilitating the combat on human trafficking.
- International Framework for Action to Implement the Trafficking in Persons Protocol (2009): It outlines detailed steps and measures that nations can adopt to meet the obligations set forth in the Protocol, adhering to the "4Ps" mechanism.
- Anti-Human Trafficking Manual for Criminal Justice Practitioners (2010): Consisting of fourteen modules, this manual offers guidance to criminal justice practitioners on how to effectively combat human trafficking, in line with the standards set by the Palermo Protocol.
- Needs Assessment Toolkit on the Criminal Justice Response to Human Trafficking (2010): Tailored to support governments, civil society, the international community, and other pertinent stakeholders, the toolkit enables both comprehensive and specific assessments of various facets of a country's criminal justice response to human trafficking through its criminal justice system.

(2) ***International human rights instruments***

Within the UN human rights framework, eight out of nine core human rights treaties contain provisions related to human trafficking. Among these treaties, the Optional Protocol to the Convention on the Rights of the Child on the Sale of Children, Child Prostitution, and Child Pornography, also adopted in 2000, stands as a crucial complement to the Palermo Protocol in the global fight against child trafficking. This Protocol augments the Convention on the Rights of the Child by providing a focused legal framework specifically targeting the sale of children, child prostitution, and child pornography, all of which are often intrinsically linked to child trafficking. More importantly, the CRC-OPSC focuses on the unique vulnerabilities of children in these crimes. Its emphasis on the protection and assistance of victims underscores the importance of addressing the physical, psychological, and social impacts of exploitation on children. It also establishes mechanisms for monitoring its implementation, thereby aiding countries in their efforts against child trafficking and related abuses. The CRC-OPSC, therefore, plays a crucial role in reinforcing the international legal architecture for the protection of children against trafficking and exploitation, complementing other key instruments such as the Palermo Protocol.

Another equally important human rights instrument is the Convention on the Elimination of All Forms of Discrimination against Women, adopted in 1979. Although the CEDAW does not explicitly reference child trafficking, its relevance is established through its exhortation to States parties to "suppress all forms of traffic in women" in Article 6, as well as its broader commitment to combatting discrimination and violence against women and girls, which implicitly includes trafficking. More specifically, in 1992, the CEDAW Committee elucidated the nexus between "trafficking in women" and "violence against women" through General Recommendation No. 19.[1] In 2020, the CEDAW Committee reaffirmed the obligations of States parties to combat all forms of trafficking in the context of global migration, as detailed in General Recommendation No. 38.[2]

Although CRC-OPSC and CEDAW are treaties primarily focused on human rights, rather than on crime control, they exhibit considerable synergy with the Palermo Protocol in various aspects. For instance, both treaties oblige ratifying states to adopt legal measures for criminalising and combating specific offences related to trafficking, thereby aligning with the broader objectives of the Palermo Protocol to prevent, suppress, and punish trafficking in persons. Vice versa, the Palermo Protocol and its supplementary documents all adopt a human rights-sensitive approach, thus demonstrating a mutual reinforcement between human rights and anti-trafficking legislation.

The most important "soft law" instruments relevant to the issue of child trafficking, issued by the OHCHR, therefore, within the human rights framework, include:

- OHCHR (2002), Recommended Principles and Guidelines on Human Rights and Human Trafficking[3]
- UN (2022), Basic Principles and Guidelines on the Right to a Remedy and Reparation for Victims of Gross Violations of International Human Rights Law and Serious Violations of International Humanitarian Law[4]

(3) ***Other international and instruments***

Another series of binding conventions at international level regards the labour rights. The International Labour Organization (ILO) categorises human trafficking as a form of modern slavery, intricately linked with issues such as forced labour, child labour, and migrant labour. The ILO has set forth standards for States to adhere to, notably the Minimum Age Convention (C138)[5] and Worst Forms of Child Labour

[1] See Footnote 19 above.

[2] See CEDAW (1992) CEDAW General Recommendations No. 19: Violence against Women, 1 February 1992, A/47/38, pp. 3–5.

[3] UN Office of the High Commissioner for Human Rights (OHCHR) (2002) *Recommended Principles and Guidelines on Human Rights and Human Trafficking*, 20 May 2002, E/2002/68/Add.1.

[4] UN General Assembly (2006) Basic Principles and Guidelines on the Right to a Remedy and Reparation for Victims of Gross Violations of International Human Rights Law and Serious Violations of International Humanitarian Law: resolution/adopted by the General Assembly, 21 March 2006, A/RES/60/147.

[5] ILO, Convention concerning Minimum Age for Admission to Employment, Geneva, 1973, Entry into force: 19 Jun 1976.

Convention (C182).[6] Ratification and implementation of these pivotal conventions by State Parties are instrumental in preventing exploitation and diminishing the demand that drives human trafficking. These labour rights conventions, together with the 1926 Convention on Slavery and the 1956 Supplementary Convention on the Abolition of Slavery, the Slave Trade and Institutions and Practices Similar to Slavery, form the legal foundation for the current anti-trafficking laws.

At the regional level, countries in Africa, the Americas, Europe, and South Asia have formulated treaties akin to the Palermo Protocol or the human rights treaties of the United Nations (as detailed in Box 1 above). However, China is not a member of any of these regional institutions. This is not to imply that China has refrained from participating in any regional anti-trafficking mechanisms. Further details regarding this matter will be presented in Section C below.

The most relevant "soft law" formulated by the aforementioned international and regional institutions and pertaining specifically to child trafficking, encompasses the following:

- UNICEF (2006), Guidelines on the Protection of Child Victims of Trafficking
- ASEAN (2007), Criminal Justice Responses to Trafficking in Persons: ASEAN Practitioner Guidelines[7]
- OSCE (2003), OSCE Action Plan to Combat Trafficking in Human Beings[8]
- European Union (2005), EU Plan on Best Practices, Standards and Procedures for Combating and Preventing Trafficking in Human Beings[9]

(4) ***China's commitment***

China has been actively engaging in international and regional anti-trafficking frameworks. The nation has ratified or acceded to the majority of international human rights treaties, including specialised conventions concerning human trafficking, child abduction, and intercountry adoption (see Table 1). Notably, China has timely ratified the Palermo Protocol, the Convention on the Elimination of All Forms of Discrimination Against Women, and the Optional Protocol to the Convention on the Rights of the Child on the Sale of Children, Child Prostitution and Child Pornography. A

[6] ILO, Convention concerning the Prohibition and Immediate Action for the Elimination of the Worst Forms of Child Labour, Geneva, 1999, Entry into force: 19 Nov 2000.

[7] Criminal Justice Responses to Trafficking in Persons: ASEAN Practitioner Guidelines was developed and finalized by the ASEAN Ad-Hoc Working Group on Trafficking in Persons, 25 June 2007, Vientiane, Lao PDR; and endorsed by the 7th ASEAN Senior Officials Meeting on Transnational Crime, Vientiane, Lao PDR, 27 June 2007, retrieved from https://jica-cb-workshop.weebly.com/uploads/8/0/7/2/8072630/criminal_justice_responses_to_trafficking_in_persons.pdf, [accessed 31 July 2019].

[8] OSCE (2003) *OSCE Action Plan to Combat Trafficking in Human Beings*, 24 July 2003, PC.DEC/557, retrieved from: https://www.osce.org/odihr/23866, [accessed 31 July 2019].

[9] European Union (2005), *EU Plan on Best Practices, Standards and Procedures for Combating and Preventing Trafficking in Human Beings*, 9 December 2005, 2005/C 311/01, retrieved from: https://ec.europa.eu/anti-trafficking/eu-policy/council-eu-plan-best-practices-standards-and-procedures-combating-and-preventing_en, [accessed 31 July 2019].

significant recent development was its ratification in 2022 of the ILO conventions concerning forced labour.

By acceding to these treaties, China has assumed obligations to implement them, necessitating measures such as legislative changes, policy reforms, administrative regulations, and other essential actions. For example, in fulfillment of its commitments under CEDAW and CRC-OPSC, the Chinese government has promulgated the Programmes for the Development of Chinese Women and Chinese Children, respectively. These programmes incorporate strategies to prevent and combat human trafficking and to safeguard the rights of women and children. The ratification of these conventions has also precipitated legal reforms within China, such as the amendment in 1997 of the articles related to trafficking in persons in its Criminal Law.

B. **Human rights principles under the "3Ps" paradigm**

A pivotal element of the human rights-based approach entails respecting core principles and standards derived from international human rights law at every facet of the response, across all stages. The ensuing question is: what constitutes the principal aspects and stages in addressing child trafficking? The Palermo Protocol, along with its supplementary documents, presents a lucid and pragmatic framework, comprised of three pillars: prevention, prosecution, and protection—collectively known as the "3Ps" paradigm. These "3Ps" encompass not only the main aspects of anti-trafficking efforts but also delineate the primary stages of child trafficking. Although occasionally extended to the "4Ps", with "partnership" as the fourth "P", this extension denotes a more technical aspect in comparison to its forerunners, namely international and multisectoral cooperation and coordination across the other three stages. Therefore, it is essential to elucidate which human rights principles and standards should guide activities in the stages of crime prevention, offender prosecution, and victim protection.

(1) ***The "3Ps" paradigm for combating trafficking in persons***

The UNODC has thoroughly explained the "3Ps" paradigm—prevention, prosecution, and protection—in a technical assistance tool designed to facilitate the effective implementation of the Palermo Protocol (UNODC 2009). This paradigm outlines a holistic approach towards combating trafficking in persons, encompassing multiple strategies and interventions.

In terms of prevention, a series of comprehensive measures is required. This includes conducting systematic research to understand the root causes of trafficking and developing initiatives to reduce demand. Addressing factors that increase vulnerability to trafficking is crucial, such as strengthening national child protection systems, empowering women and working-age youth, promoting lawful migration, and regulating the labour market. Furthermore, enhancing the capacity of law enforcement officers to identify potential victims promptly and establishing rapid

Table 1 List of international treaties relevant to the issue of child trafficking and China's participation

UN core human rights instruments		
	Signature date of China	Ratification, Accession(a) Date of China
International Covenant on Civil and Political Rights (1966)	05 Oct 1998	
International Covenant on Economic, Social and Cultural Rights (1966)	27 Oct 1997	27 Mar 2001
Convention on the Elimination of All Forms of Racial Discrimination (1965)		29 Dec 1981 (a)
Convention on the Elimination of All Forms of Discrimination against Women (1979)	17 Jul 1980	04 Nov 1980
Convention against Torture and Other Cruel Inhuman or Degrading Treatment or Punishment (1984)	12 Dec 1986	04 Oct 1988
Convention on the Rights of the Child (1989)	29 Aug 1990	02 Mar 1992
Optional Protocol to the Convention on the Rights of the Child on the Sale of Children, Child Prostitution and Child Pornography (2000)	06 Sep 2000	03 Dec 2002
Convention on the Protection of the Rights of All Migrant Workers and Members of Their Families (1990)	–	–
Convention on the Rights of Persons with Disabilities (2006)	30 Mar 2007	01 Aug 2008
Specialist crime control treaties		
Convention for the Suppression of the Traffic in Persons and of the Expression of the Prostitution of Others (1949)		(A)
UN Convention against Transnational Organized Crime (2000)	12 Dec 2000	23 Sep 2003
Protocol to Prevent, Suppress and Punish Trafficking in Persons Especially Women and Children, supplementing the United Nations Convention against Transnational Organized Crime (2000)		8 Feb 2010 (a)
Other international treaties		
Slavery Convention (1926)		22 Apr 1937 (B)
Supplementary Convention on the Abolition of Slavery, the Slave Trade and Institutions and Practices Similar to Slavery (1956)		(C)
Forced Labour Convention (ILO C 29) (1930)		12 Aug 2022
Abolition of Forced Labour Convention (ILO C105) (1957)		12 Aug 2022
Minimum Age Convention (ILO C 138) (1973)		28 Apr 1999

(continued)

Table 1 (continued)

Other international treaties		
Worst Forms of Child Labour Convention (ILO C182) (1999)		08 Aug 2002
Convention of 25 October 1980 on the Civil Aspects of International Child Abduction		(D)
Convention of 29 May 1993 on Protection of Children and Co-operation in Respect of Intercountry Adoption	30 Nov 2000	16 Sep 2005

Note (A): The Convention continues to apply to the Macao Special Administrative Region only
(B): Signed on behalf of the Republic of China on 14 December 1955. In addition, upon resuming the exercise of sovereignty over Hong Kong, China notified the Secretary-General that the Convention will also apply to the Hong Kong Special Administrative Region.
(C): The Convention continues to apply to the Macao Special Administrative Region with effect from 20 December 1999.
(D): This Convention applies to the Special Administrative Regions of Hong Kong and Macao only. Date of entry into force of the Convention for Hong Kong: 1 September 1997; date of entry into force for Macao: 1 March 1999.

response mechanisms for cases of abduction and trafficking are essential components. Given the multidimensional, complex, and evolving nature of the sale of children, establishing comprehensive, proactive, and sustainable prevention strategies is imperative.[10]

Regarding the prosecution aspect, states are required to take measures to align their national legal frameworks with the Palermo Protocol and ensure effective implementation. This alignment involves bolstering national anti-human trafficking legislation and establishing relevant institutions, including specialised police units and judicial structures.

Finally, the protection of trafficking victims is contingent upon their identification. Enhancing the victim identification process is paramount, along with adopting a comprehensive protection and assistance system that can provide personalised support to victims with diverse needs. It is also necessary to implement measures for the rehabilitation and empowerment of victims, ensuring the prevention of re-victimisation. States must also guarantee that international standards are applied in a rights-based and age-sensitive approach to victim protection, regardless of the victims' cooperation with law enforcement.

The United Nations Office on Drugs and Crime (UNODC) has emphasised the importance of two additional pillars crucial for the effective implementation of the Palermo Protocol: national coordination and cooperation, and international cooperation and coordination (UNODC 2009). This approach is also echoed by UNICEF,

[10] UN Secretary-General (2013) Effective prevention strategies in combating the sale and sexual exploitation of children: note by the Secretary-General, 6 August 2013, A/68/275, at para. 7.

referring to 'partnership' as the fourth 'P' in the expanded "4Ps" paradigm (ICAT 2010). Given the multidisciplinary and transnational nature of trafficking in persons, tackling this issue extends beyond the capacity of any single country or police force. It necessitates the active involvement and participation of national institutions across various sectors and civil society organisations. Coordinated efforts are vital to prevent inefficient resource use, incoherent interventions, and other forms of ineffectiveness.

Trafficking in persons, being an international crime, demands cooperation among a range of stakeholders, including states, regional, and international organisations. Such efforts must be orchestrated by international mechanisms and structures, with the UNODC playing a pivotal role in this coordination (UNODC 2009). At the national level, cooperation involves direct engagement with relevant ministries, while at the international level, it includes collaboration with other organisations, all under the coordination of the UNODC and other international mechanisms.

The necessity for coordination and cooperation is not limited to states alone but extends to regional and international organisations. For instance, the European Commission identified "enhanced coordination and cooperation among key actors and policy coherence" as one of the five main priorities for Member States in addressing human trafficking (European Commission 2013). In the Greater Mekong Sub-region, the Coordinated Mekong Ministerial Initiative against Trafficking (COMMIT) and its Member States have integrated elements of cooperation and coordination into their key strategies.[11] Furthermore, numerous international organisations active in the field of trafficking have established partnerships with national ministries, international and regional organisations, NGOs, and other civil society entities, including UNIFEM, UNHCR, IOM, UNDP, UNICEF, UNESCO, among others (ICAT 2010).

(2) ***Human rights principles and guidelines in responding to child trafficking***

Human rights law establishes universal principles and standards that are essential in guiding state policies and programmes when addressing child trafficking, notwithstanding the issue's diversity and complexity. The OHCHR has enumerated a comprehensive list of recommended principles that encompass all facets, of trafficking-related state policies (OHCHR 2010).

In the development and implementation of anti-trafficking policies and measures, certain fundamental human rights principles must be upheld as guiding standards. These principles are essential to ensure that efforts to combat trafficking are both effective and respectful of the rights of those affected, particularly the victims. The key principles are as follows:

- **The primacy of human rights**: States and international agencies must prioritise the human rights of trafficking victims in all efforts to prevent and combat human trafficking. It is also crucial to ensure that anti-trafficking measures do not

[11] See COMMIT (2004) *Memorandum of Understanding on Cooperation against Trafficking in Persons in the Greater Mekong Subregion*, 29 October 2004, retrieved from: http://un-act.org/wp-content/uploads/2015/07/COMMIT_MoU.pdf, [accessed 31 July 2019].

adversely affect the human rights and dignity of persons, especially the rights of trafficking victims.

This principle places the welfare and rights of trafficking victims at the forefront of all anti-trafficking initiatives. It underscores the necessity for these efforts to be human-centred and rights-respecting, avoiding any actions that could further harm or demean victims. This approach ensures that interventions are not only focused on countering trafficking but also on the wellbeing and dignity of those affected by it.

- **Non-discrimination**: All laws and measures related to trafficking must be applied equally to every victim, irrespective of race, sex, language, religion, ethnic or social origin, birth, or other status, including immigration status.

The Non-Discrimination principle is pivotal in ensuring fairness and equity in the treatment of all trafficking victims. This principle serves as a safeguard against biased practices and prejudices, which could manifest in discriminatory conducts or remarks by law enforcement officials towards victims. Such biases can lead to unequal protection and assistance, exacerbating the plight of victims who might already be facing significant challenges.

- **Do no harm to established rights**: Measures to counteract trafficking should not impinge on the established human rights or dignity of individuals, particularly those who have been trafficked.

The "do no harm" principle acts as a critical check against policies or practices that might inadvertently violate the rights or worsen the conditions of trafficking victims. It serves as a reminder that while combating trafficking is essential, it should not be pursued at the expense of the fundamental rights and dignity of the individuals involved, especially the victims.

These principles are not only ethical imperatives but also legal obligations under international human rights law. They serve as a foundation upon which all anti-trafficking strategies should be built, ensuring that the response to this global issue is rooted in a commitment to the protection and promotion of human rights.

In addition, the OHCHR has put forth recommendations that incorporate human rights principles into each phase of combating human trafficking, corresponding to the "3Ps" approach: prevention, prosecution, and protection.

Principles central to the **prevention** strategies include:

- **Addressing demand as a root cause of trafficking:** Strategies and policies targeting trafficking must confront demand as a fundamental cause.

This approach involves understanding and tackling the underlying factors that cultivate the market for trafficking, primarily aiming to reduce exploitation. By focusing on these demand-side dynamics, it becomes possible to diminish the incentives that fuel trafficking operations. This reduction in demand is a critical component in the broader strategy to combat human trafficking, targeting not just the supply of victims but also the factors that drive their exploitation.

- **Interventions to address factors increasing vulnerability:** States and other stakeholders must ensure their interventions target factors that increase vulnerability of certain persons to trafficking, such as inequality, poverty, and all forms of discrimination.

This strategy acknowledges that vulnerability to trafficking frequently stems from broader socio-economic challenges. To prevent trafficking effectively, it's imperative to confront these systemic issues head-on. By doing so, the factors that compel individuals towards high-risk activities, potentially leading to trafficking, can be reduced. Similar to the previous principle, this approach not only addresses the immediate concerns of trafficking criminal activities but also the underlying conditions that facilitate such exploitation.

- **Identifying and addressing public-sector involvement in trafficking:** States are obligated to diligently identify and eradicate any involvement or complicity in trafficking within the public sector. All public officials suspected of trafficking involvement must be thoroughly investigated, prosecuted, and, if found guilty, appropriately sanctioned.

This measure emphasises the importance of integrity and accountability within the public sector. It acknowledges that corruption and complicity within state institutions can facilitate trafficking, and therefore, such malpractices must be rigorously combated to prevent trafficking effectively.

These principles underscore the importance of a proactive and holistic approach to prevention, one that goes beyond immediate measures to address the deeper, systemic issues that enable human trafficking. They highlight the need for comprehensive measures that address both the supply and demand aspects of trafficking, as well as the importance of maintaining integrity within public institutions.

Principles and guidelines central to the **protection** of and assistance to victims include:

- **No detention or prosecution for status-related offences:** Victims of human trafficking shall not face detention, charges, or prosecution for the illegality of their entry or residence in transit and destination countries, nor for their involvement in unlawful activities if such involvement is a direct consequence of their status as trafficked persons.

This guideline emphasises protecting the rights of trafficking victims by acknowledging that their involvement in illegal activities may often stem from coercion or necessity. It ensures that victims are treated with compassion and understanding, rather than being penalised for circumstances beyond their control. This principle is crucial in fostering a sense of security among victims, thereby making them more inclined to cooperate with law enforcement authorities in the fight against trafficking networks. Recognising and addressing the complex dynamics of victimhood not only upholds justice but also enhances the effectiveness of anti-trafficking efforts.

- **Protection and assistance for victims:** States shall ensure that trafficked persons are protected from further exploitation and harm and have access to adequate physical and psychological care. Legal and other forms of assistance should be provided throughout any legal proceedings against suspected traffickers.

This principle implies the inherently traumatic feature of trafficking experience and underscores the need for a holistic approach to victim assistance. It calls for the provision of both medical and psychological care, in addition to legal support, including temporary residence permits, to facilitate thorough rehabilitation and recovery. Crucially, this principle acknowledges that anti-trafficking efforts extend beyond the immediate act of rescue. This holistic method acknowledges the multi-faceted impact of trafficking on victims and aims to address their needs in a manner that encompasses all aspects of their wellbeing. Such an approach ensures that survivors receive not just immediate relief, but also long-term support, aiding in their journey towards full recovery and reintegration into society.

- **The special rights and needs of children:** Children who are victims of trafficking must be recognised as such, with their best interests being a primary consideration at all times. They should receive appropriate assistance and protection, taking into full account their specific vulnerabilities, rights, and needs.

This guideline recognises the distinct vulnerabilities of child victims and advocates for customised protective measures that place the utmost priority on their safety, well-being, and developmental needs. It underscores the necessity of crafting responses that are specifically designed to cater to the unique circumstances of children affected by trafficking. This approach ensures that interventions not only safeguard children from further harm but also support their holistic development and recovery in a nurturing and considerate environment.

- **Safe and voluntary return:** The safe and voluntary return of trafficked persons should be ensured.

This principle advocates for the rights of trafficking victims to return to their home countries safely and of their own volition, respecting their autonomy and ensuring their reintegration process is secure and dignified.

Each of these principles plays a vital role in the comprehensive protection and assistance of trafficking victims, ensuring their rights and needs are prioritized and addressed in the aftermath of their traumatic experiences.

Key principles and guidance to the **prosecution** include:

- **Criminalisation of trafficking:** States should adopt legislative and other measures to criminalise trafficking, its component acts, and related conduct.

This calls for the establishment of a comprehensive legal framework that clearly defines and penalises all forms of human trafficking. By criminalising not only trafficking itself but also its component acts and related conduct, states can more effectively combat the entire spectrum of trafficking activities.

- **Effective investigation, prosecution and adjudication**: States are tasked with effectively investigating, prosecuting, and adjudicating trafficking cases, including its component acts and related conduct, whether perpetrated by government or non-State actors.

This principle highlights the necessity for a robust legal process that ensures accountability for all perpetrators of trafficking, irrespective of their status or affiliation. Effective prosecution is a crucial deterrent against trafficking and plays a vital role in delivering justice for victims. To achieve this, it requires skilled investigations, impartial and thorough legal proceedings, and competent adjudication. In this context, specialised training for law enforcement officers becomes essential. Such training equips them with the necessary skills to identify trafficking cases, gather evidence effectively, and navigate the complexities of trafficking crimes. This, in turn, strengthens the overall capacity of the judicial system to respond to trafficking with the seriousness and expertise it demands.

- **Effective and appropriate sanctions**: States must enforce effective and appropriate sanctions against those found guilty of trafficking or related offences.

The imposition of sanctions serves as a critical deterrent and a means of justice for victims. It's important that these sanctions are proportional to the severity of the crime, sending a strong message about the seriousness of trafficking offences. Proportional sanctions not only ensure that justice is served but also reinforce the legal system's commitment to combating trafficking. Concurrently, this approach upholds the fundamental human rights of the perpetrators, ensuring that punishments are just and fair. This balanced method aids in upholding the rule of law and bolstering public confidence in the justice system's ability to effectively tackle such egregious crimes.

- **Asset confiscation and disposal**: In appropriate cases, states shall freeze and confiscate the assets of those involved in trafficking, using the confiscated assets to support and compensate victims where possible.

Asset confiscation targets the financial incentives that drive trafficking operations. By diverting these assets to aid victims, states can both disrupt the economic foundations of trafficking networks and provide essential resources for victim support and recovery.

- **Access to remedies**: States are responsible for ensuring that trafficked persons have access to effective and appropriate legal remedies.

Remedies serve to affirm the status of trafficked persons both as victims of crime and of human rights violations. This principle guarantees that victims have the opportunity to seek and obtain redress for the suffering they have endured, utilising all requisite legal procedures. Access to such legal remedies is a fundamental aspect in the restoration of the rights and dignity of trafficking victims. It provides them with a crucial pathway towards achieving justice and embarking on the journey to recovery.

Moreover, in cases involving children, states are obliged to align their decisions with the four general principles of international children's rights law as stipulated in the CRC. These principles include non-discrimination (Article 2), the best interests of the child (Article 3.1), the child's rights to life and development (Article 6), and the child's rights to be heard (Article 12).[12] Additionally, UNICEF has provided a set of guiding principles specifically tailored to protect child victims of trafficking (refer to UNICEF Regional Office for CEE/CIS 2006). These principles are vital for consideration in both international and internal trafficking scenarios involving children. The incorporation of these principles in anti-trafficking strategies ensures that responses are child-focused and rights-based, addressing the unique needs and vulnerabilities of child victims.

- **Non-discrimination** (CRC, Article 2):

  States are obligated to respect and ensure the rights of every child as outlined in the CRC, without any form of discrimination. This includes ensuring children are not discriminated against based on their own or their parents' or legal guardians' race, colour, sex, language, religion, political or other opinion, national, ethnic or social origin, property, disability, birth, or other status. Furthermore, states must take all necessary measures to protect children from discrimination or punishment that may arise from the status, activities, opinions, or beliefs of their parents, legal guardians, or family members.

- **The best interest of the child** (CRC, Article 3.1):

  In all actions concerning children, whether undertaken by public or private social welfare institutions, courts, administrative authorities, or legislative bodies, the best interests of the child must be the primary consideration. This principle ensures that the welfare of the child is always placed at the forefront in any decision-making process.

- **Right of the Child to be Heard** (CRC, Article 12):

  Every child has the right to express their views freely in all matters affecting them, and these views must be given due consideration. States Parties are responsible for ensuring that a child capable of forming their own views is given the opportunity to express those views, with the weight given to these views being proportional to the child's age and maturity.

- **Child's Right to Privacy** (CRC, Article 16):

  Children are entitled to protection from arbitrary or unlawful interference with their privacy, family, home, or correspondence, as well as protection against unlawful attacks on their honour and reputation. This principle safeguards the personal and reputational integrity of the child against any form of violation or abuse.

These principles must be upheld at every stage of combating child trafficking, and they become particularly crucial once a child victim has been identified or rescued. During these critical moments, it is essential that all actions and interventions adhere

[12] UN Committee on the Rights of the Child (CRC) (2003) *General Comment No. 5 (2003): General measures of implementation of the Convention on the Rights of the Child* (arts. 4, 42 and 44, para. 6), 27 November 2003, CRC/GC/2003/5, para.12.

strictly to these guidelines, ensuring the child's rights and welfare are at the forefront of any response. Respect for non-discrimination, prioritisation of the child's best interests, acknowledgment of their right to be heard, and protection of their right to privacy are fundamental in providing a safe, supportive, and effective environment for the child's recovery and rehabilitation. Adherence to these principles is instrumental in facilitating the healing and empowerment of child victims, and it plays a critical role in preventing secondary victimisation. By ensuring that responses to child trafficking are grounded in respect, understanding, and a child-centric approach, we can significantly reduce the risk of further trauma and harm. This approach is vital for creating a supportive environment where the child can recover and rebuild their life with dignity and security.

C. **Mechanisms in combating child trafficking**

Undoubtedly, the responsibility of combating human trafficking primarily rests with states. However, the complex and often transnational nature of this issue poses significant challenges that transcend individual national capabilities. Consequently, international cooperation becomes imperative, not only for incidents that cross borders but also for trafficking activities confined within a single nation's boundaries. Then, what are the main mechanisms dedicated to combating human trafficking, particularly in the sectors of victim protection? More specifically, what mechanisms are influencing China's efforts in combating child trafficking?

(1) ***International institutions***

The most significant institutions engaged in addressing human trafficking at the international level have been previously outlined in earlier sections. The United Nations Office on Drugs and Crime stands at the forefront of the global effort against human trafficking. Established in 1997, UNODC operates worldwide, specialising in offering legal and technical assistance to Member States. Its work spans combating organised crime, including trafficking, corruption, drug abuse, and terrorism. The assistance rendered by UNODC encompasses three main areas: capacity-building technical cooperation projects for Member States, research and analytical work to broaden understanding and disseminate knowledge, and legal assistance in the ratification, implementation of international treaties, and development of domestic legal frameworks.[13] Under Article 32 of the United Nations Convention against Transnational Organized Crime, the Conference of the Parties to the Convention was established, which functions to enhance the capacity of States Parties and oversees the implementation of the Convention and its Protocols. In 2018, an intergovernmental mechanism for reviewing the implementation of the Convention was

[13] See UNODC, "About UNODC", retrieved from https://www.unodc.org/unodc/en/about-unodc/index.html?ref=menutop [accessed on 1 July 2019].

introduced.[14] This mechanism, operating under the Conference's authority, scrutinises each State Party's adherence to the Convention and its Protocols through self-assessment questionnaires completed voluntarily by the States Parties.[15]

Another pivotal international mechanism in the fight against human trafficking is the network of UN human rights organs, led by the OHCHR. While there are no human rights treaties exclusively dedicated to human trafficking, many existing treaties address this issue as a severe form of human rights violation. Furthermore, since 2004, the appointment of a Special Rapporteur on trafficking in persons has significantly bolstered these efforts. The primary role of these human rights mechanisms is to develop principles and guidelines that address trafficking from a rights-based perspective, as introduced in the previous section. These mechanisms, complementing the work of the UNODC, which primarily focuses on crime control, place a strong emphasis on the rights of trafficking victims and those vulnerable to trafficking.

The multifaceted nature of child trafficking has led numerous UN agencies to address this issue through various non-binding documents, each contributing its unique professional perspective. The International Organization for Migration (IOM) assists States in combating migrant smuggling and trafficking through specialised programmes, training, and research. The United Nations Children's Fund (UNICEF) identifies child trafficking and the sale of children as grave violations of children's rights, addressing a broad spectrum of issues from protection against violence and exploitation to education and gender equality (refer to UNICEF 2006; UNICEF Regional Office for CEE/CIS 2006, 2009; UNICEF Innocenti Research Centre 2009; UNICEF East Asia and Pacific Regional Office 2009). The United Nations Development Programme (UNDP) plays a crucial role with a focus on prevention strategies through capacity building, local development initiatives, and gender equality promotion (UNDP 2004; Laczko and Danailova-Trainor 2009). The World Health Organization (WHO) tackles human trafficking from a health perspective, prioritising the needs of trafficking victims (WHO, Zimmerman, and Watts 2003; WHO 2012). The United Nations High Commissioner for Refugees (UNHCR) addresses human trafficking with a particular focus on people smuggling and the protection of refugees and asylum-seekers.[16]

Recognising that the battle against child trafficking is a multi-sectoral task, effective counteraction necessitates a coordinated approach among various international organisations. To meet this need, the Inter-Agency Coordination Group against Trafficking in Persons (ICAT) was established in 2007. Coordinated by the

[14] UNODC (2018) Resolution 9/1: Establishment of the Mechanism for the Review of the Implementation of the United Nations Convention against Transnational Organized Crime and the Protocols thereto, retrieved from https://www.unodc.org/documents/treaties/UNTOC/Review%20Mechanism/Resolution/English.pdf, [accessed on 1 July 2019].

[15] Ibid., at Section B and Section and para. 52.

[16] UN High Commissioner for Refugees (UNHCR), Guidelines on International Protection No. 7: The Application of Article 1A(2) of the 1951 Convention and/or 1967 Protocol Relating to the Status of Refugees to Victims of Trafficking and Persons At Risk of Being Trafficked, 7 April 2006, HCR/GIP/06/07, available at: https://www.refworld.org/docid/443679fa4.html [accessed 29 January 2024].

UNODC, ICAT brings together the efforts of diverse UN entities such as ILO, IOM, OHCHR, UNHCR, and UNICEF. This collaboration ensures a more unified and efficient approach to combating trafficking. In addition to these entities, ICAT includes members such as the Department of Peacekeeping Operations (DPKO), International Criminal Police Organization (Interpol), Joint United Nations Programme on HIV/AIDS (UNAIDS), UNDP, United Nations Educational, Scientific and Cultural Organization (UNESCO), United Nations Interregional Crime and Justice Research Institute (UNICRI), UN Women, and the World Bank. This diverse membership, again, underscores the multi-faceted nature of anti-trafficking efforts. ICAT operates with a gender and age-sensitive, human rights-based approach, providing a platform for stakeholders at national, regional, and international levels to exchange information, experiences, and best practices in anti-trafficking activities. This collaboration promotes the effective and efficient utilisation of resources and contributes significantly to the implementation of international standards and instruments vital to the prevention of human trafficking, as well as the protection and rehabilitation of its victims.

(2) ***Regional, subregional, and bilateral mechanisms***

At the regional level in Asia, while there are no binding treaties specifically dedicated to human rights or anti-trafficking, a significant anti-trafficking mechanism exists in which China participates: The Coordinated Mekong Ministerial Initiative against Trafficking (COMMIT). Established in 2004, COMMIT was formed through the signing of a Memorandum of Understanding (MoU) by six countries in the Greater Mekong Sub-region (GMS)—Cambodia, the People's Republic of China, the Lao People's Democratic Republic (Lao PDR), Myanmar, Thailand, and Viet Nam. This intergovernmental initiative aims at establishing cooperation in the implementation of international anti-trafficking standards and enhancing both bilateral and multilateral efforts among governments and NGOs in the GMS. The COMMIT Process facilitates a coordinated approach to combat human trafficking, wherein China has actively engaged in developing bilateral cooperation mechanisms with other GMS countries, details of which are outlined in Table 2.

To support governments and various stakeholders in Southeast Asia in their efforts against human trafficking, the UNDP carried out a five-year regional project, the UN Action for Cooperation against Trafficking in Persons (UN-ACT), spanning from 2014 to 2018. This project continued and expanded upon the work of the United Nations Inter-Agency Project on Human Trafficking (UNIAP), which had been operational in the Greater Mekong Sub-region since 2000. Notably, UNIAP served as the secretariat for the COMMIT up until 2013. COMMIT operates based on annual work plans and Sub-regional Plans of Actions (SPAs), which are then adapted into National Plans of Actions (NPAs) by each member country. This structured approach ensures a coordinated and comprehensive regional response to the complex issue of human trafficking.

The inaugural Sub-regional Plan of Action under COMMIT, known as COMMIT SPA I (–2007), was adopted in 2005 and included twelve Project Proposal Concepts

Table 2 Bilateral agreements on combating trafficking in persons between China and other GMS Members

Bilateral agreements	Adoption date
MoU between the Government of the Union of Myanmar and the Government of the People's Republic of China on Strengthening the Cooperation on Combating Human Trafficking	11 Nov 2009
Agreement between the Government of the Socialist Republic of Vietnam and the Government of the People's Republic of China on Strengthening Cooperation on Preventing and Combating Human Trafficking	15 Sep 2010
Agreement between the Government of the Lao People's Democratic Republic and the Government of the People's Republic of China on Cooperation in Preventing and Combating Trafficking in Persons	1 Sep 2014
MoU between the Government of the Kingdom of Thailand and the Government of the People's Republic of China on Cooperation in Prevention and Suppression of Trafficking in Persons	1 Nov 2018

(PPCs). This was followed by COMMIT SPA II (2008–2010), which received ministerial approval from the six COMMIT member countries in December 2007, representing a progression from its predecessor. The third iteration, COMMIT SPA III (2011–2013), adopted in 2010, introduced structural modifications to the action plan, adopting a less prescriptive approach to activities, acknowledging the need for flexibility in each country's approach. The fourth plan, COMMIT SPA IV (2015–2018), agreed upon in 2015 and intended to guide the COMMIT process through 2018, places a stronger emphasis on achieving tangible outcomes that enhance the competencies of individuals and institutions. It also underscores the importance of involving civil society in monitoring the activities of key institutions. However, it is noteworthy that the renewal of the SPA ceased, though other core activities of COMMIT continue to be operational.

Annually, COMMIT Senior Officials Meetings (SOM) serve as a platform for peer review, where officials from the Greater Mekong Sub-region (GMS) evaluate the progress of the past year and set objectives for the future. Additionally, every three years, the COMMIT Inter-Ministerial Meetings (IMM) convene responsible Ministers from each member country to provide overarching guidance, reaffirm their commitment to the COMMIT objectives, and endorse future Sub-Regional Plans of Action. These meetings are complemented by various workshops and trainings conducted under the COMMIT Sub-Regional Plans of Action, ensuring continuous capacity building and implementation of anti-trafficking strategies.

The COMMIT Process, as enshrined in its Memorandum of Understanding, adopts a human rights-based approach and highlights the specific vulnerability of women and children, thus advocating for their special protection. It draws upon key international human rights documents, including the Universal Declaration of Human Rights, the Convention on the Rights of the Child, the Convention on the Elimination of All Forms of Discrimination Against Women, the Palermo Convention and its Protocol, and the fundamental conventions of the International Labour Organization.

Since its establishment in 2004, the COMMIT Process has significantly contributed to the enhancement of China's efforts in combating human trafficking. This initiative has served as an essential platform for China, enabling it to build and strengthen cooperative networks with its neighbours and beyond. It has also played a pivotal role in facilitating China's accession to the Palermo Protocol. Through the COMMIT Process, China has improved its capacity to tackle cross-border trafficking, benefiting from increased cooperation with other nations and international bodies. Domestically, the initiative has spurred advancements in China's response to trafficking in persons, evidenced by substantial policy and legal reforms. Notable milestones include the issuance of China's first National Plan of Action on Combating Trafficking in Women and Children (2008–2012) in December 2007, the execution of specialised police actions targeting the trafficking of women and children during the same period, and significant legislative amendments concerning the trafficking of these vulnerable groups.

2 State's Obligations Under International Law

One of the key aspects of combating child trafficking through the human rights-based approach is the engagement of the State's obligations under international law. As the primary duty-bearer, the State is tasked with implementing and enforcing international treaties, holding the accountability for their violations. The responsibilities of the State in child trafficking scenarios can be dissected into two primary categories. Firstly, the State is explicitly mandated to prohibit child trafficking. This includes the prevention of the crime, the prosecution of perpetrators, and the imposition of suitable penalties. Secondly, the State is charged with a broader responsibility to respect, protect, fulfil, and promote human and children's rights. The infringement of these rights is frequently an underlying factor that contributes to the occurrence of child trafficking.

The basis for the State's obligations is deeply entrenched in the international legal frameworks, comprising specific treaties, conventions, general international law, customary law, and universally recognised principles. Sources of the State's obligations relevant to child trafficking include international treaties and bilateral agreements referenced in earlier sections, alongside international customary law, general legal principles, and jurisprudence from international tribunals.

The spectrum of legal obligations varies in its imperatives. Certain provisions are unequivocally mandatory, such as the criminalisation and prosecution of child trafficking offences. Others mandate States to actively engage in efforts, for example, to "endeavour to undertake measures [...] to prevent and combat trafficking in persons".[17] Additionally, some provisions are presented as considerations for States, such as measures aimed at the comprehensive recovery of trafficking victims.[18] A

[17] Palermo Protocol, at Article 9 (2).

[18] Palermo Protocol, at Article 6 (3).

State incurs legal liability upon the violation of these international duties or failure to enact preventative or responsive measures as required. Liability also extends to actions or omissions related to child trafficking carried out by State organs or entities acting with State sanction.

A. **Obligations of States in responding to child trafficking**

The Palermo Protocol and the CRC-OPSC delineate precise legal responsibilities for State Parties in combating child trafficking. These obligations are further expounded upon in the Commentary on the Recommended Principles and Guidelines on Human Rights and Human Trafficking of the OHCHR (2010), as well as in the UNICEF Reference Guide on Protecting the Rights of Child Victims of Trafficking in Europe (UNICEF Regional Office for CEE/CIS 2006). They are sorted into three main aspects corresponding to prevention, protection and prosecution, with a leading principle of the best interest of the child.

- *The obligation to make the best interest of the child a primary consideration in all actions concerning children*

First of all, in addressing the issue of child trafficking, it is imperative for States to ensure that all measures undertaken, whether by state agencies or private entities and organisations, prioritise the best interest of the child as a primary consideration (UNICEF 2006, p. 30). This principle necessitates that any potential conflicts between the interests of individual children or groups of children, and those of other children or the general child population, be meticulously resolved on a case-by-case basis. This involves a careful balancing of all interests to reach an appropriate compromise. Similarly, when the rights of others may conflict with a child's best interests, a harmonious solution should be sought. In instances where such harmonisation proves unattainable, authorities and decision-makers are required to conduct a thorough analysis and weigh the rights involved, ensuring the child's best interests remain a paramount concern.[19]

The assessment of what constitutes the child's best interest must consider various factors, including but not limited to, the child's own views, their identity, the importance of preserving the family environment and maintaining familial relations, as well as ensuring the child's protection, care, safety, development and addressing any vulnerabilities. Additionally, the child's right to education must be taken into account. These considerations may sometimes conflict in specific cases. For example, when determining whether to reunite a trafficked child with their original family, the value of maintaining the family unit may be at odds with the imperative to protect the child from potential violence or abuse by family members. In such scenarios, the decision must tilt in favour of what best serves the child's interests.[20]

Prevention of trafficking

[19] UN Committee on the Rights of the Child (CRC) (2013) General comment No. 14 (2013) on the right of the child to have his or her best interests taken as a primary consideration (Article. 3, para. 1), 29 May 2013, CRC /C/GC/14, para. 39.

[20] Ibid., para 81.

- *The obligation to prevent child trafficking*

By ratifying or acceding to the CRC, the CRC-OPSC, and the Palermo Protocol, State Parties commit to preventing child trafficking.[21] This commitment includes the adoption of preventive measures encompassing legislation, administrative actions, social policies, and programmes. Efforts must also extend to public dissemination, awareness-raising activities, and the training of relevant practitioners, including lawmakers, police officers, and medical workers (UNODC 2004, p. 295; UNICEF 2006, p. 30).

- *The obligation to address demand*

States Parties and relevant actors, where appropriate, are mandated to address the root causes of child trafficking by actively working to reduce the demand that fosters trafficking and exploitation of children.[22] According to Principle 4 on Human rights and Human Trafficking, demand is recognised as a fundamental cause of trafficking. Guideline 7 further emphasises that prevention strategies must consider demand as a primary factor and encourages States to analyse what drives demand for all forms of exploitation. Often, this demand is influenced by discriminatory practices based on gender, age, ethnicity, or other statuses. To effectively counteract this, human rights-based strategies should aim to challenge and change discriminatory attitudes, cultures, and traditions. Furthermore, the development and implementation of laws and policies are instrumental in influencing the demand for trafficked children. While neither the Palermo Protocol nor the CRC-OPSC explicitly mandates it, criminalising those who knowingly utilise the services of exploited victims emerges as a viable strategy for reducing demand (OHCHR 2010, p. 102; UNODC 2004, p. 297).

- *The obligation to address vulnerability to trafficking*

The obligation to address vulnerability to trafficking requires States and intergovernmental organisations to tackle the factors that heighten the vulnerability of individuals or groups of children to trafficking. These factors encompass, among others, inequality, poverty, and all forms of discrimination (OHCHR 2010, p. 105). To mitigate vulnerability, it is imperative for States to actively address these underlying issues, including poverty reduction, combating inequality, addressing gender-based discrimination, and protecting women from violence. Guideline 7 on Human rights and Human Trafficking recommends several specific strategies, such as the development of programmes providing livelihood opportunities for traditionally marginalised groups, enhancing access to education for children, ensuring compulsory birth registration, and revising policies that may inadvertently lead individuals to undertake risky decisions.

In particular, it is essential to recognise that the vulnerability of children to trafficking can be significantly influenced by their family situation and socio-economic background. Thus, measures to reduce vulnerability must be tailored to address

[21] CRC, at Article 35, CRC-OPSC, at Article 9, and Palermo Protocol, at Article 9.

[22] Palermo Protocol, at Article 9.5, CRC-OPSC at Preamble.

the diverse and often disproportionate impact on children from different environments. Understanding the nuanced nature of vulnerability—its specific forms and root causes—is crucial for States to devise and implement effective and appropriate responses (OHCHR 2010, p. 105).

- *The obligation to identify and eradicate public-sector involvement in trafficking*

Complicity within the public sector in the context of child trafficking significantly undermines public trust in the rule of law, contributes to the demand for and the illicit market of trafficked children, and facilitates the activities of traffickers and criminal syndicates. Therefore, under Principle 6 on Human Right and Human Trafficking, States are required to diligently exercise due diligence to identify, eradicate, investigate, and sanction any involvement or complicity in trafficking by public-sector (OHCHR 2010, p. 117).

Protection of and assistance to victims

- *The obligation to identify victims*

Accurate identification of victims is a prerequisite for providing effective protection to them. Although the major international legal frameworks on trafficking do not explicitly mandate States to undertake positive measures for victim identification, the Principles and Guidelines on Human Rights and Human Trafficking establish a clear obligation for States to do so, as specified in Guideline 2. This Guideline underscores the critical need to accurately differentiate victims of trafficking from individuals in similar situations, such as those involved in migrant smuggling. In addition, Principle 10 explicitly states that "[C]hildren who are victims of trafficking shall be identified as such". In cases where a victim's age is uncertain and there are reasons to believe the individual is a child, the default assumption should be that the victim is a child. Until the victim's age can be verified, they should be treated as a child, receiving all necessary special protection measures (OHCHR 2010, pp. 162–163; UNICEF 2006, pp. 14–15). The process for identifying child victims of trafficking should take a pro-active approach (UNICEF 2006, p. 14), that is to be independent of the identification, prosecution, or detection of traffickers or criminals,[23] and the efforts must be conducted swiftly to ensure the immediate protection of the child.[24] This distinction is vital to protect victims from further human rights abuses, to prevent their prosecution for offences committed as a direct result of being trafficked, and to provide them with adequate assistance.

- *The obligation of protection and assistance*

---

[23] Palermo Protocol, at Article 3.

[24] See, for example, UN Office of the High Commissioner for Human Rights (OHCHR), (2002) *Recommended Principles and Guidelines on Human Rights and Human Trafficking*, 20 May 2002, E/2002/68/Add.1, at Guideline 8.2. UN Human Rights Council (2009) *Trafficking in Persons, Especially Women and Children*, 17 June 2009, A/HRC/RES/11/3, at para. 3. UNICEF (2006) *Guidelines on the Protection of Child Victims of Trafficking*, p. 33.

Under the mandates of Article 8 of the CRC-OPSC, Article 6 of the Palermo Protocol, and Principle 8 on Human Rights and Human Trafficking, States are required to safeguard trafficked persons from further exploitation and harm. This obligation extends to providing victims with safe shelter, adequate medical and psychological care, and legal as well as other forms of assistance throughout the duration of any criminal, civil, or other actions against suspected traffickers. Importantly, Principles 8 and 9 reinforce that the provision of such protection and assistance must not be contingent upon the victim's ability or willingness to participate in legal proceedings.

To effectively meet these obligations, the measures of protection and assistance must be specifically tailored to address the unique needs and vulnerabilities of children. In line with this, UNICEF (2006, p. 16) stipulates that upon the identification of a child victim, a guardian should be promptly appointed by a competent authority. This guardian is tasked with supporting the child throughout the entire process, ensuring a durable solution that aligns with the child's best interests is both identified and implemented. Furthermore, UNICEF (2006, p. 30) and UNODC (2004, p. 290) highlight the necessity for States to adopt proactive measures facilitating the recovery of children from abuse experienced during trafficking or in other contexts. Such measures include providing child victims with accommodation that is both safe and appropriate for their age and specific needs. Additionally, throughout legal proceedings, it is imperative that any direct contact between child victims and suspected offenders is strictly avoided to protect the child's well-being (UNODC 2004, p. 290).

- *The obligation of no prosecution for status-related offences*

The obligation to refrain from prosecuting trafficked persons for status-related offences is clearly articulated in Principle 7 of the Human Rights and Human Trafficking guidelines. It stipulates that trafficked individuals should not face detention, charges, or prosecution for illegal entry or residence in transit or destination countries, nor for their involvement in unlawful activities if such involvement is a direct result of their being trafficked. This principle is further supported by Guideline 2.5, which underscores the importance of swiftly and accurately identifying trafficked persons to ensure they are not wrongfully prosecuted for immigration breaches or forced activities stemming from their trafficking circumstances.[25] This approach, advocating for legal measures to eliminate prosecution for status-related offences, is endorsed by UNICEF (2006, p. 20) and other relevant UN entities,[26] reinforcing the call for protective legislation tailored to the unique conditions of trafficked persons.

Prosecution

- *The obligation of criminalisation*

---

[25] UN Office of the High Commissioner for Human Rights (OHCHR) (2002) *Recommended Principles and Guidelines on Human Rights and Human Trafficking*, 20 May 2002, E/2002/68/Add.1, at Guideline 4.5.

[26] See, for example, UN General Assembly (2009) *Trafficking in Women and Girls*, 30 January 2009, A/RES/63/156, at para. 12.

A central and non-negotiable obligation for all State parties to the Palermo Protocol, as highlighted by UNODC (2004, p. 269), is to "adopt appropriate legislative and other measures necessary to establish, as criminal offences, trafficking, its component acts and related conduct" within their domestic legal frameworks.[27] This includes a clear and comprehensive definition and criminalisation of trafficking in children, aligning with the definition provided in Article 3 of the Protocol, regardless of its transnational nature or the involvement of an organised criminal group (Gallagher 2010; OHCHR 2010, p. 186). The domestic legal definition need not be identical to that of Article 3 of the Protocol but should be sufficiently similar to facilitate effective international cooperation in investigations and prosecutions (UNODC 2004, p. 269). A parallel requirement for criminalising the sale of children is detailed in Article 3.1 of the CRC-OPSC.

Criminal liability extends to both natural and legal persons involved in trafficking, including those who commit, attempt, assist as an accomplice, or orchestrate the trafficking offences.[28] Relevant offences encompass exploitation of prostitution or other forms of sexual exploitation, forced labour or services, slavery or practices akin to slavery, servitude, debt bondage, and enforced prostitution.[29] It is stipulated that only intentional actions be subject to criminalisation (UNODC 2004, p. 276).

In addition, Article 3.1 of the CRC-OPSC mandates the criminalisation of specific offences directly associated with trafficking and the sale of children. These offences include offering, delivering, or accepting a child for sexual exploitation, organ transfer for profit, and forced labour; intermediating in the illegal adoption of a child under false pretenses; and engaging in the procurement or provision of a child for prostitution.

- *Effective investigation, prosecution, and adjudication*

Principle 13 on Human Rights and Human Trafficking mandates States to conduct effective investigations, prosecutions, and adjudications of trafficking crimes, inclusive of its component acts and related conduct. This obligation, underscored by international law, compels States to approach trafficking cases with "due diligence" (Gallagher 2010, p. 382). Furthermore, Principle 2 reinforces this mandate, asserting that States bear the responsibility to diligently investigate and prosecute traffickers as part of their international obligations.

Moreover, Principle 13 extends the duty of investigation and prosecution to offences associated with trafficking. This includes sexual exploitation, forced labour or services, slavery or practices akin to slavery, servitude, debt bondage, the worst

[27] UN Office of the High Commissioner for Human Rights (OHCHR) (2002) *Recommended Principles and Guidelines on Human Rights and Human Trafficking*, 20 May 2002, E/2002/68/Add.1, at Principle 12.

[28] Palermo Protocol, at Article 5.2. See also, the UN Office of the High Commissioner for Human Rights (OHCHR) (2002) *Recommended Principles and Guidelines on Human Rights and Human Trafficking*, 20 May 2002, E/2002/68/Add.1, at Guideline 4.2. Also, CRC-OPSC, at Article3.2.

[29] Palermo Protocol, at Article 3. See also, the UN Office of the High Commissioner for Human Rights (OHCHR) (2002) *Recommended Principles and Guidelines on Human Rights and Human Trafficking*, 20 May 2002, E/2002/68/Add.1, at Guideline 4.1.

forms of child labour, and forced marriage (OHCHR 2010, p. 193). The principle explicitly stipulates that the obligation for an effective investigation applies not only to violations perpetrated by government entities but also to those committed by non-state actors.

- *The obligation to impose sanctions*

Effective sanction is a key component of prosecution. According to Principle 15 on Human Rights and Human Trafficking, sanctions must be effective and proportionate, applicable to both individuals and legal persons found guilty of trafficking or of its component or related offences. This requirement is further detailed in Guideline 4.3, urging States to enact laws that prescribe "effective and proportional criminal penalties". Moreover, Guideline 4.3 advises States to consider imposing harsher penalties for cases involving aggravating circumstances, such as the trafficking of children or offences conducted by or with the involvement of State officials. This layered approach underscores the necessity for a comprehensive legal framework that not only penalises trafficking activities but also escalates sanctions in instances of severe exploitation or state complicity.

- *The obligation to seize and confiscate assets derived from trafficking*

Principle 16 on Human Right and Human Trafficking mandates that States must "freeze and confiscate the assets of individuals and legal persons involved in trafficking". Further elaborated by Guideline 4.4, this principle not only requires the seizure and confiscation of assets but also directs States to allocate these confiscated proceeds towards supporting and compensating victims of trafficking. Additionally, it encourages the consideration of establishing "a compensation fund for victims of trafficking", with the utilisation of confiscated assets to finance such a fund. This obligation ensures that the consequences for trafficking are stringent and that the victims receive necessary compensation through the assets derived from these illicit activities.

- *The obligation to provide remedy*

States are required to provide remedies to victims of trafficking as a means of addressing the human rights violations and harms they have endured. This obligation encompasses several dimensions, particularly in the context of child trafficking, which inherently constitutes a violation of human rights. International law firmly establishes that States must "provide a domestic legal remedy to victims of violations of international human rights and humanitarian law norms committed in its territory" (OHCHR 2010, p. 224). States are held legally accountable for any human rights violations within their jurisdiction, whether these arise from direct involvement in such offences or from a failure to prevent misconduct by private actors (OHCHR 2010, pp. 223–224). Indeed, the entitlement to an effective remedy is a core human rights principle, explicitly acknowledged in various international human rights instruments, such as the Universal Declaration of Human Rights (Article 8), the ICCPR (Article 2), the CERD (Article 14), the European Convention on Human

Rights (Article 13), and the Basic Principles and Guidelines on the Right to a Remedy and Reparation.

Furthermore, the right to access remedies is also enshrined in treaties specific to trafficking. Legal frameworks within both human rights treaties and international criminal law stipulate the State's duty to provide remedies to trafficking victims. Principle 17 on Human Rights and Human Trafficking and Guideline 9 specifically state that "States shall ensure trafficked persons have access to effective and appropriate legal remedies". Such remedies encompass restitution, compensation, rehabilitation, satisfaction, and guarantees of non-repetition (OHCHR 2010, p. 230). The Palermo Protocol (Article 6.6) and the CRC-OPSC (Article 9.4) further obligate States to facilitate compensation for victims within their domestic legal systems, underscoring the importance of remedies for the sale of children and related offences. Thus, the failure of a State to offer remedies not only constitutes a violation of human rights but also represents a breach of its treaty obligations under the Palermo Protocol and the CRC-OPSC.

B. **Responsibility of States**

States have a responsibility under international law in three circumstances (Gallagher 2010). First of all, it is a general principle of international law that "every internationally wrongful act of a State entails the international responsibility of that State".[30] Therefore, States will be held legally responsible for actions or omissions that breach international human rights law, proving that the wrongful conduct is committed by any State organ or any person or entity which has that status, as well as when a person or entity acts with governmental authority.[31] Given that child trafficking constitutes a crime prohibited by international law, a State is directly accountable if any act or omission related to child trafficking is executed by its State organs or by any individual or entity acting under its authority.

Secondly, a State's legal responsibility is invoked upon breaching obligations stemming from binding international agreements. These obligations not only prohibit States from engaging in violations but also mandate them to actively implement measures that fulfil, respect, protect, and promote human rights. In this context, a State's failure to prevent or combat child trafficking as mandated incurs legal responsibility (OHCHR 2014).

Lastly, the concept of "due diligence" introduces a scenario where a State could be liable for the actions of private parties if it neglects to take necessary preventative measures or to appropriately penalise the perpetrators of human rights violations. This principle emphasises the State's obligation not only to act against direct violations by its organs or those acting with governmental authority but also to prevent, investigate, and respond to human rights abuses committed within its jurisdiction by private actors (ILC 2001, p. 38). A failure to avert a foreseeable human rights violation

---

[30] UN General Assembly (2002) "Responsibility of States for Internationally Wrongful Acts", *Resolution adopted by the General Assembly [on the report of the Sixth Committee (A/56/589 and Corr.1)]*, 28 January 2002, A/RES/56/83, at Article 1–2.

[31] Ibid., Article 4–5.

or to rectify it signifies a breach of the due diligence standard (Gallagher 2010, pp. 237–242). In cases of child trafficking, the "due diligence" principle serves as the criterion for evaluating whether a State has exerted all requisite efforts to prevent and respond to child trafficking. A State could be accountable for offences committed by private actors if it has not exhaustively endeavoured to prevent such misconduct or to administer suitable punishment to the offender.

3 Human Rights Issues in the Child Trafficking Cycle

Child trafficking stands as a vicious violation of human rights, an assertion made unequivocal through its categorisation as a criminal offence under international law. The dignity and humanity of victims are profoundly compromised by the inhumane and dehumanising nature of this crime. Such violation is explicitly prohibited by various international and regional human rights instruments, including Article 6 of the CEDAW, Article 35 of the CRC, the CRC-OPSC, the Charter of Fundamental Rights of the European Union, the Council of Europe Convention on Action against Trafficking in Human Beings, and the African Charter on the Rights and Welfare of the Child.

Yet, the essence of its violation extends beyond its legal definition, touching upon the serious human rights issues that emerge throughout the intricate process of child trafficking. This process typically unfolds into three critical phases: recruitment and transportation, exploitation, and release and recovery. As demonstrated in Fig. 1, the trafficking cycle often precedes the actual act of trafficking, rooted in the vulnerabilities of potential victims. These vulnerabilities, encompassing child abuse, gender-based discrimination, poverty, and inequality, set the stage for the subsequent phases of trafficking: the recruitment, abduction, transportation, sale, and exploitation of children. It is within this phase that the egregious violations of the liberty, safety, and dignity of the victims become most apparent. The concluding phase of the cycle involves the rescue and rehabilitation of victims, ensuring their identification, liberation from traffickers, and support through their recovery journey. It's crucial to acknowledge that the trafficking cycle is not invariably linear—children may momentarily escape the clutches of trafficking, only to be ensnared once again, with some remaining vulnerable to re-entry into the trafficking cycle even post-rescue, underscoring the complex and enduring nature of the violation against their human rights.

In this cycle, two groups of individuals are primarily affected. At the forefront are the child victims themselves, who endure significant violations of their rights throughout the trafficking experience, warranting protection, assistance, and rehabilitation. Equally important are the rights of the parents or legal guardians, whose vulnerabilities can significantly impact the safety and well-being of their children, positioning them as crucial allies in combating and preventing trafficking. Thus, discussions surrounding this cycle must consider both the trafficked children and

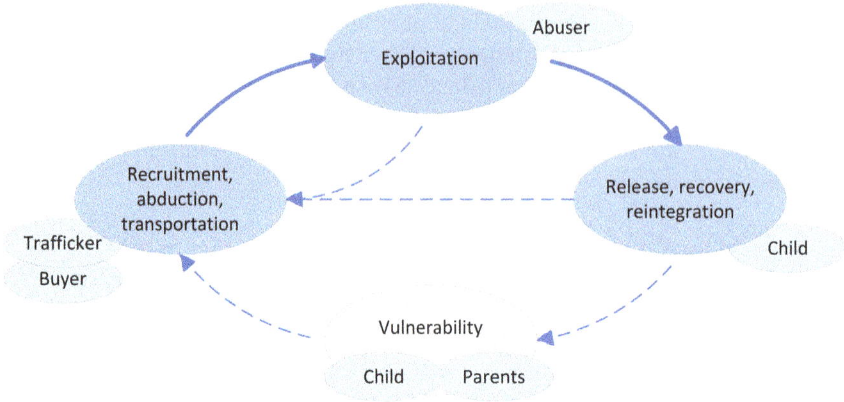

Fig. 1 The cycle of child trafficking

their parents or guardians as fundamental rights-holders and integral participants in creating effective counter-trafficking strategies.

Human rights considerations of categories of rights holders are essential at every stage of the child trafficking cycle. In fact, violations of these rights are both the underlying causes and dire consequences of child trafficking, as noted by the OHCHR (2014). Throughout the different phases of trafficking, human rights issues manifest in various forms (see Box 2). While not every cause of child trafficking directly violates children's rights, many causative factors are intricately linked to human rights concerns. These include poverty, gender-based violence, inadequate child protection systems, and corruption. The phase of exploitation particularly involves direct or indirect human rights violations of victims, with many associated offences, such as forced marriage, child prostitution, and enslavement, being expressly prohibited under international human rights law (OHCHR 2010). These offences often lead to the violation of fundamental rights, including the right to life, freedom, and security of the person, and the right of the child to know and be cared for by their parents. Post-rescue, new human rights concerns emerge, encompassing the right to privacy, the right to justice and remedy, and ongoing child protection issues.

Box 2 Relevant human rights in child trafficking cycle

Human rights most relevant to trafficking in persons:

- The prohibition of discrimination on the basis of race, colour, sex, language, religion, political or other opinion, national, ethnic or social origin, property, disability, birth or other status
- The right to life
- The right to liberty and security of person
- The right to justice

- The right to remedy
- The right to privacy
- The right not to be submitted to slavery, servitude, forced labour or bonded labour
- The right not to be subjected to torture and/or cruel, inhuman, degrading treatment or punishment
- The right to be free from gender-based violence
- The right to freely choose a spouse and to enter into marriage only with free and full consent;
- The right to freedom of movement
- The right to adequate standard of living
- The right to the highest attainable standard of physical and mental health
- The right to benefit from social security
- The right to just and favourable conditions of work

Specific rights of children relevant to child trafficking:

- The right of the child to survival and development
- The right of the child to special protection
- The right of the child to freedom from all forms of violence
- The right of the child to know and be cared for by his or her parents
- The right of the child to preserve his or her identity, including nationality, name and family relations as recognised by law

A. **Human rights issues as causes of child trafficking**

The genesis of child trafficking is deeply rooted in human rights challenges that precede the actual criminal offences. A human rights-based approach sheds light, firstly, on the vulnerabilities of potential victims and the factors amplifying their risk of falling into trafficking networks. It is critical to dissect how breaches or insufficient protection of human rights pave the way to child trafficking scenarios. Such insights are crucial for crafting prevention policies that are both targeted and effective.

Child trafficking, similar to the complexities of human trafficking at large, manifests in diverse forms and is influenced by varying factors across different settings (Kragten-Heerdink et al. 2018). At the heart of vulnerability to child trafficking lies a nuanced interplay between widespread structural issues and personal circumstances. Socio-economic deprivation is pinpointed as a fundamental and structural vulnerability, playing a pivotal role in predisposing individuals to trafficking (Cameron and Newman 2008). Beyond systemic issues, the personal attributes of potential victims also significantly contribute to their susceptibility. These attributes, often influenced or inherited from their familial backgrounds or dictated by the social environments they inhabit. These vulnerabilities encompass a broad spectrum, ranging from immediate to enduring, and can be economic, social, or political in nature (OHCHR 2014, p. 39).

Despite gaps in our comprehensive understanding of all underlying causes, several pervasive factors have been consistently identified. These include broader human rights concerns such as poverty and inequality, alongside more specific violations like gender-based violence and discrimination against women (OHCHR 2014). Acknowledging and addressing these root causes are essential steps towards mitigating the risk of trafficking and ensuring the protection of vulnerable individuals.

Poverty stands as a prevalent factor that significantly increases the risk of child trafficking (see, for instance, Cameron and Newman 2008; Ebbe Obi Ni 2007; Gallagher and Skrivankova 2015). Acknowledged as a key driver behind trafficking, especially from the victims' countries of origin, poverty extends beyond mere economic deprivation to represent a critical human rights issue that compromises human dignity. Individuals living in extreme poverty often find themselves deprived of basic economic and social rights, lacking access to essentials such as food, safe water, healthcare, adequate housing, and education (Roth 2004). The scarcity of opportunities forces many to seek better living conditions elsewhere, frequently exposing them to considerable risks.

Poverty manifests in two forms: absolute and relative. While absolute poverty denotes a sheer lack of basic necessities, relative poverty points to the inequities in wealth, income, and opportunities, both within and across regions or countries. These inequities frequently motivate migration towards more affluent areas in pursuit of improved prospects (Cottingham et al. 2013; UNICEF East Asia and Pacific Regional Office 2009), thereby influencing a child's vulnerability to trafficking in diverse manners.

In impoverished regions, for example, the lack of access to basic needs and education can precipitate a child's premature entry into the labour market or drive people to migrate in search of better opportunities. Such migration, whether internal or cross-border, can profoundly affect young children, leading to situations where they become unaccompanied minors or are left unsupervised at home. These unaccompanied or left-behind children lack adequate guardianship, making them particularly vulnerable to violence, exploitation, and human trafficking. Additionally, children of migrants may become victims due to the violation or inadequate protection of the rights their parents. Sometimes, economic hardships within families can create environments where children are at increased risk of exploitation, regardless of the broader economic status of the region they reside in. Within low-income families, children are frequently viewed as economic burdens or potential income sources. This perception may lead to grave circumstances where children are compelled into labour, prostitution, or marriages for financial gain, at times facilitated by their own parents. These scenarios starkly underscore the heightened vulnerability of children to trafficking, rooted in the context of familial poverty.

Discrimination, manifesting across various dimensions such as race, colour, sex, language, religion, national, ethnic or social origin, property, disability, birth, or other status, plays a significant role in exacerbating the vulnerability of individuals to child trafficking. Notably, discrimination against women and gender-based violations are prominently linked to human trafficking, particularly influencing sex trafficking and the sexual exploitation of female victims. The most recent global data on trafficking reveals a continuing trend: while the detection of male victims is on the rise, the majority of identified victims worldwide remain female (UNODC 2018), underscoring the heightened susceptibility of women and girls to trafficking due to gender-based discrimination and violence (ICAT 2016). For example, situations like family violence or the prospect of an arranged marriage can drive women and young girls to undertake risky migrations as a means of escape (Kaye and Winterdyk 2011; Winterdyk et al. 2011; OHCHR 2014). In societies where patriarchal values prevail, girls frequently face pressure to drop out of school to contribute to family income, further limiting their opportunities and increasing their risk of being trafficked (Kaye and Winterdyk 2011, p. 58). Moreover, when gender discrimination intersects with other factors of disadvantage, such as poverty or belonging to a minority ethnic or language group, women and girls' vulnerability to trafficking is compounded. Discrimination's link to child trafficking is not always direct. Children can suffer from the discriminatory treatment directed at their parents, for instance, those born out of wedlock or under circumstances that diverge from societal norms, highlighting how deeply entrenched discriminatory practices can indirectly facilitate the trafficking of young children.[32]

The neglect or violation of children's rights to special care and protection significantly contributes to their vulnerability to trafficking. Given their physical and mental immaturity, children require enhanced safeguards, legal protection, and social welfare. A pivotal example of such neglect is an inadequate birth registration system, which heightens children's vulnerability to trafficking by complicating the identification and tracking of criminal activities involving them. Furthermore, children who work or live on the streets embody a stark illustration of unmet needs for care, education, and protection from inhuman and degrading treatment. These children, often referred to as "street children", find themselves at a heightened risk of violence and exploitation, including trafficking, due to the absence of adequate protection measures (OHCHR 2012).

While poverty, discrimination, and inadequate child protection are not the sole human rights issues leading to child trafficking, they represent prevalent causes that significantly impact China. Various studies have identified these factors, among others, as key contributors to the rise in child trafficking within the country, including poverty, discrimination against women, and a fragile child protection framework (Li et al. 2017; Xing 2017; Shen et al. 2013; ILO/IPEC and Yunnan Province Women's Federation 2002; Yuan and Yang 2001). These commonalities lay the groundwork for an in-depth analysis of the human rights challenges that foster child trafficking in specific regions of China.

B. **Human rights issues as consequences of trafficking**

Undeniably, child trafficking leads to a multitude of direct and indirect human rights violations. First of all, the international consensus categorises trafficking in persons

[32] UN Committee on the Rights of the Child (CRC) (2005) *General comment No. 7 (2005): Implementing Child Rights in Early Childhood*, 20 September 2006, CRC/C/GC/7/Rev.1, para. 12.

per se, including child trafficking, as a grave infringement on fundamental human rights, regardless of the forms of exploitation it entails. This stance is not solely upheld by the United Nations General Assembly and the Human Rights Council, which have repeatedly emphasised that trafficking violates and impairs human rights,[33] but also by numerous international and regional human rights mechanisms. For instance, the prohibition of trafficking in women and children is explicitly stated in Article 6 of the CEDAW, Article 35 of the CRC, and the CRC-OPSC, and is echoed in regional human rights statutes like the Charter of Fundamental Rights of the European Union (Article 5), the Council of Europe Convention on Action against Trafficking in Human Beings, and the African Charter on the Rights and Welfare of the Child (Articles 24 and 29), along with the Protocol to the African Charter on Human and Peoples' Rights on the Rights of Women in Africa (Article 4).

Moreover, numerous practices associated with child trafficking are explicitly prohibited under international human rights law (OHCHR 2010, p. 37). Notably, the exploitation phase of trafficking is where the most prevalent human rights violations occur. Forced marriage, for instance, is prohibited by the Universal Declaration of Human Rights (Article 16), the International Covenant on Civil and Political Rights (Article 23), and CEDAW (Article 16). As a form of violence and harmful practice, it is also prohibited by the CRC (Articles 19 and 24.3). Likewise, international human rights law forbids other practices such as, among others, slavery, debt bondage, child marriage, enforced prostitution, and the exploitation of prostitution.

Violations of human rights also extend throughout and beyond the trafficking process as consequences of various criminal offences associated with child trafficking. First of all, child trafficking infringes upon the right to freedom from all forms of violence.[34] Moreover, the right to liberty and security of person and the right to freedom of movement are systematically undermined in the cycle of trafficking committed in the form of child abduction and illicit imprisonment of the victim. Trafficking for illegal adoption, for instance, leads to violations of children's right to know and be cared for by their parents and the right to preserve their identity, including family relations (de Boer-Buquicchio 2017, pp. 7–8). Furthermore, human rights challenges persist after the rescue, particularly if the State's response to trafficking falls short, thereby failing to uphold the right to justice and remedy for victims.

In summary, a human rights-based approach offers a holistic lens through which to view the issue of child trafficking, a complex phenomenon that unfolds in three

---

[33] For instance, Resolution 11/3 on Trafficking in persons, especially women and children, 17/06/2009, A/HRC/RES/11/3; Resolution 14/2 on Trafficking in persons, especially women and children: regional and subregional cooperation in promoting a human rights-based approach to combating trafficking in persons, 23 June 2010 A/HRC/RES/14/2; Resolution 23/5 on Trafficking in persons, especially women and children: efforts to combat human trafficking in supply chains of businesses, 19 June 2013, A/HRC/RES/23/5; and Resolution 32/3 on Trafficking in persons, especially women and children: protecting victims of trafficking and persons at risk of trafficking, especially women and children in conflict and post-conflict situations, 30 June 2016, A/HRC/RES/32/3.

[34] UN Committee on the Rights of the Child (CRC) (2011) *General comment No. 13 (2011): The right of the child to freedom from all forms of violence*, 18 April 2011, CRC/C/GC/13, para. 7.

distinct phases: recruitment and transportation, exploitation, and finally, release and recovery. Human rights issues serve as both the root causes and the dire consequences of trafficking and its associated offences. This perspective is embraced by the prevailing international anti-trafficking frameworks, which underscore the critical importance of human rights in all facets of their operations. These frameworks are structured around the "3Ps" paradigm: prevention of the crime, prosecution of the perpetrators, and protection of the victims. At the heart of this approach lie human rights values and principles, guiding and informing each aspect of the anti-trafficking response.

References

Cameron, Sally, and Edward Newman. 2008. *Trafficking in Humans: Social, Cultural and Political Dimensions*. Tokyo: United Nations University Press.

Cottingham, Marci, Thomas Nowak, Kay Snyder, and Melissa Swauger. 2013. 'Sociological Perspective: Underlying Causes'. In *Human Trafficking: Interdisciplinary Perspectives*, edited by Mary C. Burke, 51–72. New York and London: Routledge.

de Boer-Buquicchio, Maud. 2017. 'Before the Inter-American Court of Human Rights Expert Opinion by the United Nations Special Rapporteur on the Sale and Sexual Exploitation of Children: RAMÍREZ BROTHERS AND FAMILY VS. GUATEMALA'. https://www.ohchr.org/sites/default/files/Documents/Issues/Children/Submission/Opinions28April2017.PDF.

Ebbe, Obi Ni. 2007. 'Causes of Trafficking in Women and Children'. In *Global Trafficking in Women and Children*, 47–51. CRC Press.

European Commission. 2013. *EU Strategy towards the Eradication of Trafficking in Human Beings 2012–2016*. Brussels.

Gallagher, Anne T. 2010. *The International Law of Human Trafficking*. Cambridge: Cambridge University Press.

Gallagher, Anne T., and K. Skrivankova. 2015. 'Human Rights and Trafficking in Persons –15th Informal ASEM Seminar on Human Rights (Background Paper)'.

ICAT. 2010. 'An Analytical Review: 10 Years on from the Adoption of the UN Trafficking in Persons Protocol'. In.

ICAT. 2016. *Providing Effective Remedies for Victims of Trafficking in Persons*. Issue Paper. UNODC. https://www.unodc.org/documents/human-trafficking/ICAT/ICAT_Policy_Paper_3._Providing_Effective_Remedies_for_Victims_of_Trafficking_in_Persons_2016.pdf.

ILC. 2001. *Draft Articles on Responsibility of States for Internationally Wrongful Acts, with Commentaries*. UN.

ILO/IPEC, and Yunnan Province Women's Federation. 2002. *Yunnan Province, China Situation of Trafficking in Children and Women: A Rapid Assessment*. Bangkok, Thailand: ILO & IPEC.

Kaye, Julie, and John Winterdyk. 2011. 'Explaining Human Trafficking'. In *Human Trafficking: Exploring the International Nature, Concerns, and Complexities*, edited by John Winterdyk, Benjamin Perrin, and Philip Reichel, 57–78. Boca Raton, FL: CRC Press.

Kragten-Heerdink, Suzanne L. J., Corinne E. Dettmeijer-Vermeulen, and Dirk J. Korf. 2018. 'More Than Just "Pushing and Pulling": Conceptualizing Identified Human Trafficking in the Netherlands'. *Crime & Delinquency* 64 (13): 1765–1789. https://doi.org/10.1177/0011128717728503.

Laczko, Frank, and Gergana Danailova-Trainor. 2009. 'Trafficking in Persons and Human Development: Towards a More Integrated Policy Response'. *Human Development Research Paper*, Human Development Research Paper, 51. https://mpra.ub.uni-muenchen.de/19234/.

Li, Gang, Ran Tan, Huijuan Wang, Xiang Yan, and Yan Shao. 2017. 'Geographic Characteristics of Child Trafficking Crime in China [中国拐卖儿童犯罪的地理特征研究]'. *Scientia Geographica Sinica [地理科学]* 37 (7): 1049–1058. https://doi.org/10.13249/j.cnki.sgs.2017.07.010.

McConnell, Lee, and Rhona Smith. 2018. *Research Methods in Human Rights*. Milton, UNITED KINGDOM: Routledge. http://ebookcentral.proquest.com/lib/uwsau/detail.action?docID=5358373.

OHCHR. 2002. *Recommended Principles and Guidelines on Human Rights and Human Trafficking: Report of the United Nations High Commissioner for Human Rights to the Economic and Social Council*. E/2002/68/Add.1. ECOSOC.

OHCHR. 2006. *Frequently Asked Questions on a Human Rights-Based Approach to Development Cooperation*. New York and Geneva: United Nations.

OHCHR. 2008. 'A Human Rights Approach to Tackling Climate Change'. *OHCHR*. https://www.ohchr.org/en/stories/2008/11/human-rights-approach-tackling-climate-change.

OHCHR. 2010. Commentary on the Recommended Principles and Guidelines on Human Rights and Human Trafficking. New York and Geneva: United Nations Publication.

OHCHR. 2012. *Report of the United Nations High Commissioner for Human Rights on the Protection and Promotion of the Rights of Children Working and/or Living on the Street*. Human Rights Council.

OHCHR. 2014. *Human Rights and Human Trafficking*. Fact Sheet 36. New York & Geneva: United Nations.

Roth, Kenneth. 2004. 'Defending Economic Social and Cultural Rights: Practical Issues Faced by an International Human Rights Organization'. *Hum. Rts. Q.* 26: 63–73. https://doi.org/10.1353/hrq.2004.0010.

Shen, Anqi, Georgios A. Antonopoulos, and Georgios Papanicolaou. 2013. 'China's Stolen Children: Internal Child Trafficking in the People's Republic of China'. *Trends in Organized Crime* 16 (1): 31–48. https://doi.org/10.1007/s12117-012-9167-z.

UN. 2022. 'United Nations Disability Inclusion Strategy'. United Nations. https://www.un.org/en/content/disabilitystrategy/assets/documentation/UN_Disability_Inclusion_Strategy_english.pdf.

UNDP. 2003. 'Poverty Reduction and Human Rights: A Practice Note'. UNDP. https://www.undp.org/sites/g/files/zskgke326/files/publications/HRPN_(poverty)En.pdf.

UNDP, Europe and the CIS. 2004. *Trafficking in Human Beings: A Guidance Note*. UNDP.

UNICEF Regional Office for CEE/CIS. 2006. *Reference Guide on Protecting the Rights of Child Victims of Trafficking in Europe*. Geneva: UNICEF.

UNICEF. 2006. *Guidelines on the Protection of Child Victims of Trafficking*. https://www.refworld.org/docid/49997af727.html [accessed 25 January 2024.

UNICEF and UNESCO, eds. 2007. A Human Rights-Based Approach to Education for All. New York: UNICEF.

UNICEF East Asia and Pacific Regional Office. 2009. *Child Trafficking in East and South-East Asia: Reversing the Trend*. Bangkok: UNICEF East Asia and Pacific Regional Office.

UNICEF Innocenti Research Centre. 2009. *Handbook on the Optional Protocol on the Sale of Children, Child Prostitution and Child Pornography*. New York: The United Nations Children's Fund.

UNICEF Regional Office for CEE/CIS. 2009. *Risks and Realities of Child Trafficking and Exploitation in Central Asia*. UNICEF.

UNODC. 2004. *Legislative Guides for the Implementation of the United Nations Convention against Transnational Organized Crime and the Protocols Thereto*. UN,. https://digitallibrary.un.org/record/543728.

UNODC. 2009. *International Framework for Action To Implement the Trafficking in Persons Protocol*. Vienna.

UNODC. 2018. *Global Report on Trafficking In Persons 2018*. Global Report on Trafficking in Persons. Vienna, Austria.

WHO, Cathy Zimmerman, and Charlotte Watts. 2003. *WHO Ethical and Safety Recommendations for Interviewing Trafficked Women*. WHO. https://iris.who.int/bitstream/handle/10665/42765/9241546255.pdf?sequence=1.

WHO. 2012. *Understanding and Addressing Violence against Women: Human Trafficking*. WHO/RHR/12.42. https://iris.who.int/bitstream/handle/10665/77394/WHO_RHR_12.42_eng.pdf?sequence=1.

Winterdyk, John, Benjamin Perrin, and Philip Reichel. 2011. *Human Trafficking: Exploring the International Nature, Concerns, and Complexities*. Boca Raton, FL: CRC Press.

Xing, Hongmei. 2017. 'Study on Rime of Selling of Children by Parents [出卖亲生子女犯罪研究]'. *Journal of People's Public Security University of China (Social Sciences Edition) [中国人民公安大学学报: 社会科学版]* 33 (4): 17–24.

Yuan, E., and Zhenyu Yang. 2001. 'An Analysis of the Crime of Abducting and Selling Women in Frontier Ethnic Areas in China: A Case Study of Wenshan Zhuang and Miao Autonomous Prefecture in Yunnan Province [当前我国边疆民族地区拐卖妇女犯罪活动分析研究——以云南省文山壮族苗族自治州为例]'. *Collection of Women's Studies [妇女研究论丛]* 2001 (2): 17–22.

Chapter 3
Status Quo of Child Trafficking in China as Reflected in Judicial Cases

This chapter offers a unique and unmatched examination of child trafficking in China, drawing on data from judicial cases across the country. Beyond the official statistical figures mentioned in the review section, the majority of the data were thoroughly gathered from "China Judgements Online", the official database for China's legal rulings and judgements. This chapter commences with a comprehensive statistical overview that underscores the prevalence and routes of child trafficking throughout China. This preliminary analysis lays the groundwork for a more thorough exploration of trafficking patterns and marks the beginning of an in-depth investigation. A particularly innovative aspect of this work is the creation of an original classification system designed to categorise the various forms of child trafficking identified within the country. Building upon this framework, I employ descriptive analyses and crosstabulations to cast light on the intricacies of these crimes, including the profiles of the perpetrators and the characteristics of the victims. This meticulous approach not only illuminates the complex nature of child trafficking in China but also enhances our understanding of its dynamics, offering a more nuanced perspective on this pressing issue.

1 Scale and Routes of Trafficking in China

The clandestine nature of human trafficking significantly complicates efforts to estimate the number of victims, both on a global scale and within individual countries. However, certain official sources offer a glimpse into the extent of the issue. Internationally, the UNODC annually releases the Global Report on Trafficking in Persons, offering an overview of global and regional trends in the crime based on cases detected and reported by Member States. Within China, both official statistical data and information from NGOs contribute to a more detailed understanding of the gravity of the situation.

L. Han, *Child Trafficking in China*, https://doi.org/10.1007/978-981-97-3717-8_3

A. **Statistical and literature review**

(1) *The scale of trafficking in China*

According to the UNODC's annual reports, the incidence of human trafficking detected in East Asia and the Pacific had been on a steady rise for several years, culminating in 2020 when the closure of borders by most Asian countries in response to the global pandemic led to a noticeable change in trends. In 2020, children accounted for approximately 25% of all trafficking victims identified globally (UNODC 2023, p. 25). However, specific data from the UNODC indicate that in China, victims of trafficking under the age of 17 were identified only during the years 2013–2015, with each year recording fewer than five victims.[1]

The periodic reports submitted by China to the human rights treaty bodies of the United Nations also shed light on the issue of child trafficking within the country. Notably, the third and fourth periodic reports to the Committee on the Rights of the Child reveal that in 2009 alone, the police rescued 704 minors from child prostitution.[2] Furthermore, these reports (specifically in Annex XVIII) disclose that between 2000 and 2008, public security organs in China detected 12,937 cases of child trafficking, indicating a similar number of victims were rescued or identified. Additionally, from 2003 to 2009, a total of 20,314 suspects were arrested for involvement in child trafficking, with 18,828 of these individuals subsequently brought to trial.

The variation in data between UNODC reports and China's submission to the CRC Committee could arise from several key issues: first, the inherent difficulty in accurately compiling statistics on child trafficking presents a substantial challenge. Second, discrepancies may also be due to differing definitions and criteria used in data collection by the UNODC compared to those utilised in China's CRC report. Lastly, the reports may suggest a marked decrease in child abduction and trafficking cases in China, attributed to a range of anti-trafficking measures or alterations in reporting methodologies, a scenario that seems improbable.

Similar challenges in compiling accurate reports and research findings on child trafficking have been encountered at the national level in China as well. While this study does not seek to determine precise figures for child trafficking within China, gaining a general, albeit somewhat indistinct, overview of the situation remains valuable. The China Statistical Yearbook, published by the National Bureau of Statistics of China, offers yearly data on criminal cases filed by public security organs. According to these official statistics, from 1997 to 2022, there were over 203 thousand cases filed under the category of "abduction and sale of women or children." (see Table 1).[3] However, these figures do not specify the cases detected and lack disaggregation by age and gender. Additionally, certain cases involving missing children,

---

[1] See the UNODC data portal, available at https://dataunodc.un.org/dp-trafficking-persons.

[2] UN Committee on the Rights of the Child (2012) *Consideration of reports submitted by States parties under article 44 of the Convention: Third and fourth periodic reports of States parties due in 2009—China*, 6 June 2012, CRC/C/CHN/3–4, para. 256.

[3] National Bureau of Statistics of China, *China Statistical Yearbook*, retrieved from http://data.stats.gov.cn/publish.htm?sort=1, [accessed: 7/2/2024].

Table 1 Number of filed cases of abduction and sale of women or children by public security organs (1997–2022)

Year	No. of filed cases	Year	No. of filed cases
1997	6425	2007	2378
1998	6513	2011	13,964
1999	7257	2012	18,532
2000	23,163	2013	20,735
2001	7008	2014	16,483
2002	5684	2015	9150
2003	3712	2016	7121
2004	3343	2017	6668
2005	2884	2018	5397
2006	2569	2019	4571
2007	2378	2020	3035
2008	2566	2021	2860
2009	6513	2022	2287
2010	10,082		
Total			203,278

Source China Statistical Yearbooks (1999–2023)

potentially linked to trafficking, may not be filed as criminal cases if the informants, mainly the parents, lack evidence of criminal conduct. Hence, even with this data, estimating the actual number of child trafficking victims in the country is challenging.

Over the past two decades, there were two significant spikes in the number of filed cases related to the abduction and sale of women and children: the first in 2000 and the second in 2013. While the surge in 2000 lacks a clear explanation, the second peak can be attributed to a concerted effort by the state, including China's ratification of the Palermo Protocol in 2010, the implementation of the National Plan of Action (NPA) for 2008–2012, the special police actions of combating human trafficking,[4] and amendments to legislation concerning the trafficking of women and children.[5] As per a State Council report, police anti-abduction efforts between

[4] Ministry of Public Security (2009) 公安部部署打击拐卖儿童妇女犯罪专项行动 [Ministry of Public Security deploys a special campaign against crimes of trafficking in children and women], *全国公安机关打击拐卖儿童、妇女犯罪专项行动 [National Public Security Organs' Special Action to Combat Trafficking in Children and Women]*, retrieved from http://www.mps.gov.cn/n2255079/n2255231/n2255233/c3579140/content.html, [accessed on 19/07/2018].

[5] In specific: Standing Committee of the National People's Congress, Standing Committee of the National People's Congress (2009) 全国人大常委会关于严惩拐卖、妇架妇女、儿童的犯罪分子的决定(2009修正) [Decision of the Standing Committee of the National People's Congress Regarding the Severe Punishment of Criminals Who Abduct and Traffic in or Kidnap Women or Children (2009 Amendment)], Order No. 18 of the President of the People's Republic of China, issued and entered in force on 27 August 2009, retrieved from https://flk.npc.gov.cn/detail2.html?ZmY4MDgwODE3NzRjNzJiMzAxNzc3MTE0ZGIwMTFkY2M%3D. And Supreme People's Court, Supreme People's Procuratorate, Instrumentalities of the State Council, All Ministries, Ministry of Public Security, Ministry of Justice (2010) 最高人民法院、最高人民检察院、公

2009 and 2011 resulted in the rescue of 36,369 women and children, with children comprising 36.5% (13,284) of those rescued.[6] Assuming the proportion of child victims remained consistent over the years, we can roughly estimate that more than 74 thousand children could have been trafficked between 1999 and 2022, based on police filings.

Judicial authorities also serve as a crucial official source for data and cases related to child trafficking. While the information released by the judiciary may not explicitly state the annual count of child abduction and trafficking cases processed, it still offers valuable insights into the issue. Notably, a substantial number of child trafficking incidents involve the victims' own parents, who sell their children for financial gain.[7] Research by Xing (2017) indicates that approximately 35% of child trafficking cases are conducted by parents. Furthermore, a news report by Gong (2017) highlights an even more alarming statistic, suggesting that up to 72.4% of victims were sold by their own parents. This points to a deeply troubling aspect of child trafficking, where those who are supposed to protect their children become the perpetrators of this egregious violation of human rights.

In addition to official data, independent researchers have sought information from non-governmental sources to gain further insight into child trafficking within China. For example, Li Gang and colleagues have examined the issue from 1980 to 2015, utilizing data from the BBHJ, an online public platform operated by an NGO (Li et al. 2017a, b). Their research indicates that over these 35 years, 14,352 children were trafficked in China—a figure significantly lower than those cited in official reports. This discrepancy may arise because not all police-reported victims are recorded on the BBHJ platform, and the BBHJ data might not account for cases that have been resolved. The study also sheds light on the demographics of the victims, noting a pronounced gender imbalance with 10,236 boys trafficked versus 4,116 girls. Alarmingly, 60% of these victims (8,998 children) were trafficked at under 4 years of age, with this percentage increasing to 80% (12,166 children) for those under 6 years of age. The majority of these young children were trafficked for the purposes of illegal adoption. In contrast, older children were subjected to various forms of exploitation, including criminal activities, forced labour, forced marriage, servitude, and forced prostitution.

安部、司法部印发《关于依法惩治拐卖妇女儿童犯罪的意见》的通知 [Notice of the Supreme People's Court, the Supreme People's Procuratorate, the Ministry of Public Security and the Ministry of Justice on Issuing the Opinions on Legally Punishing the Crimes of Abducting and Trafficking in Women and Children], Documents of Judicial Interpretation Nature, No. 7 [2010] of the Supreme People's Court, issued and entered in force on 15 March 2010, retrieved from http://en.pkulaw.cn/display.aspx?cgid=095d828db4ce796bbdfb&lib=law.

[6] State Council of China (2011) "公安部公布"打拐"专项行动十大典型案例 [The Ministry of Public Security communicated the ten typical cases of the special action against the crime of "abduction and trafficking"], retrieved from: http://www.gov.cn/fwxx/sh/2011-04/02/content_1836946.htm, [accessed on 26/06/2018].

[7] People.cn (2015) "最高人民法院:大多被拐儿童系被父母出卖遗弃 [Supreme People's Court: Most trafficked children were sold out by their parents]", retrieved from http://bj.people.com.cn/n/2015/0228/c14545-24015042.html, [accessed on 26/06/2018].

The discrepancy in data underscores the intricate challenges involved in monitoring and documenting child trafficking cases, emphasising the crucial need for standardised definitions and effective data collection strategies to accurately assess the prevalence of this issue. Moreover, it brings to light the multifaceted dynamics of child trafficking in China, particularly the significant impact of familial situations. These findings reveal how deeply entrenched socio-economic factors and family structures contribute to the vulnerability of children to trafficking, stressing the importance of addressing these root causes in efforts to protect children's rights and prevent trafficking.

(2) *The flow of trafficking*

The trafficking of persons typically follows a trajectory from regions with lower levels of development to those with higher standards of living. For example, countries in Western and Southern Europe report high numbers of trafficking victims from various regions and identify victims from a broader array of global origins (UNODC 2018, p. 9). Nevertheless, globally, most of trafficking are domestic and subregional. While cross-border trafficking is prevalent globally, a considerable portion of trafficking victims are also trafficked within their own countries (UNODC 2016, pp. 40–41).

From the perspective of international trafficking, China is recognised as a source, destination, and transit country (UNODC 2012, pp. 49–51; UNODC 2016, pp. 9, 105). Trafficking from China involves men, women, and children who are mainly exploited for forced labour and sexual purposes across various countries, including Argentina, the United States, several European countries, and Japan (UNODC 2016, pp. 58, 76, 105). Moreover, China serves as a destination or transit point for trafficking victims, predominantly women and girls, from South Asian, Southeast Asian, and African countries (U. S. Department of State 2018, p. 141).

Actually, China also faces significant challenges with domestic trafficking, particularly involving children trafficked for illegal adoption and women and girls trafficked for forced marriage (UN-ACT 2012). Reports indicate that child trafficking occurs in every province of China. Certain provinces, such as Yunnan, Guizhou, and Sichuan in the southeast, are primarily known as origins of trafficking victims. In contrast, provinces in East China tend to be destinations where victims are sold for illegal adoption or exploitation. Trafficked children from the southeast are transported to East China via two main routes: a northern path leading to Henan, Hebei, and Shandong through Shaanxi Province, and a southern path to Fujian and Guangdong through Guangxi Province (Li et al. 2017b). Li et al. further highlighted the significant issue of internal child trafficking within the provinces of Fujian, Guangdong, and Henan, underscoring the multifaceted nature of trafficking within China.

B. **Mapping child trafficking routes through detected cases**

The data presented herein were collated in late 2020 from judgements nationwide, sourced from "China Judgements Online". By employing the search term "*Guǎi mài ér tóng (拐卖儿童)*", which translates to "abduction and sale of children" or "child trafficking" in the context of criminal law, a total of 1,567 records were pinpointed at the national level and consequently procured. After the exclusion of duplicates, commutation verdicts, and decisions deficient in substantive case details, the distilled dataset consists of 1,449 criminal judgements across the first, second, and final appeal stages. Records from these judgements indicate that a sum of 2,270 victims of child trafficking have been rescued or identified. These are detailed in Table 2, encapsulating cases of child trafficking that occurred between 1986 and 2020. Within the 32 provincial-level administrative divisions of mainland China, which comprise 23 provinces, 4 municipalities directly under the central government, and 5 autonomous regions, only three reported no judgements related to child trafficking. These were Heilongjiang, Tibet Autonomous Region, and Ningxia Hui Autonomous Region. These victims were from 30 provincial-level administrative regions and had been trafficked to 28 such regions, indicating the broad geographical spread of this issue. Notably, more than 60% of trafficking cases nationwide are concentrated in the top five provinces, underscoring the significant regional variations in the prevalence of this crime.

These cases span provinces, autonomous regions, and municipalities directly under the Central Government, with detections from 1986 to 2020 as depicted in Fig. 1. The data indicates that the majority of the cases examined in this study were detected predominantly between 2009 and 2017. This concentration of identified cases over nearly a decade could be attributed to two principal factors: firstly, the judgements available online pertain to cases concluded more recently, thus omitting incidents that occurred prior to the inception of the online publication system; secondly, the surge correlates with intensified police anti-trafficking efforts initiated in 2009. A subsequent decline in detected cases post-2014 may reflect the positive impact of these anti-trafficking measures, suggesting a notable reduction in child trafficking incidents. Alternatively, the decline could result from other variables, such as diminished focus on child trafficking cases or a reduction in the publication of such cases on digital platforms. Given the dataset's limited representativeness, this study can only reveal certain aspects of contemporary trafficking cases and does not provide insights into historical trends or changes in patterns over time.

The concentration of trafficking crimes in China is notably high in a select few provinces, with over half of the identified victims originating from six specific provinces: Yunnan (305), Shandong (248), Sichuan (199), Fujian (199), Henan (141), and Hebei (118), as demonstrated in Fig. 2. Regarding the destination regions for these victims, the top five provinces accounted for over 70% of the total, with Shandong, Fujian, Henan, Hebei, and Guangdong receiving 546, 385, 340, 249, and 121 victims, respectively, as shown in Fig. 3. A comparison of the maps showing origins and destinations reveals a significant discrepancy in the distribution, with origins being more widespread across the country and destinations predominantly located in the wealthier eastern and southeastern provinces. Fujian, Guangdong, Henan, Hebei, and Shandong notably function as both significant sources and destinations of child trafficking cases.

Actually, determining the final destination of a child victim proves challenging, even if they were rescued by police. Often, children are trafficked multiple times before reaching the end buyer. If a crime is uncovered before the child is sold to this

Table 2 Overview of child trafficking case judgments in China: Analysis of data from "China Judgements Online" (collected in late 2020)

Jurisdiction of the case	No. of judgements	No. of cases	NO. of offenders	NO. of victims
Shandong	257	233	820	470
Fujian	211	194	678	318
Henan	197	181	680	328
Hebei	150	147	441	206
Guangdong	81	79	198	122
Yunnan	63	61	154	126
Jiangsu	56	50	162	52
Sichuan	58	51	190	81
Guangxi	51	40	103	98
Zhejiang	50	38	123	91
Shaanxi	44	32	112	42
Shanxi	33	32	75	44
Guizhou	35	34	143	49
Jiangxi	27	25	65	59
Anhui	35	33	123	39
Hubei	19	14	28	19
Chongqing	16	13	48	15
Gansu	13	11	43	13
Hunan	12	11	27	28
Tianjin	9	51	190	14
Shanghai	7	10	37	18
Inner Mongolia	6	9	24	11
Liaoning	5	4	15	6
Beijing	7	6	37	7
Xinjiang	2	5	10	5
Jilin	2	4	8	5
Hainan	2	2	13	2
Qinghai	1	1	1	1
Total	1449	1371	4548	2270

final buyer, traffickers in possession of the child at the time of detection frequently claim they had no intention of selling the victim further. In such instances, the destination is recorded as the location where the child was found. Additionally, there are situations where a child victim is resold after being kept or raised for an extended period, sometimes spanning months.

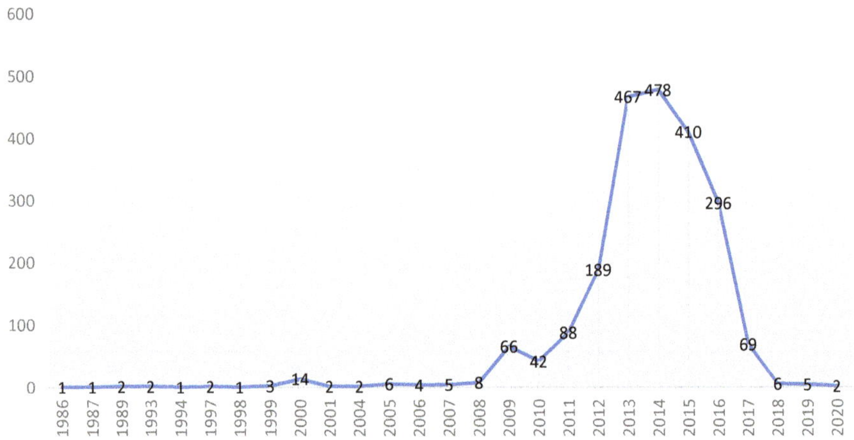

Fig. 1 Chronological analysis of documented child trafficking case detections in the present study (n = 2172)

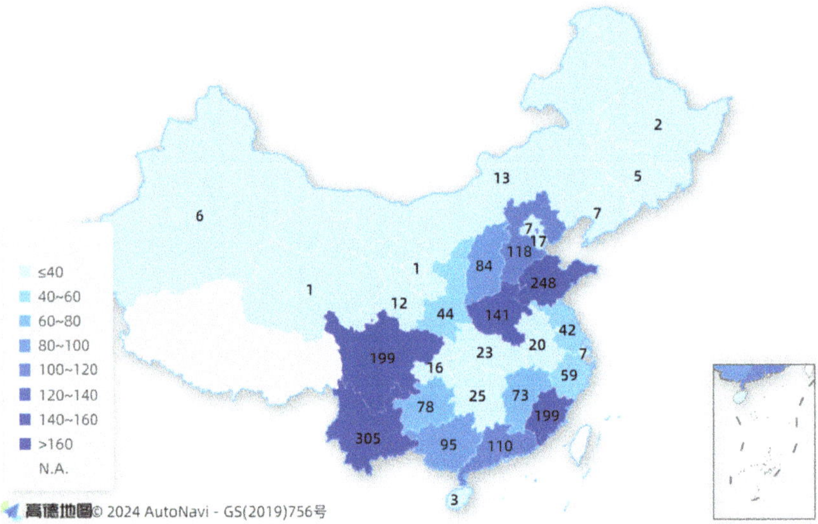

Fig. 2 Distribution of the origins of trafficked children in China (N = 1960)

Remarkably, these detected cases are predominantly domestic trafficking. Only 19 child victims were identified as foreign nationals, all hailing from Vietnam. Furthermore, there was at least one instance where a child was documented as being trafficked from China to a foreign country, also Vietnam in this case. Many of these children were trafficked together with their mothers. This information suggests that the true scale of international trafficking victims might be greater than what is initially

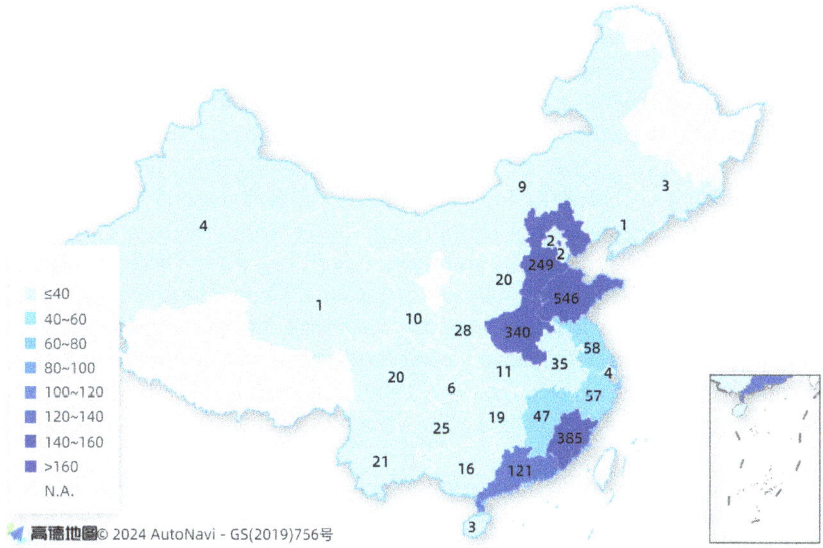

Fig. 3 Distribution of the destination for trafficked children in China (N = 2043)

apparent. The geographical proximity of Yunnan Province to Vietnam, Laos, and Myanmar is particularly noteworthy in this context, indicating a potential corridor for cross-border trafficking activities. These instances of international trafficking were marked by violence and the involvement of criminal networks, highlighting the complex and perilous nature of cross-border child trafficking. This situation underscores the complexity of child trafficking networks and the imperative need for a nuanced understanding of both domestic and international dimensions of this grave issue.

It's critical to acknowledge that not all judgements offer comprehensive details regarding the victims' origins and destinations. For 291 children, information about their place of origin was missing, and for 226, the details of their intended destination were not provided. This gap in information is primarily due to a few key reasons. As previously mentioned, in many cases, children were trafficked several times by different traffickers. Sometimes, even the traffickers did not know where exactly the victim was from. Moreover, a significant number of victims were too young to communicate their origins. In cases where criminal networks were involved, pinpointing their exact origin or intended destination posed a significant challenge. There were tragic cases where some victims did not survive the trafficking ordeal or remained missing by the time legal actions were initiated against the traffickers. Lastly, a considerable amount of information was simply not recorded in the judgements.

Analysing child trafficking solely at China's national level is akin to studying the crime across Europe—a perspective that may prove too broad and general given the vast geographic and demographic diversity of the country. A detailed examination at the provincial level, however, reveals more nuanced insights and patterns, some of which mirror observations made in international contexts. According to the UNODC's annual reports, a significant portion of human trafficking occurs within national borders. A similar trend also evident in China where approximately half of the child trafficking cases are intra-provincial. Notably, this rate exceeds 80% in provinces such as Henan (82%), Fujian (88%), and Shandong (93%). The chord diagram of Fig. 4 illustrates top 15 trafficking flows within the country, predominantly showing intra-provincial movements of child victims. There are only six significant flows, namely from Sichuan to Shandong, Guangxi to Fujian, and from Yunnan to Guangdong, Henan, Fujian, and Shandong. In addition, when it comes to inter-provincial trafficking, there is a marked trend of victims being moved from economically poorer areas, like Yunnan, Sichuan, and Guangxi, to wealthier regions, showcasing another parallel between the dynamics of domestic and international trafficking.

Nevertheless, it would be misleading to generalise that child trafficking solely occurs from impoverished to affluent areas. In the analysis of the origin and destination of trafficking cases, particular attention was given to whether the incidents took place in urban or rural settings. While many case files lack explicit mention of the

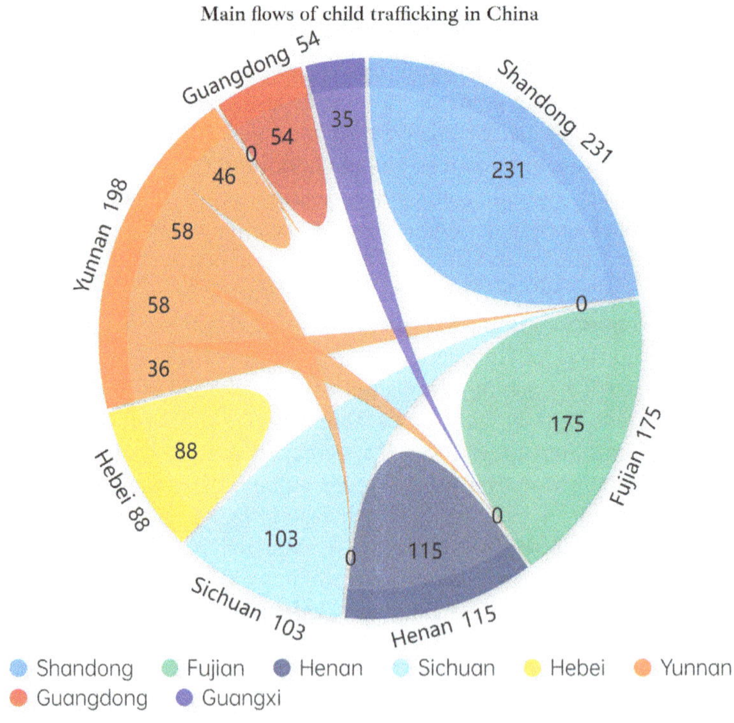

Fig. 4 Victim flows of child trafficking in China: main regional nexus

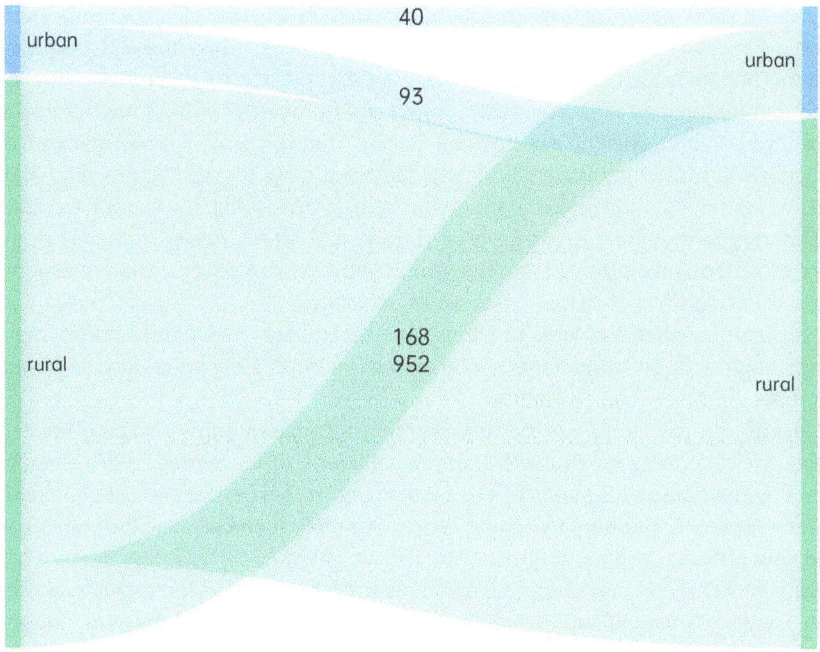

Fig. 5 Victim flows of child trafficking in China: the rural–urban nexus (n = 1253)

incidents' locale as rural or urban, over half of the cases provide sufficient details to discern this aspect. In this context, "rural area" encompasses all locales beyond city centres, including urban villages and suburbs, areas that frequently house individuals facing economic hardships. The Sankey diagram depicted in Fig. 5 reveals that a substantial majority of child trafficking cases transpire within rural areas for both the origins and destinations of the victims. Put it in other words, most of the buyers are not economically strong This observation is very different from international trafficking patterns, indicating that the dynamics of child trafficking in China are influenced by factors beyond mere economic disparities between urban and rural areas.

2 Modern Patterns of Child Trafficking in China

Mapping crime patterns is fundamentally important for criminologists, as it offers vital insights into the nature of criminal activities. According to Siegel (2008, p. 47), a thorough comprehension of the patterns of child trafficking within a nation is essential for identifying the myriad human rights violations that lead to trafficking. This knowledge plays a critical role in guiding the formulation of policies designed to prevent such crimes and protect the victims. Annually, the UNODC publishes a Global Report on Trafficking in Persons, providing insights into global and regional patterns of human trafficking. These reports highlight that trends in human trafficking can vary significantly across different regions and from one year to the next. However, there are some consistent patterns, for instance, in terms of the victims and the directions of trafficking flows. Typically, there are more female victims than male, and the individuals trafficked often come from poorer countries or regions, being transported to wealthier areas such as Europe and North America. Lured by the hope of bettering their living conditions, these individuals frequently find themselves trapped in situations of sexual or labour exploitation.

Turning our attention back to China, questions arises: does child trafficking in China align with global patterns? Who are the victims? How were they trafficked? For what purpose? And by whom?

Identifying the victims is the first step in understanding this complex issue. In China, victims can range from newborns to teenagers, often coming from vulnerable social or economic backgrounds. The methods of trafficking vary widely, including abduction, deceit, coercion by acquaintances or family members, and through organised networks that exploit the trust of parents or guardians. The actors in these trafficking rings can be just as varied, encompassing not only criminal syndicates but also parents or guardians selling children under duress or for financial gain, intermediaries, and individuals seeking to exploit children for personal profit. This complex web of how, why, and by whom children are trafficked in China is essential for policymakers and law enforcement to make effective strategies to prevent and crack down on the crime.

A. **Dominant modes of child trafficking in China**

While meticulously examining and codifying hundreds to thousands of cases across China, with the ultimate goal of uncovering the underlying human rights issues, it became evident that the crime of child trafficking is not uniform. Typically, classifications of child trafficking within China are predicated on the intended outcomes, such as whether the child ends up in exploitative industries or is targeted for illegal adoption. However, such a results-based framework comes with notable shortcomings.

First and foremost, a substantial portion of the child trafficking cases examined in this study do not pertain to sexual or labour exploitation, a point that will be elaborated upon towards the end of the next section. Moreover, classifying trafficking based solely on its intended outcome is impractical. The true purpose behind trafficking can be difficult to ascertain, especially in instances where victims are rescued before they reach the supposed final buyer. Additionally, the assumption that all trafficking operations are orchestrated by criminal organisations is flawed; traffickers may not always be aware of the final buyer's intentions. Focusing exclusively on the outcomes also means neglecting the complexities of the trafficking process and the unique vulnerabilities of the victims—oversimplifying a deeply intricate issue that requires a comprehensive and multifaceted investigative approach. Crucially, it simplifies the complex motivations and mechanisms behind the trafficking operations, potentially overlooking the nuanced and varied experiences of the victims and the specific contexts from which these crimes emerge.

An alternative and perhaps more insightful method of categorising child trafficking is by examining the specific actions involved. While the prevalent view in China predominantly equates child trafficking to the violent abduction and sale of children from streets and public spaces, the actual scope of this crime extends much further. Child trafficking encompasses a broad range of activities that transcend straightforward acts of violence. It involves various non-violent actions, including the purchasing, selling, transporting, and transferring of children, all undertaken with the clear objective of selling the child. Crucially, a notable portion of "non-violent" trafficking operations involves the participation of the victims' parents or legal guardians, indicating that the dynamics of child trafficking can also encompass complex familial and guardian relationships, thereby adding another layer of complexity to the understanding and categorisation of these crimes.

Therefore, taking into account the motivations of the parents or legal guardians of the child victims, child trafficking in China can essentially be classified into two primary types: (1) the abduction and sale of children, and (2) the sale of children by parents. The former entails the removal of children from their parents or guardians by means of abduction, physical violence, coercion, deception, abuse of power, or other forms of actions against the will of parents. The latter scenario occurs when one or both parents or guardians consent to sell their children.

Upon further examination of parental intentions, the sale of children by parents can be subdivided into two categories. In the first, parents actively decide to sell their children, driven by a variety of motivations. In contrast, the second category, organised trafficking of children, involves parents being enticed or coerced into selling their children, often by professional traffickers who exploit their vulnerabilities or mislead them with fraudulent promises. The degree of parental concern for the welfare of trafficked children often varies markedly between these scenarios.

Additionally, the research identified a distinct category, pre-arranged child trafficking, wherein the intentions of the biological parents are rendered inconsequential. This category, which surfaced unexpectedly during the codification process of the research, encompasses instances where the child was "booked" in advance by the buyer through the traffickers. Facilitated by corrupt medical workers, the buyers are able to secure a birth certificate for the newborn, listing themselves as the parents. This revelation adds a complex dimension to child trafficking that was not initially foreseen in the study's design, indicating a sophisticated and deeply entrenched network that manipulates legal and medical systems to validate the trafficking process.

To sum up, to categorise child trafficking, at least four critical elements need to be taken into consideration: the key actors involved, their actions and means, the role of the parents or legal guardians of the victim, and the experiences of the victims themselves. Utilising these criteria, the detected child trafficking cases in China can be divided into three main modes: abduction and sale of children, parental sale of children, organised child trafficking, and pre-arranged child trafficking (see Table 3).

Table 3 The main child trafficking modes in China

	Key actor(s)	Action and means of the key actor(s)	Role of parent(s) or legal guardian	Victims' experiences
Abduction and Sale of Children (M1)	Trafficker(s)	Threat or use of force or other forms of coercion, abduction, fraud, deception, the abuse of power or of a position of vulnerability, etc.	Victims as well; actively looking for the missing child	Sold very quickly by the trafficker; may be traumatised; go back to parents once rescued
Parental Sale of Children (M2)	Father and/or mother, or legal guardian	Sale	Active perpetrator, taking the initiative to sell the child	May be sold to traffickers and then resold
			Selecting suitable buyer (for adoption)	May be sold directly to the adoptive family
Organised Child Trafficking (M3)	Traffickers	Recruitment, purchase, and sale	Passively participating: lured by trafficker	Sold, transported, and resold
Pre-arranged Child Trafficking (M4)	Traffickers	Recruitment, corruption and complicity	Mother actively participating; may be confined during the pregnancy	Sold to and adopted by the buyer

Abduction and Sale of Children (M1) involves taking children away from their parents against their will, through abduction, violence, coercion, deception, abuse of power, or other violent means. In these instances, both the children and their parents are victims, with the latter suffering directly from the violence and indirectly from the trauma and loss. The range of perpetrators is wide, including strangers, acquaintances, family friends, and sometimes even relatives. Following the abduction, victims are often quickly sold for exploitative activities or illegal adoption. Typically, family members report these incidents to the police soon after the abduction occurs. Upon rescue, the children are generally returned to their parents.

In **Parental Sale of Children (M2)**, children are sold by one or both parents or guardians, either directly to another family or through a middleman. The parents themselves initiate and facilitate this transaction, seeking out potential buyers or intermediaries. These middlemen can include professional traffickers, but more commonly, they are known individuals to the family such as relatives, friends, neighbours, or medical professionals in contact with the family. In most cases within this mode, parents are concerned about their child's welfare. Thus, they tend to consider the economic stability and family environment of the potential buyers before proceeding with the sale, indicating a nuanced perspective on the motivations behind such actions. Despite these considerations, the parents in this mode are essentially acting as perpetrators, often leading to the sale of the unwanted children. Such cases typically remain hidden until uncovered by external parties or law enforcement, and the children involved frequently encounter complex challenges related to their protection after being rescued.

In **Organised Child Trafficking** (**M3**), the involvement of parents is notably passive, with them being induced or recruited by intermediaries who are part of a loose trafficking network. This recruitment process targets parents at particularly vulnerable times, possibly shortly after or even before the birth of a child, with traffickers presenting incentives to persuade parents to part with their newborns. The distinguishing factor between M2 and M3 is the level of parental initiative; in M3, parents do not actively seek out buyers or intermediaries for their children. Instead, they are approached by traffickers, highlighting a more coercive or manipulative aspect of recruitment. Once ensnared in these networks, children undergo repeated transactions and are transported across vast distances, often with measures taken by traffickers to avoid detection, such as sedating the children or hiding them in luggage. Similar to the challenges faced in M2, the clandestine nature of M3 trafficking operations makes them difficult to uncover, typically relying on intervention by external parties or law enforcement. The depth and reach of these networks, coupled with a marked indifference or inability of the parents to protect their children, significantly hinder efforts to trace and reunite rescued victims with their original families.

Pre-arranged Child Trafficking (**M4**) is identified as a distinct trafficking mode, wherein recruiters organise for women who are several months into pregnancy to reside in a designated apartment with restricted freedom of movement. During the period leading up to the childbirth, the trafficker initiates contact with prospective buyers interested in "adopting" the soon-to-be-born infant. These traffickers meticulously plan for the admission of the pregnant women into selected hospitals, where they have already secured the complicity of hospital staff through bribery. This corrupt arrangement allows the pregnant woman to register a medical file using the identity of the intending buyer's spouse, leading to the issuance of a birth certificate that names the buyer as the parent, thereby erasing the biological mother's link to the child. By colluding with hospital insiders, traffickers effectively "launder" the child's identity from the moment of birth. It is crucial to note that the pregnant women involved are fully aware of the illicit nature of this operation and willingly participate in the sale of their unborn children. They typically adhere to the recruiters' directives, moving from their home province to another, predetermined province, where they live under austere conditions alongside other pregnant women in similar situations. During their confinement, they are denied the liberty to move freely and lack access to essential prenatal care and nutritional supplements, posing significant risks to both their health and that of their unborn children.

Fortunately, most of the judgments reviewed provided detailed accounts of the crimes, with only eight cases lacking specific details about the trafficking incidents. This comprehensive documentation has shed light on the inadequacy of the traditional Chinese term "abduction and sale" to encompass the range of trafficking practices

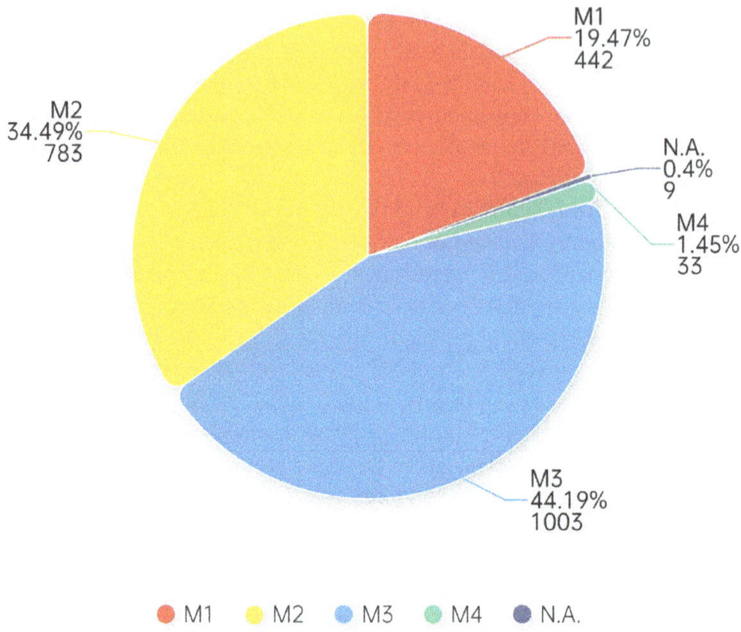

Fig. 6 Modes of child trafficking: distribution of victims in China (n = 2270)

currently observed. As depicted in Fig. 6, at the national level, the classic case of child abduction and sale (M1) represents less than 20% of the total instances, marking a significant departure from past trends. Instead, organised child trafficking (M3) has become the most widespread form, with the parental sale of children (M2) not far behind. This evolution in trafficking dynamics indicates a profound shift in the nature of child trafficking across China, moving beyond simple abduction scenarios to more complex networks of trafficking. Among these, pre-arranged child trafficking (M4) is the least reported, comprising less than 1.5% of the total cases, reflecting its relatively rare occurrence within the broader context of trafficking activities.

However, the prevalence of the four modes of trafficking varies significantly across different regions (see Fig. 7). A closer look at the top 15 regions with reported trafficking victims[8] reveals the abduction and sale of children (M1) is predominantly observed in Guizhou province alone, accounting for 59% of the victims rescued there. Conversely, in seven regions—Fujian, Henan, Hebei, Yunnan, Sichuan, Jiangxi, and Shanxi—less than 20% of the victims were abducted and then sold. In the remaining seven provinces, instances of M1 account for from 23 to 33% of the cases. This distribution further underscores that the traditional method of abduction and sale of children no longer constitutes the majority of trafficking instances.

[8] They are: Shandong (470), Henan (329), Fujian (318), Hebei (206), Yunnan (126), Guangdong (122), Guangxi (98), Zhejiang (91), Sichuan (81), Jiangxi (59), Jiangsu (52), Guizhou (49), Shanxi (44), Shaanxi (42), and Anhui (39).

Parental sale of children (M2) emerges as the predominant mode in only four provinces: Jiangsu (71%), Shanxi (48%), Shaanxi (67%), and Anhui (46%), each marked by a considerable presence of less developed areas. In the remaining regions, M2 accounts for 21–35% of the victims. Organised child trafficking (M3) exhibits a polarised distribution trend across different regions. In eleven out of fourteen provinces, more than 35% of trafficking victims fall under M3, with Yunnan and Henan leading at 67% each. In contrast, in the remaining provinces, the percentage of children trafficked by criminal groups falls below 15%, highlighting a stark dichotomy in the prevalence of organised child trafficking within China. Pre-arranged child trafficking (M4), the least reported form of trafficking, has been identified mainly in the provinces with the highest overall numbers of trafficking incident—Shandong, Fujian, Henan—and also in Sichuan province, with 12, 9, 4, 8 infants reported respectively (Fig. 7).

B. Profile of the victims

Drawing the profile of the victims of child trafficking elucidates those targeted by traffickers and identifies the groups of children most vulnerable to such exploitation. Details concerning the victims' gender, age, methods of trafficking, and outcomes of rescue efforts are instrumental in guiding the processes of crime prevention and victim protection.

Contrary to the global pattern of child trafficking, where the majority of victims are female (UNODC 2016), in China, there is a higher incidence of male victims. Among 2270 recorded instances, there are 1345 boys compared to 894 girls (refer

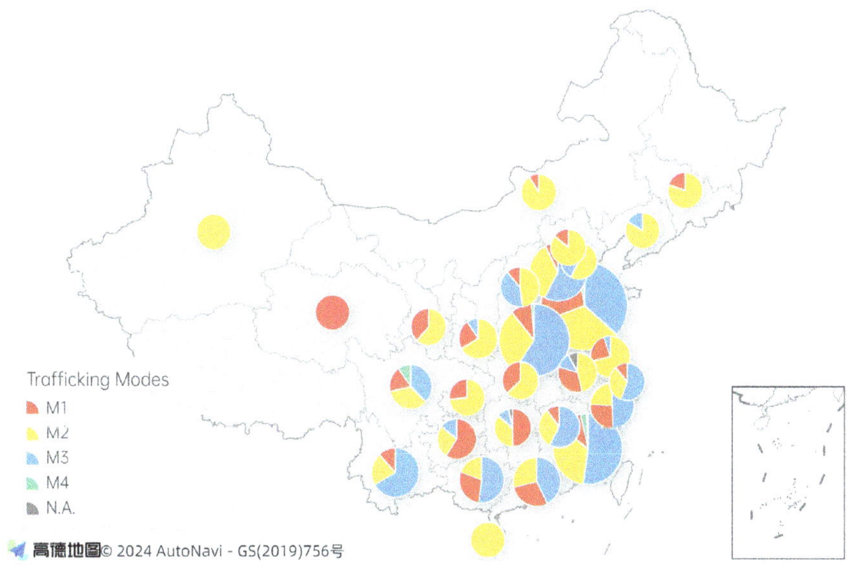

Fig. 7 Modes of child trafficking: distribution of victims in cases detected in each region of China (n = 2270)

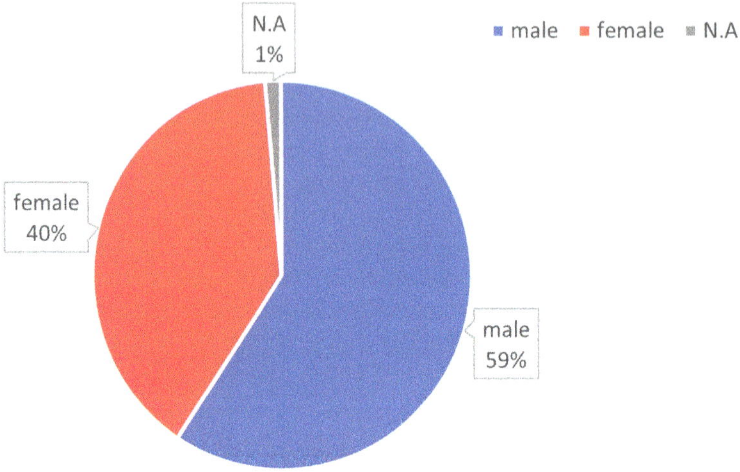

Fig. 8 Demographic distribution of trafficked children in China by gender (n = 2270)

to Fig. 8). This tendency is consistent across all age brackets, save for those aged 12–14 years (as shown in Fig. 9). The gender ratio of victims across the four modes of trafficking mirrors this general trend, albeit with minor variations in proportion. As depicted in Fig. 10, the ratio of male to female victims in modes M1, M2, and M4 is nearly double, whereas in M3, the ratio of male victims slightly exceeds that of females. This suggests that boys and male infants are at a much higher risk of being abducted or sold directly by their parents, while infants of either gender are equally vulnerable to resale and neglect during organised child trafficking.

Upon examining the data from each province, marked disparities in the gender of victims become evident (see Fig. 11). An analysis of the top ten regions with the highest incidences of trafficking (refer to Table 2) reveals that only in three regions—Hebei, Henan, and Yunnan—does the number of female victims exceed that of male victims, with sex ratios of 0.93, 0.95, and 0.94, respectively. Conversely, a pronounced gender imbalance is noted in Fujian province, where there are 266 male victims to 50 female victims, resulting in a sex ratio of 5.32. This is followed by Guangdong and Shandong provinces, with sex ratios of victims at 1.75 and 1.41, respectively. Such disparities in the gender of victims may be indicative of differing patterns and motivations among buyers, reflecting the cultural nuances of these provinces.

Regarding the age of the victims, as detailed in Fig. 12, an overwhelming majority of the victims, accounting for 85%, are younger than 6 months. Alarmingly, newborn infants aged less than 1 month constitute nearly half of the total number of victims. Children aged between 6 months and 5 years number 247, representing 12.4% of the total victims, while merely 50 victims (2.5%) had attained school age (6 years old) at the time of their trafficking. Furthermore, only 28 victims were over 9 years old, indicating that a minimal portion (1.6%) of child trafficking victims were subjected to

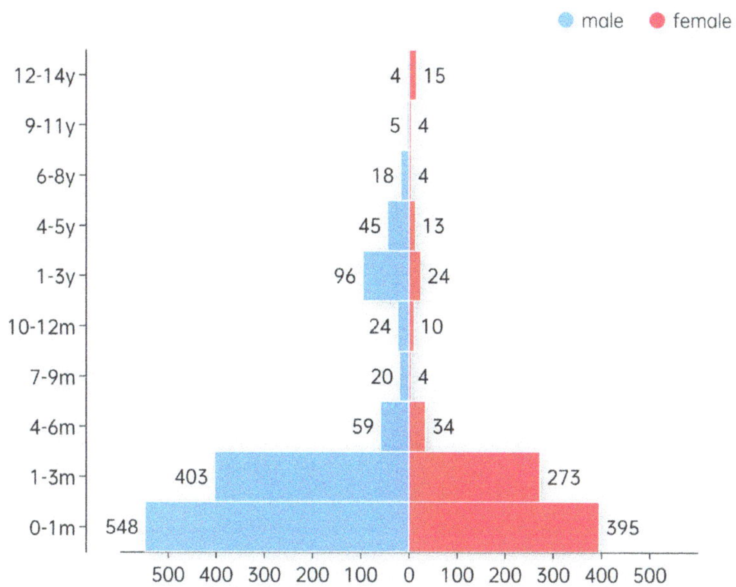

Fig. 9 Demographic distribution of trafficked children in China by gender and age group (n = 1998)

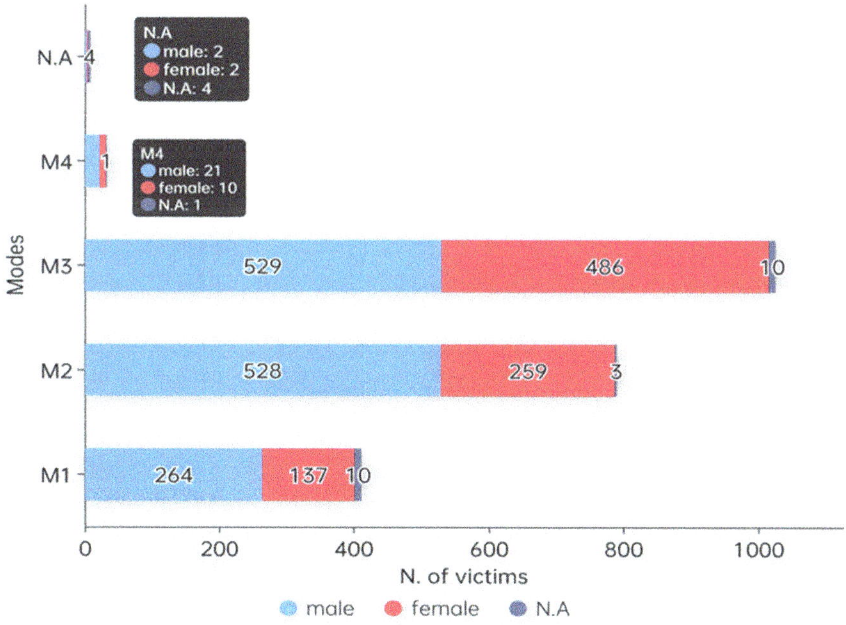

Fig. 10 Gender distribution of victims across different trafficking modes

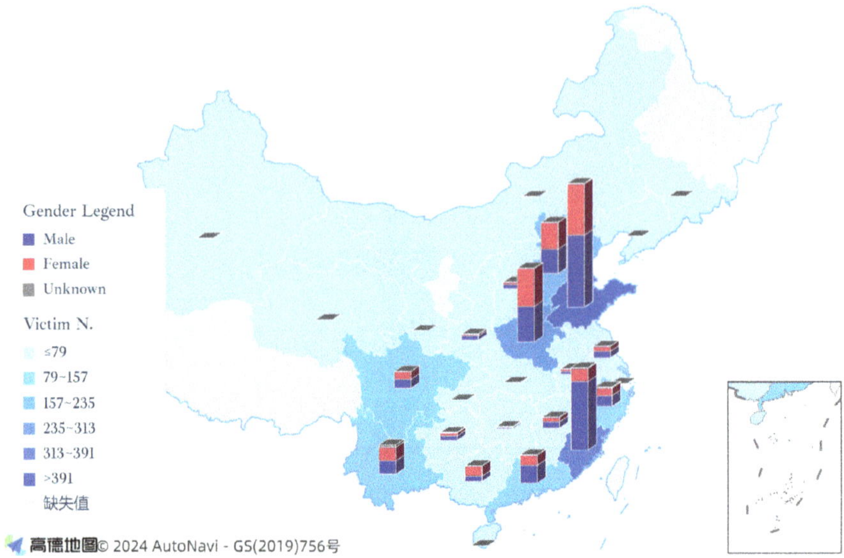

Fig. 11 Regional distribution of detected child trafficking victims in China by gender

conventional forms of exploitation recognised internationally, such as forced prostitution, forced marriage, and forced labour. However, considering that the legal definition of child trafficking victims in Chinese legislation encompasses individuals under 14 years of age, this proportion would ostensibly increase were victims between 15 and 18 years old to be included.

Upon examining the age distribution within each trafficking mode (refer to Fig. 13), Mode 1 exhibits a broad range across all age categories. Whilst the proportion of children under 1 year old remains predominant, a significantly higher proportion of older children, compared to other trafficking modes, is observed. This suggests that children from every age group are susceptible to being victims of abduction and the sale of children. For Modes 2 and 3, children under the age of 1 year constitute the overwhelming majority of victims, suggesting that the sale of children by parents predominantly occurs when the children are very young. Nonetheless, at least 25 school-aged children were sold with their parents' involvement, making them among the most pathetic victims as they are cognisant of being abandoned by their parents and placed in exploitative conditions. The chart also underscores potential gaps in data (labelled as "N.A" segment) in Mode 3, highlighting traffickers' disregard for the specifics and welfare of the children.

In certain instances, particularly with parental sales of children (M2), these transactions involve the direct sale of children to the ultimate buyer, who often claims or intends to adopt the purchased child. In Mode 2, middlemen are typically remunerated by either the parents (who are also the sellers) or the buyers, and occasionally by both parties. There also exist scenarios wherein middlemen either decline any form of compensation or do not request it. Contrastingly, in situations involving child

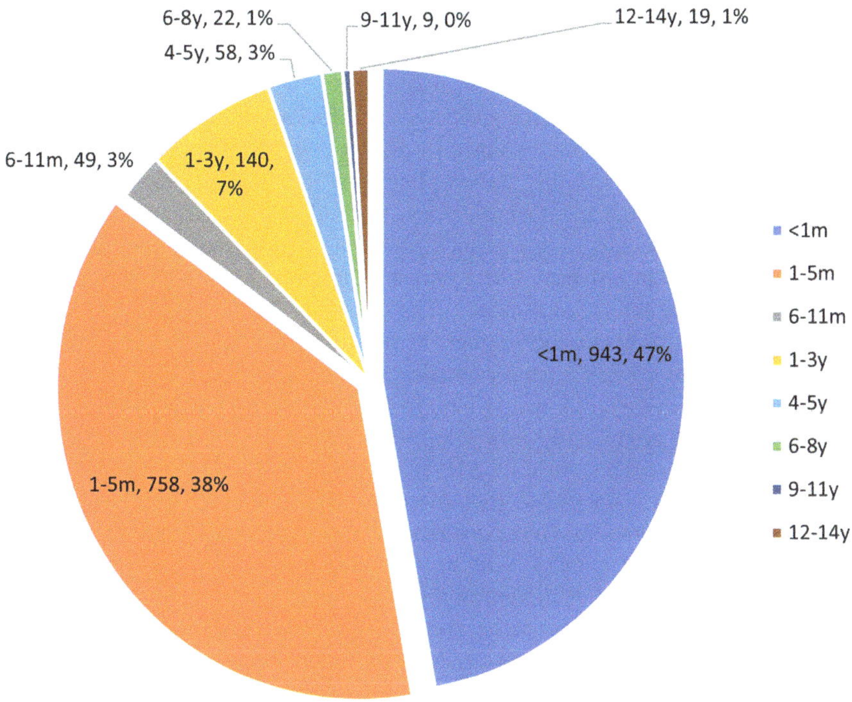

Fig. 12 Demographic distribution of trafficked children in China by age (n = 1998)

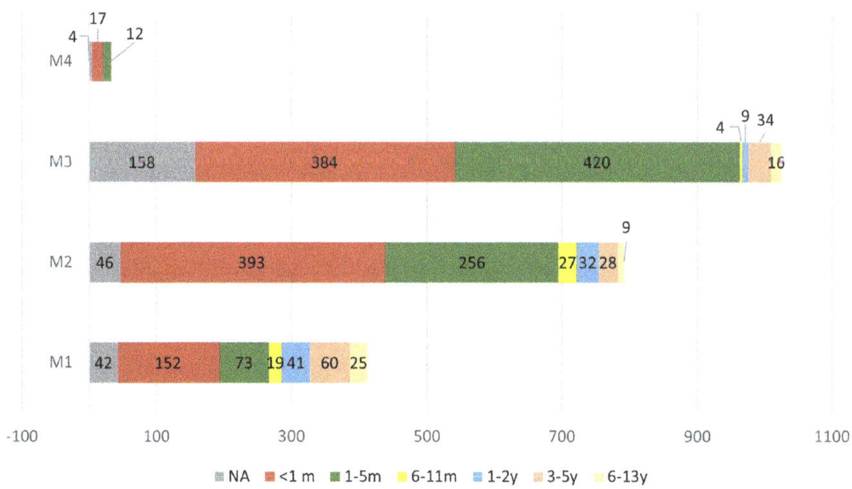

Fig. 13 Age-specific distribution and modes of child trafficking in China (n = 2261)

trafficking by criminal networks (M3), children may be sold multiple times, with the price for the same child escalating from a few thousand to in excess of a hundred thousand Chinese Yuan.

To ascertain the financial value attributed to trafficked children within the black market and to understand the variance in pricing, two distinct price points were documented for each child: the "lowest price" and the "highest price". Generally, these represent the initial and final sale prices of children in cases categorised under Mode 3. Prices encountered at intermediary stages of the trafficking chain were not recorded, while in instances where only a single price was available, this figure was documented as the "highest price". The overall prices span from 360 Yuan to 160,000 Yuan. On average, the "highest price" for male victims stands at 48,433 Yuan, in contrast to 29,339 Yuan for female victims.

The box plot depicted in Fig. 14 offers an analytical perspective on the distribution of the "highest prices"—the final sale prices—for trafficked children, segmented by mode and gender. This illustration reveals that the prices for trafficked children are subject to variation not only across different trafficking modes but also between genders within these modes. Generally, the sale price for female victims is significantly lower than that for males. With the exception of the M1 category, where the mean prices for male and female victims are nearly identical, in all other modes, male victims command considerably higher mean prices than female. The price range for both male and female victims in M1 is the broadest, whereas the price fluctuations for victims fall within a narrower range in cases of pre-arranged child trafficking (M4). Moreover, the mean sale prices for male victims across the four modes differ, with M1 registering the lowest mean price and M4 the highest. The scenario diverges for female victims; the mean prices for M1 and M3 are quite similar, approximately 25,000 Yuan, while for M2 and M4, they are marginally higher, around 30,000 Yuan and 40,000 Yuan respectively. Notably, in M3—the mode with the most documented cases—the prices for female victims are the lowest amongst the four modes.

Figure 15 presents a box plot that elucidates the disparities in the "highest prices" for trafficked children, segregated by age and gender. Generally, the mean prices for females across various age groups remain relatively stable, with the notable exception of the 6–11 months age group. Conversely, the mean prices for male victims tend to decrease as they age, except for boys aged 6–13 years. For victims younger than 6 months, the mean price for male infants is approximately 50,000 Yuan—considerably higher than that for females. The mean prices for females do not exhibit substantial fluctuations across most age groups, maintaining a degree of consistency. However, there is an exception in the age group of 6–11 months, where we observe a distinct peak in prices, which surpasses that of males. This anomaly warrants further investigation due to the small sample size—only seven cases—which may affect the accuracy of the data representation for this particular group. For males, the trend shows a general decline in mean prices with increasing age, though there is an uptick for the group aged between 6 and 13 years. In contrast, in the age groups of 6–11 months and 3–5 years, females command higher mean prices than males. This could potentially be attributed to two factors: a limited sample size skewing the data or a specific demand dynamic for females in these age brackets

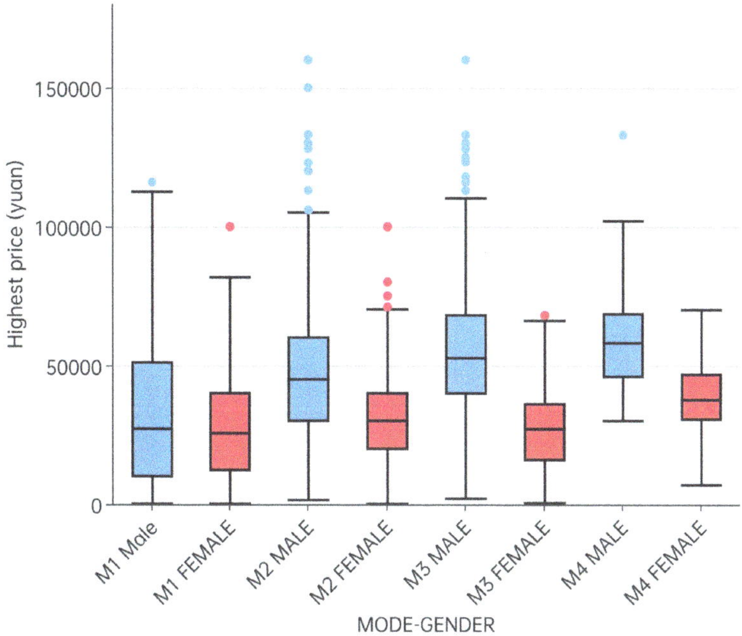

Fig. 14 Comparative analysis of highest prices of victims by mode and gender (n = 2065)

within the black market, which appears to be particularly applicable to the 3–5-year age group.

C. **Profile of the cases**

As anticipated previously, child trafficking in China does not predominantly revolve around exploitation. Among all the cases reviewed, only 17 victims were definitively identified as being exploited, of which 14 were female. These girls were subjected to sexual exploitation, either through forced marriage or prostitution. Conversely, the male victims were compelled into engaging in criminal activities, specifically theft and robbery. The relatively low incidence of trafficking cases involving exploitation could be attributed to the age limit of victims defined in China's Criminal Law, which is set at 14 years old. This legal stipulation likely excludes many instances of the trafficking of young females and males for exploitation from being categorised as child trafficking for the purposes of this research.

As illustrated in Fig. 16, of the 2270 identified victims, 1716 have been rescued or released from the trafficking chain, representing 75% of the total. Nevertheless, 445 victims (20%) remained unlocated by the time of the traffickers' prosecution. The percentages of victims still missing across the four trafficking modalities are 13, 15, 26, and 12%, respectively. This underscores the clandestine nature of this crime and the challenges inherent in its detection, particularly for organised child trafficking. Most distressingly, 23 victims perished during their ordeal: 5 were abducted, 4 sold by their parents, 13 ensnared by organised trafficking networks, and 1 was the result

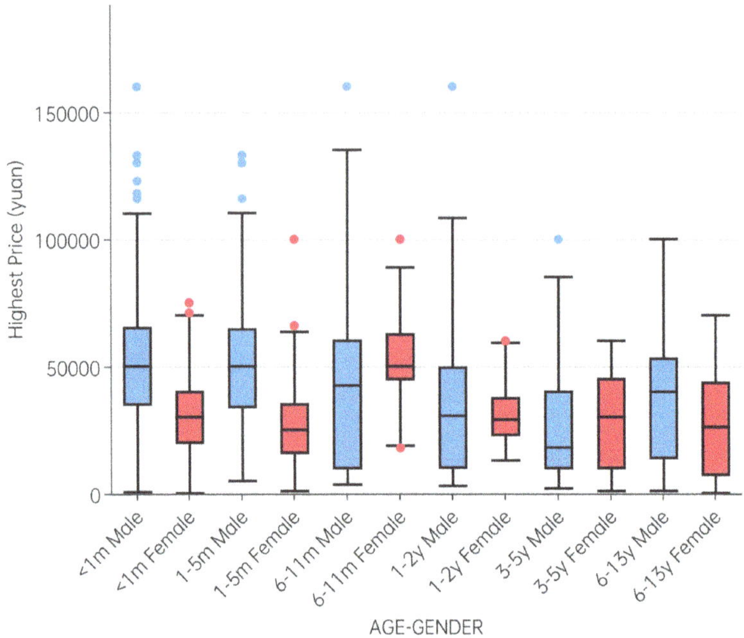

Fig. 15 Comparative analysis of highest prices of victims by age and gender (n = 1703)

of a pre-arranged pregnancy. It is crucial to highlight that these statistics pertain solely to cases that have been detected, suggesting that they may represent merely the tip of the iceberg.

Child trafficking cases can emerge at several critical points: before the sale of the victim, during the process of transportation, or after the victim has been deeply entangled in the trafficking network. This variability means that the window for rescuing a victim spans from the immediate moments of trafficking to years, or even decades, after their separation from their original family. Central to the efficacy of these rescue efforts is the timeliness of reporting the incident to the police; prompt action significantly raises the probability of the victims' recovery. Illustrated by Fig. 17, among 1792 victims who were rescued by police, a significant majority, 75%, of the victims were rescued within the first year. Furthermore, 19% of the victims were extricated from the trafficking cycle within 1–5 years. Alarmingly, almost 5% had been alienated from their families for more than 5 years, within which, 30 individuals had been subjected to trafficking for over a decade. This data, while revealing, also hints at a broader issue: these figures only account for cases that have been detected. Given that many undetected cases are often those that occurred years earlier, the actual number of victims either still under the control of traffickers or living within the purchasers' families is likely to be substantially higher. This stark reality underscores the imperative for swift reporting and robust investigative efforts to unearth and disrupt these trafficking networks.

Fig. 16 Rescue results (n = 2270)

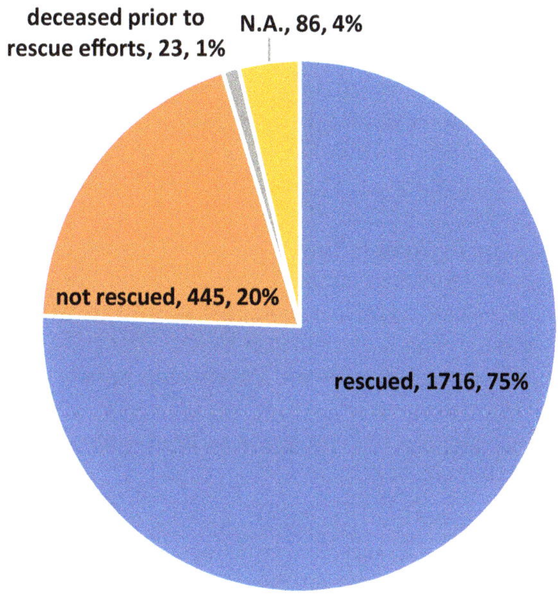

Fig. 17 Number of cases by duration of trafficking (n = 1792)

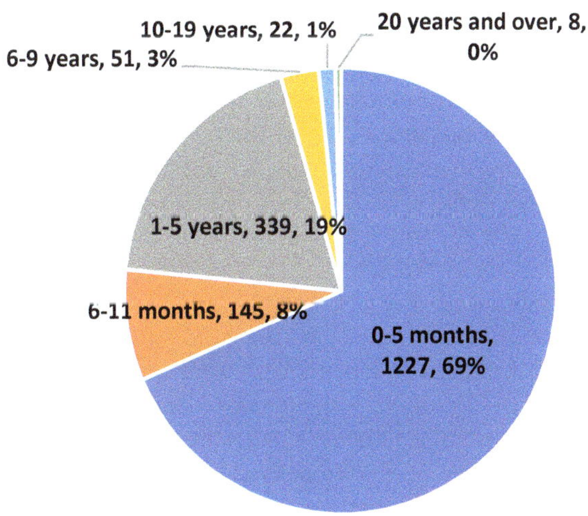

Following their rescue or identification by the police, child victims must be safeguarded. The study, informed by judicial outcomes, delineates five types of resettlement options available to the victims:

1. **Return to Non-complicit Parent(s)**: The child victim is returned to the parent(s) who were either unaware of or opposed to the trafficking, typically being the initial reporters of the crime to the police.

2. **Return to Complicit Parent(s)**: In cases where the parent(s) had been involved in selling the child, either through direct action, assistance, or passive consent, the police may still return the child to these individuals.
3. **Resettlement with Extended Family**: There are instances where both parents are either unwilling or unable to assume custody due to financial, health, or legal constraints, resulting in the child being placed with other relatives, such as grandparents, uncles, and aunts.
4. **Care in Welfare Homes or Foster Families**: When it is challenging or impossible to locate a child's biological parents, or if the parents and extended family are deemed unfit to resume care, the child may be sent to a welfare home or foster family. This is common for children trafficked by criminal networks.
5. **Continuation with the Purchasing Family**: The children continued residing with the purchasers, whether by their own volition, decision made by their biological parents, or determinations from authorities, including the police and local welfare institutions.

In over 60% of the total trafficking cases analysed, information pertaining to post-rescue outcomes is conspicuously absent, either not applicable or unspecified in the judgements, suggesting a potential lapse in the safeguarding of child victims' rights. As indicated in In cases categorised as M1, numerous victims, by the time of their rescue, had either reached adulthood or were mature enough to make their own decisions, opting to stay with their "adoptive parents". In M2 scenarios, the biological parents, lacking either the willingness or the means to care for the victims, might return the children to the buyers post-rescue. For many M3 cases, a shortage of welfare resources has led the police to temporarily entrust the children to the purchasing families, or for local welfare institutions to designate these families as foster caregivers. Nevertheless, it is paramount to acknowledge that such practices contravene the principles outlined in the China National Plan of Action on Combating Trafficking in Women and Children (2013–2020), as decreed by the State Council of China.

As illustrated in Table 4, a mere 245 victims (representing 10.8% of those rescued) were reunited with parents who were not implicated in the trafficking. This figure diminishes to 1.9% in instances involving criminal networks. Welfare homes or foster families provided refuge for 237 victims (10.4%), the majority of whom (173 victims) were M3 victims. Additionally, 24 victims sold by their parents found a haven with their extended families.

A particularly alarming aspect is the risk of re-victimisation: at least 41 children were returned to parents who had previously expressed a disinterest in their upbringing and had actively participated in selling them. Furthermore, it is concerning that 271 children continued to reside with the purchasers' families, with the rationale behind such arrangements varying across different trafficking scenarios. Commonly, many trafficked children are sold to families seeking to adopt, albeit through illegal channels. Before the crime came to light, these families may have already assumed a parental role, caring for the children as if they were their own.

Table 4 Post rescue situation by trafficking modes

		Trafficking mode					
		N.A	M1	M2	M3	M4	Total
N.A	Count	6	73	128	312	8	527
	% within mode	66.7%	17.7%	16.2%	30.4%	24.2%	23.2%
Return to non-complicit parent(s)	Count	1	118	107	19	0	245
	% within mode	11.1%	28.6%	13.5%	1.9%	0.0%	10.8%
Return to complicit parent(s)	Count	0	3	**32**	6	0	41
	% within mode	0.0%	0.7%	4.0%	0.6%	0.0%	1.8%
Resettlement with extended family	Count	0	0	24	0	0	24
	% within mode	0.0%	0.0%	3.0%	0.0%	0.0%	1.1%
Care in welfare homes or foster families	Count	0	16	39	173	9	237
	% within mode	0.0%	3.9%	4.9%	16.9%	27.3%	10.4%
Remained in the buying family	Count	0	31	76	**163**	1	**271**
	% within mode	0.0%	7.5%	9.6%	15.9%	3.0%	11.9%
Unspecified	Count	2	171	385	352	15	925
	% within mode	22.2%	41.5%	48.7%	34.3%	45.5%	40.7%
Total	Count	9	412	791	1025	33	2270
	% within mode	100.0%	100.0%	100.0%	100.0%	100.0%	100.0%

In cases categorised as M1, numerous victims, by the time of their rescue, had either reached adulthood or were mature enough to make their own decisions, opting to stay with their "adoptive parents". In M2 scenarios, the biological parents, lacking either the willingness or the means to care for the victims, might return the children to the buyers post-rescue. For many M3 cases, a shortage of welfare resources has led the police to temporarily entrust the children to the purchasing families, or for local welfare institutions to designate these families as foster caregivers. Nevertheless, it is paramount to acknowledge that such practices contravene the principles outlined in the China National Plan of Action on Combating Trafficking in Women and Children (2013–2020), as decreed by the State Council of China.

D. **Profile of the perpetrators**

Although the profile of victims in this study diverges from those noted in international research, the characteristics of the perpetrators conform to the general attributes of traffickers recognised both globally and within the East Asia and Pacific region. In the 1449 criminal judgements analysed in this study, 3339 individuals were convicted of trafficking crimes for their direct involvement in the abduction, kidnapping, purchase, sale, transportation, or transfer of 2270 children for the purpose of selling them. The majority of the traffickers are male. After excluding 695 offenders due to the lack of relevant information, it emerged that 57% of the convicted individuals are male, 43% are female, and there is one case involving a female minor (see Fig. 18). This gender distribution is consistent with the demographics of traffickers observed in the East Asia and Pacific region and globally (UNODC 2023, p. 58).

However, the perpetrators involved in child trafficking within China demonstrate a notably higher maturity level than the global average cited by the UNODC. Whereas the international average age of traffickers is 37 (UNODC 2023, p. 59), the average age of traffickers in China is 41 (as shown in Fig. 19). The discrepancy between the average ages of male and female offenders is minimal, with figures of 40.91 and 41.09 years, respectively. Furthermore, the age range of traffickers in China is broader, spanning from 16 (the minimum age of legal responsibility prior to 2020) to 79 years, in contrast to the global span of 23–36 years. Among the 2186 convicted individuals, those younger than 35 years constitute less than 40%, whereas middle-aged traffickers represent 50%, and individuals over 65 years old make up more than 3%, totalling 68 persons.

Despite a significant proportion of the traffickers not being young, and older individuals typically possessing lower levels of education in China, the educational background of traffickers is disproportionately low. Based on the details extracted from the judgements, merely one third of the perpetrators have completed the 9-year compulsory education (as shown in Fig. 20). A scant 6% have attained higher secondary education or beyond, while a notable 24% of 1711 convicted individuals were found to be illiterate. This pattern suggests that bolstering formal or vocational education could serve as an effective strategy to mitigate the incidence of child trafficking.

Another trend in the profiles of offenders, which aligns with findings from international research, is the predominance of national traffickers in child trafficking cases within China. The UNODC's research indicates that approximately 94% of traffickers convicted in the East Asia and Pacific region were nationals of the country where they faced conviction (UNODC 2023, p. 124). This study reveals an even higher proportion within China, with 98% of the offenders holding Chinese nationality. Among the 3339 individuals convicted of child trafficking in the three selected provinces of China, merely 60 were not Chinese citizens. Additionally, given China's

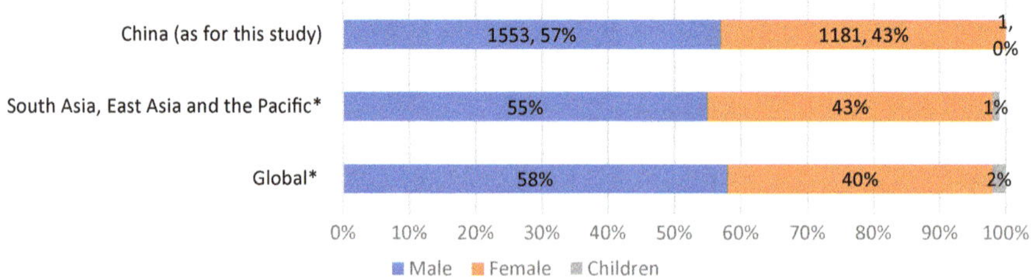

Fig. 18 Gender distribution of convicted offenders: comparative data (n = 2735). **Source* UNODC, Global Report on Trafficking in Persons 2022, p. 58

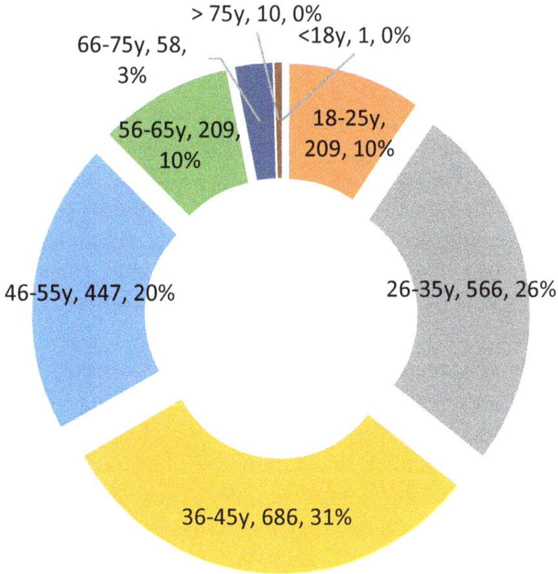

Fig. 19 Age Distribution of individuals convicted for child trafficking (n = 2186)

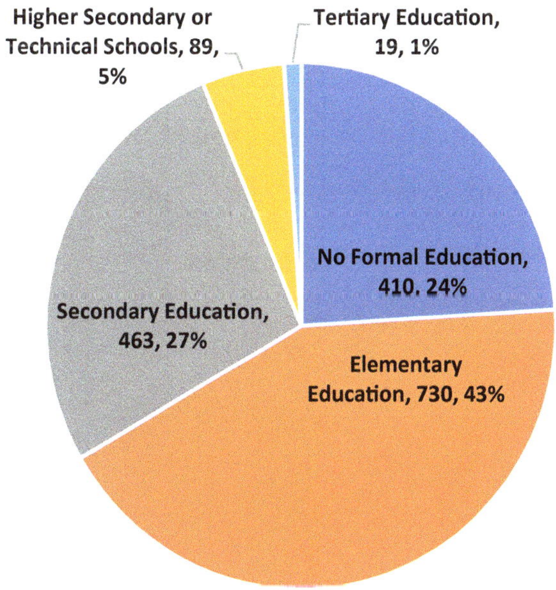

Fig. 20 Educational levels of individuals convicted in child trafficking cases (n = 1711)

vast territory and its unique household registration system, it is pertinent to examine the permanent residences of the offenders in greater detail.

In addition, the data highlights a notable disproportion in the representation of ethnic minorities among individuals convicted of child trafficking. According to valid data, approximately 18% of convicted offenders are from ethnic minorities. Illustrated in Fig. 21, the proportion of offenders identified with the Han majority (82%) is notably higher than that of any single ethnic minority group. However, when this is compared to the proportion of Han Chinese within the overall population, the representation of Han offenders is considerably lower. Data from the latest National Population Census (Census Office of the State Council 2021) reveals that Han Chinese constitute 91.11% of the national populace. In contrast, ethnic minorities, making up just 8.89% of the national population, account for 18% of all convicted offenders. This disparity becomes even more pronounced in certain provinces, such as Yunnan and Sichuan, where the proportion of offenders from ethnic minorities is higher.

Finally, regarding the relationship between perpetrators and the victims, according to the details reported in the judgements, 60% of the convicted persons are strangers to the victims, while 30% are those who were supposed to provide care and guardianship to the victims. In addition, 9% of the perpetrators were friends, neighbours, or colleagues of the victims' families. There are also 29 medical staff, including obstetricians, gynaecologists, nurses, and midwives, who were found guilty of committing the crime of child trafficking. Nevertheless, the number of medical workers who have assisted in the offence and those who have ignored the criminal activities taking place in their work place is much higher (Fig. 22).

E. **Operation and organisation**

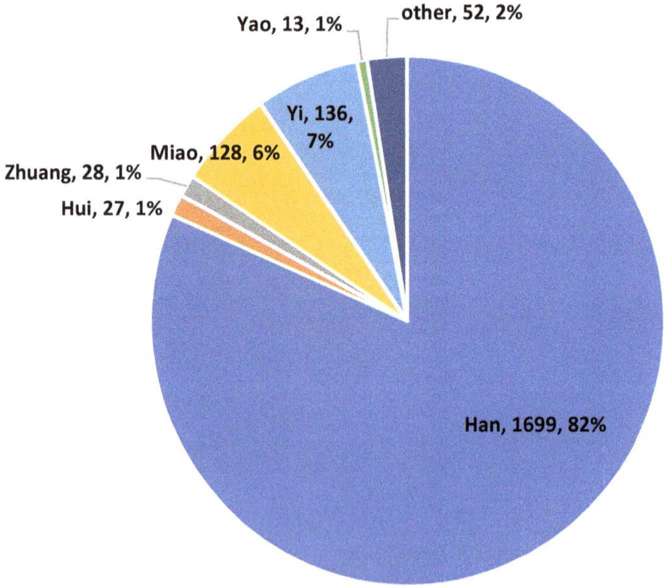

Fig. 21 Ethnic composition of convicted traffickers (n = 2083)

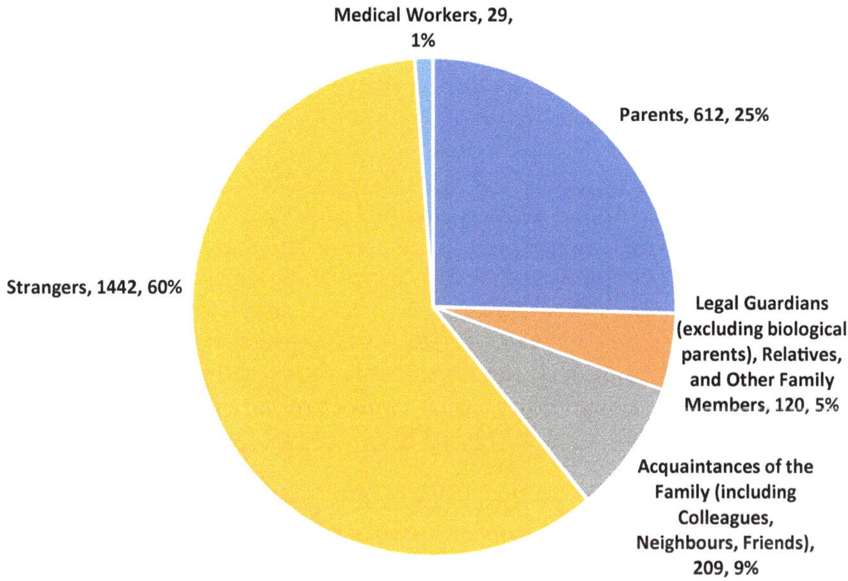

Fig. 22 Relationships of traffickers to their victims (n = 2412)

It is frequently observed that incidents of trafficking involve multiple victims, and intriguingly, the average number of traffickers involved in these cases is double that of the victims (refer to Table 2 above). This statistic highlights the organised and widespread nature of trafficking networks across the country. However, the high number of perpetrators involved does not necessarily indicate the existence of highly organised criminal groups. Regrettably, a significant number of judgements lack detailed information about the structure of these trafficking networks. Nonetheless, through the testimonies of defendants and witnesses, it is possible to approximately sketch the operational and organisational patterns characterising the criminal activities associated with the four modes of child trafficking. This approach provides insight into the complex dynamics underpinning these illicit networks, despite the limited direct evidence of their organisational frameworks.

(1) *Abduction and sale of children*

Criminal operations of abduction and sale of children (M1) are the simplest ones among all the four modes. The number of perpetrators directly involved in the crime is not very high, usually one or two people. Some so-called "professional" traffickers first look for buyers and go about finding and abducting suitable children according to the buyer's requirements on the gender and age of the child. In contrast, for some offenders, child trafficking is just one of the many criminal activities from which they derive their income. They first find a child playing in their neighbourhood and decided to abduct the child before finding a buyer. Then they abduct the child on a whim and then sell the victim at will for a relatively low price. In any case, the victim of M1 will not be harboured for a long time by the traffickers. Most of the buyers intend to "adopt" the child though illegally, but it also happens that buyers find the child "difficult to keep" with them, or has mental or physical health conditions, then they resell the victim to other buyers.

Within the spectrum of child trafficking, the abduction and sale of children (M1) are characterised by relatively straightforward operations. The crimes typically involve a small number of perpetrators, usually one or two, who directly engage in the trafficking activities. Some "professional" traffickers, start by securing potential buyers. They then actively seek and abduct children who meet specific criteria requested by these buyers, such as gender and age preferences. Conversely, there are offenders for whom child trafficking is merely one among many criminal activities from which they derive income. These traffickers might identify a child in any area, impulsively decide to abduct them without a prior buyer in mind, and subsequently selling the child at a relatively low price, seizing the opportunity rather than acting on a preconceived plan.

Furthermore, traffickers can sometimes be individuals familiar to the victim's family, including neighbours, coworkers, friends, or even relatives. This adds a layer of complexity to the crime, as the trust placed in these individuals by the family can be exploited to facilitate the abduction and sale of children. In any case, the criteria for selecting victims are not arbitrary; there is a preference for young boys who are neither too young to be difficult to care for nor too old to remember their abductors or their original families. Young girls with mental disabilities are also targeted due to their sexual maturity and ease of manipulation, making them particularly vulnerable to sexual exploitation. In fact, the few cases of trafficking for the purpose of exploitation identified in this study were predominantly associated with M1.

In numerous cases, the offender is a relative of the victim, such as grandparents, uncles, aunts, or other distant relatives. This introduces scenarios where the child is sold under the pretext of "protecting" the family or a single parent, often targeting young single mothers unable to marry due to age or family opposition. The societal stigma surrounding out-of-wedlock births can prompt relatives to sell the child against the parents' wishes, complicating the victim's chance of being reported to the police by their own reluctant parents. Therefore, the parents of the victims of M1 are also victims of violence, physical, or psychological, that may come from strangers, friends, or their own families.

Victims in M1 scenarios are rarely held by traffickers for extended periods. While the majority of purchasers seek to illegally adopt these children, there are instances where a child deemed "difficult to manage" due to behavioural or health issues is resold. However, the trafficking cycle often ceases and does not recur once a victim is rescued. This break in the cycle is largely attributed to the cooperative nature of the victims' parents, who, being victims themselves, typically report the crime promptly and collaborate with the police in the search and identification of their missing children. Furthermore, victims in M1 cases are seldom traded by multiple traffickers, making the tracing and rescue of abducted children relatively less complicated compared to other forms.

(2) *Parental Sale of children*

The core issue at the heart of the parental sale of children (M2) revolves around abandonment and profiting from one's children. The primary perpetrators—the victim's parents—proactively seek out potential buyers. Among these parents, attitudes vary significantly; some diligently search for a suitable adoptive family for their newborn, prioritising the child's future well-being, while others are indifferent, treating their own children as mere commodities.

A notable procedure in M2 involves conducting medical examinations for the child, serving as a sort of quality assurance for prospective buyers about the infant's health. Transactions commonly take place in the vicinity of hospitals, including within the facilities, on adjacent roadways, or in close-by accommodations such as residences or hotels. This setting underscores the transactional nature of these exchanges, blending the lines between healthcare and illicit trade.

Intermediaries often play a role in facilitating transactions between parents and buyers. These go-betweens can range from acquaintances to strangers encountered in hospitals (who are often professional traffickers) and even hospital staff like gynaecologists. Many of them believe they are performing a service that benefits all involved: aiding the child in finding a loving home, alleviating the economic pressures on the parents, and fulfilling the desires of individuals unable to have biological children. These intermediaries often steer clear of direct involvement in the transactions to avoid potential legal repercussions, though they may receive commissions from one or both parties after the fact. However, there are instances where parents directly sell their child to a middleman, who then sells the child to the final buyer at a significantly increased price.

This form of trafficking is particularly challenging to uncover since all involved parties, except for the victim, have a vested interest in the transaction's success, making them unlikely to initiate contact with law enforcement. Even when such cases come to light, the trafficking cycle may not necessarily conclude with the child's return to their original family.

(3) *Organised child trafficking*

Organised child trafficking is marked by well-defined yet loosely organised criminal networks, encompassing at least two main groups of traffickers within the victim's trafficking chain. At the origin, the group typically includes a recruiter, several transporters, and often a babysitter. Similarly, in the destination region, the composition again involves transporters, a babysitter and a seller. The trafficking process may also engage intermediary traffickers or groups.

The recruiter and seller usually play central roles as the organisers and main perpetrators, directly engaging in the buying and selling of infants. They coordinate the logistics of harbouring, babysitting, and transporting the children, often hiring others to assist in these tasks. Within these networks, traffickers frequently share familial ties or come from the same locality, which may contribute to the cohesion and operational secrecy of the group.

Victims of M3 frequently undergo multiple transactions and are transported over extensive distances. Similar to the operations in M2, the initial sale often takes place in proximity to hospitals or at the child's original home. During the transportation phase, traffickers employ various means such as trains and private vehicles to transport the infants. To ensure secrecy and minimise detection, traffickers often resort to sedating the babies with sleeping pills during train journeys or concealing them in luggage or under blankets in cars when traveling by road, aiming to keep the infants quiet and avoid the scrutiny of others. Typically, the transactions involving babies are conducted separately from the exchange of money, with the latter usually managed by the leading traffickers.

Upon reaching the final buyers, the infants may be several months older, with the sale price significantly inflated. While the transportation segment of the trafficking chain is the most visible and hence the most susceptible to detection, tracing the child back to their original family poses a formidable challenge, highlighting the intricate and clandestine nature of these trafficking operations.

(4) *Pre-arranged child trafficking*

The dynamics and structure of pre-arranged child trafficking (M4) distinctly differ from other trafficking forms. In this scenario, the typical role of a trafficker—who abducts, transfers, and sells a victim—is absent. Instead, the traffickers perform dual roles: on one hand, they recruit women who are several months pregnant; on the other, they engage with prospective buyers interested in "adopting" the newborn.

Upon arriving at the location managed by the traffickers, the pregnant women face severe restrictions on their personal freedom. To avoid detection, traffickers house these women in secluded settings, cutting off any contact with the external world. Such isolation often results in poor living conditions and inadequate healthcare, adversely affecting both the pregnant women and their unborn children.

A pivotal aspect of this form of trafficking is the involvement and complicity of medical personnel. Traffickers establish illicit connections with hospitals, enabling a range of unlawful activities, including determining the sex of the foetus and falsifying birth certificate details. Corrupt medical workers, bribed by the traffickers, play a crucial role in this process. They ensure that the pregnant women are admitted to hospitals under the identities of the buyers, which results in the buyers' names being listed as the parents on the birth certificates. Consequently, the biological mothers leave no hospital records of their admission and childbirth.

The transaction in such cases is not a direct purchase of a child but encompasses payment for an extensive array of services. This suite of services includes compensation for the biological mother, agency fees, and expenses related to medical care, which is registered under the names of the adoptive parents. For the biological mothers involved in this arrangement, disengaging from the agreement or retaining any custody of the child becomes an insurmountable challenge, effectively entrapping them in a cycle of exploitation and deprivation. This system not only commodifies the childbirth process but also severely limits the rights and options of the biological mothers, deepening the ethical and humanitarian concerns associated with such trafficking practices.

3 Conclusion

Although the data presented in this chapter is based on all the judgements available in current situation, yet they are just a slide of the tip of the iceberg of child trafficking crimes. Given that the "China Judgements Online" database was established only in 2013, it does not encompass all judgments. More critically, these judgments reflect only the cases that have been detected, leaving a potentially vast number of undetected cases beyond the scope of our analysis. Despite these limitations, judgments stand out among various sources for their ability to provide relatively comprehensive details of the cases from multiple perspectives, including those of the victims' parents, traffickers, witnesses, and prosecutors. As such, despite the inherent limitations in the scope of the data, judgments are an invaluable resource for analysing the dynamics of child trafficking in China, offering insights into the complexity and multifaceted nature of this issue.

Based on this data, we have delineated some key trends of child trafficking in China. First of all, there are four distinct modes of child trafficking in the country: abduction and sale of children, parental sale of children, organised child trafficking, and surrogacy-related trafficking. Our findings reveal that the prevalence of these modes varies across different regions, with the traditional abduction and sale of children no longer being the most common form. Regrettably, a significant number of children find themselves handed to traffickers by their own parents. It raises a question for further exploitation: what are the main reasons that push some parents to sell their children?

The crime of child trafficking spans virtually every region of the country, with nearly half of the incidents being intra-provincial. Predominantly, the main destination regions are the economically prosperous coastal areas such as Guangdong, Fujian, and Shandong, whereas the primary source regions are the economically disadvantaged areas like Yunnan, Guangxi, and Sichuan. This pattern of interprovincial flow suggests that poverty plays a crucial role in driving child trafficking. Yet, poverty alone does not fully explain the phenomenon, as the majority of cases occur in rural areas, indicating that children are not only sourced from but also transported to rural locales. This raises questions about the factors that fuel demand in rural areas and the reasons behind the purchasing of children in regions like Guangdong, Fujian, and Shandong, necessitating further exploration.

The financial transactions documented in this study, which include only the initial sale and the final transaction, already exceeded 90.71 billion Chinese Yuan. Another notable trend is the higher market demand for boys in illegal adoptions, as evidenced by both the greater number and higher prices of male victims compared to females. This trend may be partly attributed to gender-based discrimination, with a preference for male offspring in certain areas. However, this preference prompts a perplexing question: if boys are more desired, why do some parents opt to sell their sons? This contradiction highlights the complex interplay of cultural, economic, and social factors influencing child trafficking in China and underscores the need for a deeper understanding of the underlying causes and motivations.

A common pattern observed is that children are often sold multiple times before reaching their final buyer. This cycle not only underscores the deeply exploitative nature of trafficking networks but also illuminates the challenges involved in dismantling such chains. The process of detecting child trafficking cases can span months, years, or even decades, underscoring the complex and protracted nature of addressing this issue. In certain cases that have been uncovered, victims remained missing even as the offenders were prosecuted and brought to trial. This situation leaves some parents in a state of agonising wait for their children's return, whereas other child victims find themselves awaiting reunion with their biological parents after being rescued. However, new issues arise when victims of M2 and M3 are rescued, raising significant concerns for their future safety and well-being.

The demographic makeup of those perpetrating these crimes is predominantly male, with a notable overrepresentation of individuals from ethnic minority groups. Unanswered questions linger regarding the dynamics within families involved in trafficking: the specific roles that mothers play in both M2 and M3 modes, and whether fathers and mothers contribute equally to the decision to sell their children.

In the following chapter, we will delve into specific cases to seek answers to these questions that remain elusive when relying solely on quantitative data. Through this qualitative exploration, we aim to unravel the human rights issues interwoven throughout the process of child trafficking, whether they are overtly manifested or lie hidden beneath the surface. This approach will provide a deeper understanding of the personal, familial, and societal factors that fuel this grievous violation of children's rights.

References

Census Office of the State Council. 2021. '第七次全国人口普查公报 [Seventh National Census]'. China Statistics Press. https://www.gov.cn/guoqing/2021-05/13/content_5606149.htm.

Gong, Longfei. 2017. '追踪"7·14"特大贩婴案'.

Li, Gang, Huijuan Wang, Ran Tan, and Ying Fu. 2017a. 'Spatiotemporal Characteristics and Formation Mechanism of Child Trafficking in China Based on "successful Cases" [中国拐卖儿童犯罪的时空特征与形成机制 ——基于"成功案例"的管基]'. *Geographical Research [地理研究]* 36 (12): 2505–2520. https://doi.org/10.11821/dlyj201712019.

Li, Gang, Ran Tan, Huijuan Wang, Xiang Yan, and Yan Shao. 2017b. 'Geographic Characteristics of Child Trafficking Crime in China [中国拐卖儿童犯罪的地理特征研究]'. *Scientia Geographica Sinica [地理科学]* 37 (7): 1049–1058. https://doi.org/10.13249/j.cnki.sgs.2017.07.010.

Siegel, L. 2008. *Criminology: Theories, Patterns, and Typologies*. 10th ed. Wadsworth.

U. S. Department of State. 2018. *2018 Trafficking in Persons Report*. U.S. Department of State,.

UN-ACT. 2012. 'China: National Trafficking Trends'.

UNODC. 2012. *Global Report on Trafficking in Persons 2012*. New York: United Nations.

UNODC. 2016. *Global Report on Trafficking in Persons 2016*. Global Report on Trafficking in Persons. Vienna, Austria.

UNODC. 2018. *Global Report on Trafficking In Persons 2018*. Global Report on Trafficking in Persons. Vienna, Austria.

UNODC. 2023. *Global Report on Trafficking in Persons 2022*. E.23.IV.1. Vienna. https://www.unodc.org/documents/data-and-analysis/glotip/2022/GLOTiP_2022_web.pdf.

Xing, Hongmei. 2017. 'Study on Rime of Selling of Children by Parents [出卖亲生子女犯罪研究]'. *Journal of People's Public Security University of China (Social Sciences Edition) [中国人民公安大学学报: 社会科学版]* 33 (4): 17–24.

Chapter 4
Child Trafficking in China as Human Rights Issues

The previous chapter provided an overview of child trafficking in China, addressing the question of "what is the situation of child trafficking in China". This chapter advances the discourse by utilising anecdotal evidence from case law to explore the emergence of human rights issues throughout the trafficking cycle. Focus is given to elucidating how human rights violations manifest at various stages—before, during, and after the trafficking of children—while identifying the pertinent rights holders, and delineating their entitlements.

It is universally acknowledged that child trafficking constitutes a grave violation of human rights. Numerous studies have explored the human rights dimensions of human trafficking, categorising the underlying factors as either "push" or "pull" (Gallagher and Skrivankova 2015; Kragten-Heerdink, Dettmeijer-Vermeulen, and Korf 2018; Bales 2007; Tavcer 2007). However, this binary framework proves inadequate for trafficking scenarios involving infants or very young children, as predominantly observed in this study. Contrary to the majority of trafficking research, which focuses on adult victims capable of decision-making, the subjects of our investigation lack the autonomy to influence their circumstances directly. Thus, the concept of "affective factors" as either push or pull becomes irrelevant. Moreover, the notion of "push factors" influencing the victims' parents does not extend to cases involving the abduction and sale of children. Additionally, while certain factors may foster the demand for trafficked children, they scarcely qualify as 'pull factors'. Notably, in the majority of child trafficking incidents in China, there are no discernible factors enticing victims or their families to relocate to a specific region. Consequently, the "push and pull" paradigm fails to provide a comprehensive framework for analysing child trafficking in China.

The structural-proximate factors framework proposed by Cameron and Newman (2008) offers a more suitable analytical lens for examining child trafficking cases in China. While certain factors, such as poverty, are structural and prevalent in most

L. Han, *Child Trafficking in China*, https://doi.org/10.1007/978-981-97-3717-8_4

cases, others are proximate, for instance, inadequate and poorly enforced child protection laws. The interplay between these two categories of factors renders specific children more vulnerable to trafficking. These factors, pertinent both at the origin and the demand side, hold equal significance. Additionally, it is imperative to incorporate a temporal dimension into this framework, as the analysis should not be confined to the period preceding the trafficking but should encompass the entire child trafficking cycle.

Human rights violations serve not merely as the catalysts for child trafficking but also as its dire consequences. From the initial separation of a child from their family to their eventual liberation by law enforcement, fundamental human rights and dignity are egregiously compromised. Moreover, specific rights inherent to children are also breached. These infringements include, but are not limited to, the right to life, the right against separation from parents, the right to maintain one's identity, and the right to be registered immediately after birth, among others. Challenges to human rights persist beyond the trafficking ordeal and the rescue of victims. In the aftermath, new complexities arise concerning the care of the victims, underscoring the imperative for effective rehabilitative measures and the enforcement of their right to reparation. Even in instances where a trafficked child is embraced as a cherished member of the buyer's family, it does not preclude them from experiencing harm as a consequence of their status as an "adopted child". This thorough investigation aims to illuminate the complex web of human rights issues intertwined with the phenomenon of child trafficking, tracing from its underlying causes through to the consequences following rescue efforts.

1 Human Rights Issues as Causative Factors

The analytical framework proposed by Cameron and Newman (2008) delineates the human rights issues precipitating child trafficking through the lens of structural and proximate factors. Structural factors encompass economic, social, ideological, and geopolitical dimensions that influence the broader societal context, whereas proximate factors pertain to legal and policy frameworks, the rule of law, and partnership dynamics that exert a more immediate effect on the victims. While certain elements, such as geopolitical factors, may not directly pertain to our study, we do not discount the potential relevance of specific factors unique to the context of child trafficking in China. Furthermore, these factors are not isolated; rather, it is the interaction of various elements that predisposes certain children to become victims of trafficking.

A. **Poverty**

Poverty represents a pressing human rights concern that the international community has endeavoured to address for decades. From the inception of the 1993 Vienna Declaration and Programme of Action, through to the United Nations Millennium Declaration of 2000 and the subsequent Millennium Development Goals, and culminating in the 2030 Agenda for Sustainable Development, poverty has consistently been a central issue that all United Nations member states have pledged to tackle. It acts as a significant barrier to the enjoyment and realisation of numerous human rights, giving rise to additional human rights challenges such as the right to life, the right to an adequate standard of living, the right to education, and the rights to equality and freedom from discrimination. Poverty, coupled with a lack of livelihood opportunities and illiteracy, fundamentally exacerbates the vulnerability of families and children to trafficking.

Poverty undeniably constitutes a structural factor in child trafficking within China. As evidenced by the flow trends outlined in the preceding chapter, a significant majority of the child victims originated from economically disadvantaged regions, including Yunnan, Sichuan, Guizhou, and Shanxi. Moreover, the vast majority of incidents occurred in rural areas. Poverty not only compels parents to sell their offspring for profit but also heightens the vulnerability of children to abduction. However, poverty need not be absolute; in numerous instances, it is relative poverty, or the perception of poverty, that prompts parents to make ill-judged decisions.

(1) *Poverty and Residential Security*

Although abduction and sale of children (M1) are reported in urban areas as well, a significant number of detected M1 cases occur in rural regions. This disparity is likely due to rural areas being less densely populated and having lower levels of surveillance compared to urban regions. It is a common practice in rural communities for children to play unmonitored in front of their homes or in local neighbourhoods, which often lack video surveillance coverage. Although the victims' family might not have been impoverished, residing in comparatively poorer regions rendered their children susceptible to traffickers. The Case of Yao Chao, as detailed in Box 1, exemplifies a typical instance of child abduction and sale. Both the perpetrators and the victim resided in villages within the same county, where the victim girl was accustomed to playing without any supervision from her family members. Similarly, Case of Fan detailed in Box 2 also occurred in a village setting where the young victim girl and her brother were playing unsupervised by adults. These calamitous incidents might have been avoided had the children been under adult supervision. The absence of such supervision could be attributed to adults being preoccupied with household tasks or work, or possibly due to a perception that their village was inherently safe.

Box 1 Case of Yao Chao, M1, 2012-SX-CZ-Final Criminal Trial-No. 69 2012-SX-CZ-Final Criminal Trial-No. 69 [(2012)长刑终字第069号]

Date: 7 February 2012.

Before: Intermediate People's Court, Changzhi City of Shanxi Province.

Public Prosecution Agency: People's Procuratorate of Qinyuan County, Shanxi Province.

Appellant (defendant in the first instance):

Yao Chao (male, born on 10 August 1989. Residence: Qinyuan County, Shanxi Province).

Case summary:

On 2 June 2010, *Yao Chao*, the accused in the initial trial, shared his plan to traffic children with co-accused *Shi Pengfei*, *Guo Chouchou*, and *Liu Wei* (born 21 September 1994) inside the billiards hall he owned, and all three agreed to the plan. On the afternoon of June 3, *Yao Chao* called *Shi Pengfei* to rent a car. That afternoon, Shi Pengfei, driving the rented car with *Yao Chao*, *Guo Chouchou*, and *Liu Wei*, searched for a target in Liyuan Village, Liyuan Town, Qinyuan County. They identified *Liu Ying* (a girl born on 12 December 2007) in front of *Liu Junmin*'s house in the village as their target, but due to the crowded street, they failed to abduct her.

At 4 p.m. on 4 June 2010, *Yao Chao*, *Shi Pengfei*, *Guo Chouchou*, and *Liu Wei* gathered outside *Yao Chao*'s billiard hall in Liyuan Village and assigned their roles inside the rented car. *Guo Chouchou* and *Liu Wei* were to lure the child (*Liu Ying*), while *Shi Pengfei* drove the car, and *Yao Chao* provided backup near the village's railway crossing. After abducting *Liu Ying*, Shi Pengfei drove the car carrying *Yao Chao*, *Liu Wei*, and *Guo Chouchou* to Changzhi City. Upon arrival, *Yao Chao* sent *Shi Pengfei* and *Liu Wei* back to Qinyuan County. *Yao Chao* and *Guo Chouchou* took *Liu Ying* to *Qin Guiying*'s home at No. 106, Gudian Village, Jinzhuang Town, Huguan County, and handed her over, receiving 16,600 RMB from *Qin* and an additional 100 RMB for fuel. *Yao* and *Guo* returned to Changzhi City that night and stayed in a hotel in Zhuoma Village. The next morning, *Yao Chao* gave *Shi Pengfei* 3300 RMB, *Liu Wei* 300 RMB, and kept 13,100 RMB for himself. Later, citing the child's mother's dissatisfaction with the payment, *Yao Chao* extorted an additional 3000 RMB from *Qin Guiying*.

Box 2 Case of Fan, M1, 2016-AH-1222-Preliminary Criminal Trial-No. 228

2016-AH-1222-Preliminary Criminal Trial-No. 228 [(2016)皖1222刑初228号]

Date: 23 August 2016.

Before: The People's Court of Taihe County, Anhui Province.

Public Prosecution Agency: People's Procuratorate of Taihe County, Anhui Province.

Defendant:

Fan (male, born on 5 December 1973. Residence: Taihe County, Anhui Province).

Case summary:

The accused, *Fan*, met *Wang Lan* online. By the end of 2015, *Wang Lan* learned that *Lv*'s cousin, *Sang*, wanted to adopt a girl and was willing to pay 50,000 yuan in compensation. On December 31 of the same year, *Wang Lan* informed *Fan* that someone was willing to pay 50,000 yuan for a girl. They agreed that *Fan* would go to Taihe County, Anhui, to find a girl to sell. *Fan* stated that he was not able to do it alone, so *Wang Lan* brought in another accused, *Wang Jun*, to accompany *Fan* to Taihe. On the same day, *Fan* and *Wang Jun* drove a red Suzuki motorcycle to Taihe County. On 2 January 2016, *Fan* told *Wang Jun* about the plan to abduct and sell a girl in Taihe. *Wang Jun* then called *Wang Lan*, who instructed to follow *Fan*'s arrangements and promised *Wang Jun* a reward of 5000 yuan afterwards.

Around 3 p.m. on 3 January, *Fan* and *Wang Jun*, while riding the motorcycle, targeted *Wu X*, a 5-year-old girl, and her brother *Wu Y*, an 8-year-old boy, playing by the roadside in Guomiao Township, Taihe County. Distracting the boy by asking for directions, *Wang Jun* grabbed *Wu X*, and they fled on the motorcycle. The boy tried to stop them but was dragged for about four to five meters before he had to let go. *Fan* and *Wang Jun*, with *Wu X* in tow, passed through several places, including Shangqiu, Xinxiang, and Linzhou in Henan, and reached She County in Hebei overnight. Along the way, *Fan* kept in touch with *Wang Lan*, indicating that they had the child. On 4 January, led by *Wang Lan*, the three accused brought *Wu X* to *Lv*'s house, where, after a call with *Sang*, the *Sang* couple refused to buy the girl due to her age (too old) and lack of household registration. On the evening of January 5, *Fan*, *Wang Lan*, and *Wang Jun* were arrested, and the victim, *Wu X*, was rescued.

(2) *Tangible and Perceived Poverty*

In M2 and M3 cases, poverty is frequently cited as either a reason or an excuse. Yet instances of absolute poverty constitute only a minor fraction. In many scenarios, poverty serves merely as a pretext for the grievous decision to sell one's child. The causes of financial distress vary widely. In some instances, individuals bring about their own economic predicament through choices like unwillingness to work, gambling, drug addiction, or violating birth-control regulations. For example, in the Case of Dai and Zheng (referenced in Box 3), the defendant Dai and his spouse, already parents to two children, proceeded to have a third. They could have opted for contraceptive measures to avert the additional financial burden and significant fines incurred from breaching the prevailing birth control policy. Conversely, in certain cases, economic hardship arises from factors beyond the defendant's control, such as disability or illness, exemplified by the Case of Chen detailed in Box 4. Diagnosed with a mental illness since 2005, and with both of his parents also suffering from health issues, Chen's family faced understandable financial difficulties. However, they too had the option of employing contraceptive measures to prevent further pregnancies if they were financially unprepared for additional children.

Box 3 Case of Dai and Zheng, M2, 2016-SD-0832-Preliminary Criminal Trial-No. 126
2016-SD-0832-Preliminary Criminal Trial-No. 126 [(2016)鲁0832刑初126号]

Date: 29 June 2016.

Before: People's Court of Liangshan County, Shandong Province.

Public Prosecution Agency: People's Procuratorate of Liangshan County, Shandong Province.

Defendants:

Dai (Male).

Zheng A (N/A).

Case summary:

After the Spring Festival of 2007, the defendant *Dai*'s wife was pregnant. Since they already had two children and faced financial difficulties, *Dai* conspired with another defendant, *Zheng A*, to arrange for the sale of the baby upon birth. *Zheng A* subsequently contacted *Zheng B* and his wife to negotiate the sale. On 24 April 2007, at around 8:00 p.m., *Dai*'s wife, Zhang, gave birth to a baby boy at a health centre in Liangshan County. The next day, under *Zheng A*'s mediation, Dai sold the newborn to *Zheng B* and his wife for 28,000 yuan. An additional 1000 yuan was paid to *Dai* for handling the discharge procedures of the mother and covering the hospitalization costs.

Box 4 Case of Chen, M2, 2014-SX-ZZ-Preliminary Criminal Trial-No. 148
2014-SX-ZZ-Preliminary Criminal Trial-No. 148 [(2014)泽刑初字第148号]

Date: 20 October 2014.

Before: People's Court of Zezhou County, Shanxi Province.

Public Prosecution Agency: People's Procuratorate of Zezhou County, Shanxi Province.

Defendants:

Chen

Case summary:

On 16 May 2013, the wife of the defendant, *Chen*, gave birth to a baby girl at the health clinic of Dadonggou Town in Zezhou County. Due to financial hardships, *Chen* decided to give the baby girl up for adoption. *Li*, an employee at the Dadonggou Town health clinic, learned of this and informed *Tian*. On the afternoon of 17 May 2013, *Tian*, along with a couple, *Du* and *Wang*, who wanted to adopt a baby girl, came to the health clinic. After seeing the baby, the couple decided to adopt her. On 18 May 2013, *Chen* sold the baby girl to *Du* and *Wang* for 42,000 yuan.

After the case was solved, the baby girl was rescued, and *Chen* returned the 42,000 yuan to *Du*. According to the forensic psychiatric assessment by the Shanxi Provincial Centre for Mental Disease and Judicial Expertise, *Chen* suffers from schizophrenia and possesses partial criminal responsibility capacity.

Beyond the impact of tangible poverty, which drives individuals to sell their offspring, perceived poverty plays a crucial role in prompting parents to part with their children. This phenomenon is particularly pronounced in regions experiencing more robust economic development. For instance, Guangdong Province, despite being among China's most affluent provinces, reported in 2016 that 1.79 million individuals were living below the provincial relative poverty line, defined as having a disposable income of less than 4000 yuan annually (Cheng 2016), showcasing a stark contrast between highly developed urban centres and the most isolated rural locales. A comparable scenario is found across various other regions within China (refer to, for example, Shi 2016). The modernisation process has exacerbated the wealth divide, and advancements in communication technology have broadcasted the allure of urban lifestyles to secluded areas. The aspiration for a superior or even luxurious existence has become a widespread ambition among many Chinese, particularly among rural youth. Nonetheless, the absence of adequate education can lead to a distortion of values. Children may be perceived as hindrances in the pursuit of affluence or as means to generate income. For instance, in the Case of Fan (referenced in Box 5), the 24-year-old defendant Fan sold his newborn son for 56,000 yuan in the hospital merely two days post-delivery by his girlfriend. Despite Fan asserting his inability to financially support the newborn or afford his girlfriend's medical expenses, he subsequently squandered the proceeds on hotel accommodations, a second-hand car, and other expenditures, depleting the entire sum within a month. The reverence for material wealth, coupled with his incapacity to secure a high income through personal endeavour, compels him to exploit his children as a means to generate income. A similar mindset is observed in M1 cases, where the abductor aims to make a quick profit through the abduction of a child.

Box 5 Case of Fan, M2, 2014-SD-F-Preliminary Criminal Trial-No. 79
2014-SD-F-Preliminary Criminal Trial-No. 79 [(2014)费刑初字第79号]

Date: 27 February 2014.

Before: People's Court of Fei County, Shandong Province.

Public Prosecution Agency: People's Procuratorate of Fei County, Shandong Province.

Defendant:

Fan (Male, born on 20 April 1989. Residence: Fei County, Shandong Province).

Case summary:

On 4 October 2013, *Fan*'s partner, *An*, gave birth to a son at People's Hospital of Fei County. By 2 p.m. on October 6, leveraging connections with *Dr. Wang C* from the hospital's obstetrics and gynaecology department and *Wang A* from Xichan Village, Tanyi Town in Fei County, *Fan* facilitated the sale of the newborn. The baby was sold for 56,000 yuan to *Wang B*, a resident of Shanghe Village, Mazhuang Town in Fei County, who agreed to raise the child.

Based on the statements and testimonies provided, *Fan* initially set the price for the child at 70,000 yuan. However, the negotiation process led to a reduced final sale price of 56,000 yuan, after the buyer expressed concerns regarding the child's health, specifically a diagnosis of heart disease.

Fan utilised the proceeds to purchase a second-hand car and cover various other costs. The relationship between *Fan* and *An* subsequently ended due to *Fan*'s repeated instances of domestic violence against her.

Economic hardships are often intertwined with other forms of social disadvantage, such as non-traditional marital statuses. This is exemplified in both the Case of Fan, as mentioned in Box 5, and the Case of Lin and Lian, detailed in Box 6, where financial strains were either precipitated or exacerbated by unconventional relationships. In the case of Lin and Lian, the couple had a child outside of marriage. Their relationship, particularly noted for Lian being 5 years Lin's senior, was not endorsed by Lin's family, contravening traditional Chinese customs. At the time of the offence, Lin was 21, a year shy of the legal age for marriage in China. In their defence, both Lin and Lian cited unemployment and lack of family support—stemming from opposition to their relationship and the birth of the child—as critical factors in their decision-making. The accumulated challenges faced by this young couple ultimately compelled them to make a misguided decision to sell their child.

Box 6 Case of Lin and Lian, M2, 2014-GD-HD-Preliminary Criminal Trial-No. 271

2014-GD-HD-Preliminary Criminal Trial-No. 271 [(2014)惠东法刑一初字第271号]

Date: 9 September 2014.

Before: People's Court of Huidong County, Guangdong Province.

Public Prosecution Agency: People's Procuratorate of Huidong County, Guangdong Province.

Defendants:

Lin (Male, born on 8 August 1992).

Lian (Female, born on 16 March 1987).

Case summary:

Defendants *Lin* and *Lian*, who were living together, faced opposition from *Lin*'s family regarding their relationship. In early 2013, upon learning of *Lian*'s pregnancy, *Lin*'s family refused to support the upbringing of the child, and *Lian*'s family was financially incapable of doing so. Consequently, the couple resolved to seek an "adoptive family" for their unborn child. *Lin* advertised online for an "adoptive family," requesting 50,000 yuan for the adoption. Several individuals expressed interest in purchasing the child, but a person from Shanghai, named *Ni*, agreed to pay 70,000 yuan for the child, a proposal that *Lin* accepted and *Lian* was apprised of.

In late October 2013, *Ni* visited *Lian*, contributing towards the hospital deposit for her necessary medical treatment. *Lian* gave birth to a son on 7 November 2013. The following day, *Ni* visited the hospital, paid *Lian* 70,000 yuan, and presented three gold necklaces as gifts to *Lian*, her mother, and her aunt. After *Lian* signed an adoption document, *Ni* took the baby boy to Shanghai. Although *Lin* was not present at the time of the birth and the subsequent transaction, he withdrew 35,000 yuan from Lian's bank account upon being informed about the sale.

(3) *Child Poverty*

Child poverty directly impacts on children's education. This impact is not only on the enrolment rates in schools and higher education but also compromises the quality of education available, thereby increasing the vulnerability of children from low-income families. A lower rate of school enrolment signifies a heightened risk of children being exploited—physically, sexually, or being coerced into criminal activities (UNICEF East Asia and Pacific Regional Office 2009).

Instances exist where children, constrained by their family's economic difficulties, are forced to abandon their education in search of a better life, subsequently falling victim to trafficking. This scenario closely mirrors the pattern observed in the transnational trafficking of women and girls. Victims, driven by their families' financial distress, are enticed by traffickers with promises of well-paying jobs and improved living conditions. In the Case of Long Qingliu, detailed in Box 7, the victim's family faced severe hardships after losing their primary caregiver and emotional support: her father became paralysed and bedridden, and her mother subsequently left the family. Learning of job opportunities from the trafficker, the girl, merely 13 years old, decided to drop out of school to earn a livelihood for herself and her family. She had not even finished her compulsory education and started working below the legal minimum age of sixteen. While her peers might have been pursuing higher education, she was already a mother of two. Had there been any support from her local community, the government, or her school, her life might have taken a different path.

Box 7 Case of Long Qingliu, M1, 2014-GZ-2627-Preliminary Criminal Trial-No. 59

2014-GZ-2627-Preliminary Criminal Trial-No. 59 [(2017)黔2627刑初59号]

Date: 28 April 2014.

Before: People's Court of Tianzhu County, Guizhou Province.

Public Prosecution Agency: People's Procuratorate of Tianzhu County, Guizhou Province.

Defendants:

Long Qingliu (Male, born on 19 March 1956).

Case summary:

In the autumn of 2008, the defendant *Long Qingliu* discovered that a child from his village, *Long X* (female, born on 1 September 1995), had experienced a family crisis (her mother had abandoned the family, and her father, *Long Guoji*, was paralysed and bedridden). Luring *Long X* to leave the village to work, *Long Qingliu* brought her to Jiqing Town, Xinhua County, Hunan Province, and sold her for 38,000 yuan to *Cao* from to be his wife.

Long X attempted to flee from *Cao*'s home but was recaptured by him. Subsequently, *Cao* returned *Long X* to *Long Qingliu* and received a refund. Afterwards, *Long Qingliu* sold *Long X* to a different individual, who then took her to Guangzhou in search of employment. In 2010, at the age of 15, *Long X* began cohabiting with a man she met through her job, and they had two children together. In 2016, *Long X* returned to her hometown once with her children.

(4) *Poverty and Legal Illiteracy*

Poverty frequently results in a low level of education and a lack of legal awareness, which in turn exacerbates the vulnerability of children in several respects. Initially, when poverty affects parents, it not only heightens the likelihood of them engaging in child trafficking but also diminishes their capacity to protect their offspring. Primarily, individuals in these situations often lack proper sex education, leading to a significant number of children born from unintended pregnancies. These births can further destabilise the already precarious financial conditions of their parents or place single mothers in dire straits. As a result, these children face an increased risk of being neglected or sold. Moreover, the illiteracy and insufficient education of parents hinder their ability to safeguard their children adequately. For example, some parents might not realise the importance of notifying the police when their children are kidnapped by traffickers, thereby complicating efforts to locate the victims.

Poor educational attainment emerges as a notable characteristic among child trafficking offenders. Within a cohort of 1711 perpetrators for whom educational data was accessible, a substantial 67% had not completed their compulsory education, with 24% being illiterate, and merely 6% having achieved secondary higher education or beyond. This deficiency in educational background is conjectured to curtail their employment prospects and their understanding of law, resulting in some defendants mistakenly believing that the sale or purchase of children did not constitute a criminal act. This lack of education, therefore, not only impacts their socioeconomic status but also their comprehension of the law, illustrating a direct link between education levels and susceptibility to engaging in criminal activities like child trafficking.

(5) *Poverty Fuelling Demand*

Our research uncovered an unconventional way in which poverty fuels child trafficking: it serves as an incentive for increasing demand. As demonstrated by the data in the previous chapter, a notable number of victims were trafficked to rural areas (see Fig. 3.5 for the destination and origin areas of child trafficking victims). It was observed that many buyers originated from economically disadvantaged backgrounds. But why? The Case of Lu A (as detailed in Box 8) can provide us some explanation. The defendant Lu A procured a trafficked woman to serve as a wife for his cousin, Lu B, who was still unmarried in his fifties. The trafficker set the price at 48,000 yuan for the woman and her daughter, yet Lu B could initially afford only a 2000-yuan deposit. To cover the full amount, he borrowed 35,000 yuan from his sisters and 13,000 yuan from his cousin Lu A. Individuals living in poverty, particularly men like Lu B, often face insurmountable challenges in forming their own families, leading to prolonged bachelorhood, the absence of descendants, and disqualification from legal adoption procedures. Consequently, they turn to the black market of human trafficking in search of women or girls for marriage or boys to carry on their family names.

Box 8 Case of Lu A, M1, 2013-SD-F-Preliminary Criminal Trial-No. 325
2013-SD-F-Preliminary Criminal Trial-No. 325 [(2013)费刑初字第325号]

Date: 10 September 2013.

Before: People's Court of Fei County, Shandong Province.

Public Prosecution Agency: People's Procuratorate of Fei County, Shandong Province.

Defendant:

Lu A (Male, born on 1 February 1972. Residence: Fei County, Shandong Province).

Case summary:

In early April 2013, the defendant *Lu A* purchased a Vietnamese woman, referred to as a "wife" along with her 1-year-old daughter, for 48,000 yuan on behalf of his cousin, *Lu B*. However, the woman vehemently opposed living with *Lu B*. When *Lu A* attempted to return the woman and her daughter to the trafficker, *Zhao* (who is being prosecuted separately), his request was denied. Subsequently, he sold the Vietnamese woman's daughter to a couple in the same county for 28,000 yuan.

On 26 April 2013, *Lu A* accommodated *Zhao*, two Vietnamese women, *Yi* and *Di*, and a 13-year-old Vietnamese girl named *Na*, all of whom were trafficking victims. On 3 May 2013, *Lu A* and *Zhao* trafficked *Na* to a local man, *Yao A*.

Yao A declared that he acquired the girl intending for her to marry his son, *Yao B*, a 24-year-old with mental disabilities resulting from an accident. *Na* refused to engage in sexual relations or marry *Yao B*. During her time with the *Yaos*, she lived alongside *Yao B* but did not experience any form of violation or abuse from either *Yao B* or his father.

In conclusion, poverty emerges as a significant causative factor that facilitates trafficking, affecting all involved parties—the families of victims, the victims themselves, traffickers, and buyers. On the origin side, poverty serves as a push factor by intensifying the vulnerability of potential victims and eroding the protective capacity of their parents. On the destination side, it escalates the demand for children in illegal adoptions and women in forced marriages. Simultaneously, poverty, often accompanied by a lack of education, predisposes individuals in high-demand areas to engage in the crime of child trafficking or participate in trafficking-related activities.

B. **Discrimination**

It is a fundamental human rights principle that every individual has the right to be free from discrimination of any kind, whether it's based on race, colour, sex, language, religion, political or other opinions, national or social origin, property, birth, or any other status. This principle of non-discrimination is not only acknowledged in the Universal Declaration of Human Rights but is also integral to all core international human rights treaties. Numerous studies have pinpointed discrimination as a critical root cause of trafficking in persons (examples include Gallagher and Skrivankova 2015; Cohen 2003; Davis et al. 2003; ECOSOC 2000). Our research corroborates these findings, revealing instances where victims or their families were subjected to discrimination on various grounds, such as gender, age, health, and social status.

(1) *Gender-Based Discrimination and Violence*

Similar to many parts of the world, women and girls in China face gender-based discrimination, manifesting across various facets of everyday life. Rooted in Chinese tradition is the belief that only men can "perpetuate the family lineage". Within this framework, women are often viewed as subordinate to men, with daughters not regarded as permanent members of their birth families since they are expected to marry. As Chinese culture progresses, with feminist viewpoints making inroads, the traditional concept of marriage—whereby the bride departs from her parental home to integrate into her husband's family—still holds sway for many. Despite contemporary legislation that ensures women have rights equal to those of men, including the inheritance of property and land, the right to retain their family name, and the right to pass this name onto their children, patriarchal beliefs continue to be deeply entrenched, particularly in rural and economically less-developed regions. In these areas, a prevailing expectation exists that a man requires a wife to manage his household affairs, and families lacking male descendants often face societal disdain.

The statistical data from the Chinese population censuses of 2010 and 2020, presented in Table 1, highlight entrenched gender discrimination in birth ratios across the country, as ratios significantly exceed the natural baseline of approximately 105 males for every 100 females. This reflects a persistent preference for male offspring, especially noticeable in higher-order births. Historically, practices of sex selection were intensified by the one-child policy, inadvertently leading to a marked disparity in sex ratios (Wu et al. 2006). Remarkably, following the abolition of the one-child policy in 2016, there has been a discernible shift towards a more balanced sex ratio among newborns, indicating that the policy change may be starting to mitigate the gender disparities once amplified by restrictive reproductive policies. Nevertheless, the elevated sex ratios for births subsequent to the second child reveal that gender discrimination persists within certain segments of the population.

The data presented in this study further corroborate the entrenched preference for male children over female children within China. Figure 3.10 from the preceding chapter clearly indicates that male victims outnumber their female counterparts in all four identified modes of trafficking. This gender disparity is especially marked in the provinces of Fujian and Guangdong, where the incidence of trafficked male victims is significantly higher than that of females, regardless of whether the trafficking is into or out of these regions. Such a pronounced discrepancy highlights the persistent cultural bias favouring male children and its consequent influence on the dynamics of child trafficking in these localities.

Table 1 Comparative gender ratio of newborns by birth order in China (Female = 100)

	Gender ratio (Female = 100)					
	2019.11.1–2020.10.31			2009.11.1–2010.10.31		
	Overall	Urban	Rural	Overall	Urban	Rural
Overall newborns	112.28	112.15	111.90	121.21	118.33	122.09
First child	113.17	112.04	114.09	113.73	113.44	113.62
Second child	106.78	108.32	104.87	130.29	132.19	128.95
Third child	132.93	147.64	124.48	161.56	178.16	157.34
Fourth child	130.07	118.99	131.75	146.50	160.63	143.35
Fifth and subsequent children	127.14	163.37	120.87	143.65	147.76	140.60

Source National Bureau of Statistics

Gender-based discrimination significantly fuels the incidence of child trafficking in China. The societal preference for male children has given rise to an underground market for illegal adoption, as evidenced by the higher prices fetched by male victims, a fact substantiated by Fig. 3.14 in the previous chapter. This preference has led to a surge in demand for male infants, putting young boys at an increased risk of abduction. Traffickers, frequently employing violent tactics, tend to specifically target young boys or male infants. This is starkly demonstrated in the Case of Xie and others (refer to Box 9 for details). In this case, defendant Cheng, incentivised by an offer of 10,000 yuan for a boy, conspired with accomplices to abduct a male infant from a family, Cheng moved into a neighbouring apartment of the victim's family. After more than ten days of meticulous planning and building trust with the family, they executed their plan, abducting the infant and selling him to a buyer in the vicinity. The child was only found by the police 14 years following the abduction. The primary motivation for this crime was the buyer's wish to have a male grandchild and her attractive offer, as she only had granddaughters. Reports of similar cases from other Chinese provinces corroborate the pervasive and detrimental influence of gender preference on the phenomenon of child trafficking. Similarly, in the Case of Ding and Li (as detailed in Box 10), the traffickers initially had no intention of abducting and selling children. Their criminal plan was conceived only after learning about a buyer's specific demand for a baby boy. Subsequently, they encountered the victim, whether by chance or through deliberate search, setting the stage for their illicit act. In summary, the prevailing preference for male children in the context of illegal adoption places boys, particularly those of a young age deemed suitable for adoption, at a heightened risk of abduction compared to young girls.

Box 9 Case of Xie and others, M1, 2014-GD-SZ-Intermediary Criminal Trial -No. 650

2014-GD-SZ-Intermediary Criminal Trial-No. 650 [(2014)深中法刑一终字第650号]

Date: 16 July 2014.

Before: Intermediate People's Court of Shenzhen, Guangdong Province.

Public Prosecution Agency: People's Procuratorate of Longgang District, Shenzhen, Guangdong Province.

Defendants:

Xie (Female).

Cheng (Male).

Chen (Male).

Liu (Male).

Case summary:

In July 1999, defendants *Xie*, *Cheng*, *Chen*, and *Liu* became aware of an individual seeking to purchase a male child. Seizing this opportunity, they targeted the *Li* family, who had a newborn baby boy. Defendant *Cheng* moved into an apartment adjacent to the *Lis'* to gain their trust and establish proximity. On 20 July, *Chen* occupied the baby's mother with a diversion, enabling *Cheng* to abduct the baby undetected.

Once the child was in their custody, *Xie* liaised with the prospective buyer and arranged a medical examination for the baby at a local hospital, ensuring the child was fit for sale. The baby was subsequently trafficked for 9000 yuan.

It took over a decade, but on 31 July 2013, the abducted child was located and the case was resolved.

The buyer's son revealed in his testimony that his mother had only granddaughters and desired a male grandchild, which led to her decision to purchase a boy.

Box 10 Case of Ding and Li, M1, 2017-SAX-0728- Preliminary Criminal Trial-No. 55
2017-SAX-0728- Preliminary Criminal Trial-No. 55 [(2017)陕0728刑初55号]

Date: 18 July 2017.

Before: People's Court of Zhenba County, Shaanxi Province.

Public Prosecution Agency: People's Procuratorate of Zhenba County, Shaanxi Province.

Defendants:

Ding (Male).

Li (Male).

Case summary:

Around 1994, the defendant *Ding* engaged in work in Taibai County where he met *Yang*, with whom he subsequently cohabited. Defendant *Li* (*Yang*'s brother-in-law) was also working under *Ding* during this time. In 1996, defendant *Li* learned that a fellow villager with the same surname, *Li A*, wanted to adopt a son because his wife could no longer bear children. Li informed *Ding* of this situation. In September 1997, *Ding* took *Yang* to Zhenba County for a visit and, while at the home of the victim *Sun*, noticed Sun's son *Sun X* (born on 5 March 1997).

On 7 November 1998, *Ding* and *Li* traveled to Zhenba County. *Ding* went alone to *Sun*'s house, luring *Sun* away with the pretence of a cat business deal, and then deceitfully convinced *Sun*'s wife, *Luo*, to leave. With both parents away, *Ding* abducted *Sun X* and met up with *Li* to catch a train to Jiangsu Province. However, during their journey, at Zhengzhou Railway Station in Henan Province, *Ding* was stranded due to losing the train tickets and his money. *Li* then continued alone with *Sun X* to Feng County, Xuzhou City, Jiangsu Province, and sold the child for more than 7000 yuan to a fellow villager *Li A*. *Li A* renamed *Sun X* to *Li X* and has raised him ever since.

In addition, the cultural preference for male children also underpins the rationale for some parents deciding to sell their offspring, driven by two distinct motivations: the potential for higher profits due to the higher market price for boys, and the desire to alleviate economic burden, given the perceived higher costs associated with raising a son compared to a daughter. In the first scenario, the gender factor intersects with poverty and other factors, such as discrimination against women with disabilities, which will be discussed in the subsequent section. In such cases, one or both parents decide to sell their child before or immediately after birth. Aware of the high demand for boys, they typically set a very high price. The Case of Fan (referenced in Box 5) exemplifies this scenario.

Paradoxically, the preference for boys can render them an economic liability for the family, as observed in the second scenario. It is a widely held belief in China that, beyond regular expenses, parents are obliged to secure at least an apartment and a considerable bride price for their son's marriage. Thus, for families without a strong preference for either gender, having one child, whether a son or a daughter, is seen as ideal, and having one of each is viewed as even more favourable. However, the arrival of a second son begins to introduce financial stress, which intensifies with the birth of additional sons. In some cases, the desire for a daughter—either out of personal preference or the hope for a future caretaker for the parents and her brothers—becomes prominent. Consequently, when a family finds itself with more than two or three sons, the decision to sell one to ease the anticipated economic strain becomes a consideration. The Case of Yang Zhichun, as detailed in Box 11, exemplifies such a scenario. Yang sold his third son for 36,900 yuan after realising the immense financial pressures of raising three sons. He and his wife had hoped for a daughter as their third child, and upon the birth of another son, Yang deemed the familial burden too significant to manage, leading to the sale of the newborn.

Box 11 Case of Yang Zhichun, M2, 2014-YN-GN-Preliminary Criminal Trial-No. 98
2014-YN-GN-Preliminary Criminal Trial-No. 98 [(2014)广刑初字第98号]

Date: 13 June 2014.

Before: People's Court of Guangnan County of Yunnan Province.

Public Prosecution Agency: People's Procuratorate of Guangnan County, Yunnan Province.

Defendants:

Yang Zhichun (Male, born on 11 August 1971. Residence: Guangnan County, Yunnan Province).

Yang XX (Male, born on 11 May 1988. Residence: Guangnan County, Yunnan Province).

Case summary:

On 19 October 2013, *Yang Zhichun*'s wife gave birth to a boy, their third son. A local leader inquired if he was interested in selling the child, highlighting that the child's birth breached the birth control policy in place at the time. Reflecting on his situation, *Yang Zhichun* realised his preference for a daughter and acknowledged the substantial financial challenges of raising three sons. Consequently, he decided to sell the newborn through the mediation of an individual referred to as *Yang XX*, for a sum of 36,900 yuan. For facilitating the transaction, *Yang XX* received a commission of 1000 yuan from the buyer.

Gender-based discrimination and violence serve as significant, albeit indirect, catalysts for child trafficking. Often, the mothers of trafficked children, who are direct victims of gender-based oppression and violence, find themselves incapacitated in safeguarding their offspring. A representative illustration of this dynamic is seen in the Case of Fan (highlighted in Box 5 above), where the mother of a trafficked child fell prey to domestic abuse. In the harrowing case of 8-year-old Chen A, as outlined in Box 12, the girl was left unprotected by her mother, who was a victim of domestic violence, and subsequently became a victim of trafficking and of sexual violence. Powerless or unwilling to prevent the sale of her child, she endured physical aggression at the hands of her partner. In a substantial number of cases classified as M2 and M3, it is the father who emerges as the perpetrator, leaving the mothers disenfranchised, devoid of any decision-making power, or even knowledge regarding their children's whereabouts. While some mothers choose to remain silent, others take action by reporting their husbands to the police.

Additionally, child trafficking incidents are sometimes intertwined with the trafficking of the child's mother. The Case of Lu A (outlined in Box 8) is a stark exemplar of such circumstances. Lu A initially sought to purchase a woman under the guise of marriage, with the ulterior motive of subjecting her to sexual and physical exploitation. He subsequently sold the child of the Vietnamese woman he had bought, aiming to offset his financial expenditures. This narrative is not unique; there exist several instances where women, alongside their young children, are trafficked, only for the children to be later estranged from their mothers and sold to disparate parties. These narratives underscore the intricate relationship between gender-based violence, discrimination, and the perpetuation of child trafficking, highlighting the complexity and depth of the challenges involved.

Box 12 Case of Zhang Yanhui, M2, 2016-SC-0802-Preliminary Criminal Trial-No. 359
2016-SC-0802-Preliminary Criminal Trial-No. 359 [(2016)川0802刑初359号]

Date: 30 August 2016.

Before: People's Court of Lizhou District, Guangyuan City, Sichuan Province.

Public Prosecution Agency: People's Procuratorate of Lizhou District, Guangyuan City, Sichuan Province

Defendants:

Zhang Yanhui (Female, born in August 1972. Residence: Dabao Town, Liling City, Hunan Province).

Case summary:

On the morning of 2 August 2013, defendant *Zhang Yanhui*, after a violent altercation with her boyfriend *Chen Moumou* the night before, decided to take her two daughters, the eldest *Chen A* (8 years old) and the younger *Chen B*, to the local police station to report the incident of domestic violence. At 8:00 a.m., while en route to the station, *Zhang Yanhui* encountered *Zhang X* (convicted in another trial) and inquired about directions. Following her report at the Nanhe police station, *Zhang Yanhui*, while traversing Beijing Road within the Nanhe Office area, once again came across *Zhang X*. It was during this second encounter that *Zhang Yanhui* expressed a desire to sell her daughter, asking for a sum of 10,000 yuan. *Zhang X* consented to the price.

Zhang X brought *Chen A* back to his residence to retrieve cash, while *Zhang Yanhui* remained at their agreed-upon location, awaiting their return. Upon his return, *Zhang X* presented 10,000 yuan in cash to *Zhang Yanhui* but proposed to defer payment until after assessing whether *Chen A* could acclimate to living with him. *Zhang Yanhui* consented to this arrangement. *Zhang X* went back home and raped *Chen A*. After a prolonged wait without any sign of *Zhang X* fulfilling his promise to pay, *Zhang Yanhui*, accompanied by her younger daughter, departed for her hometown in Hunan Province.

While not the most prevalent, instances of trafficking young girls for sexual exploitation have also been noted in child trafficking cases within China. Given that the legal definition of a child in China's criminal law is capped at 14 years old, the actual number of sex trafficking cases involving children under the age of 18 is likely to be higher. In most of these cases, the victims are teenage girls who were trafficked for forced marriage, such as the Case of Long Qingliu as detailed in Box 7 above. Several instances have been recorded where girls were trafficked under the pretense of adoption, yet with the underlying intent of marrying them off to a member of the buyer's family. This practice bears resemblance to the traditional "Tongyangxi" or "Shim-pua marriage", where girls are brought into a household ostensibly as adopted daughters, but then marriage to one of the sons of the family at a young age. In the Case of Yang Yulan (detailed in Box 13), a foster caregiver trafficked a 14-year-old girl, selling her to a man with the explicit intention of having her become his son's wife upon reaching the age of 18. In a turn of events that is both fortunate and controversial, the buyer's family treated the girl with care without subjecting her to any form of violation. Remarkably, the girl herself expressed a desire to continue living with the buyer's family, indicating a complex dynamic within the situation.

Box 13 Case of Yang Yulan, M1, 2017-AH-0621-Preliminary Criminal Trial-No. 388
2017-AH-0621-Preliminary Criminal Trial-No. 388 [(2017)皖0621刑初388号]

Date: 29 November 2017.

Before: People's Court of Suixi County, Anhui Province.

Public Prosecution Agency: People's Procuratorate Suixi County, Anhui Province.

Defendants:

Yang Yulan (Female, born on 2 April 1978. Residence: Woyang County, Anhui Province).

Case summary:

In February or March of 2014, a resident of Zhanglou Village, Linhuan Town, Suixi County, identified as *Zhao B*, entrusted his niece, *Zhao A* (born on 23 April 2000), to the care of the defendant *Yang Yulan* in Linhuan Town, Suixi County, for foster care. During this period, without the knowledge of *Zhao B* or *Zhao A*'s other relatives, *Yang Yulan* arranged through *Zhang Jiling* to sell *Zhao A* to *Wu*. The arrangement was purportedly for *Wu* to foster *Zhao A* until she reached 18 years of age, at which point she would become Wu's daughter-in-law. For this transaction, *Yang Yulan* received a cash payment of 70,000 yuan.

Regrettably, amidst the various manifestations of gender-based discrimination that result in children becoming victims of trafficking, female figures often emerge among the perpetrators. In certain instances, it is the mother herself who decides to and commits the act of selling her children. In other scenarios, the perpetrator may be the child's grandmother, who, having been subjected to and influenced by patriarchal culture for her entire life, ultimately assumes the role of an oppressor. Furthermore, there are instances where women, whether they are the perpetrator's mother, sister, or wife, underpin these criminal activities either through operational or financial support. This cycle of oppression highlights a tragic dimension of gender-based discrimination, where those who have been marginalised may, in turn, perpetuate the cycle of abuse and exploitation. This perpetuation of oppression underscores a profoundly distressing aspect of gender-based discrimination, illustrating how individuals who have been victimised by societal structures can, paradoxically, contribute to the perpetuation of abuse and exploitation.

(2) *Persons with Disabilities*

Discrimination against individuals with disabilities is another factor that significantly heightens the vulnerability of children to trafficking. The challenges these individuals face in engaging fully in social life frequently result in economic hardship for both the persons with disabilities and their families. They commonly experience marginalisation or exclusion from their communities and face numerous human rights violations. This marginalisation, compounded by additional layers of discrimination such as gender, exacerbates their plight. Women and girls with disabilities, in particular, are exceptionally vulnerable to violence, abuse, and sexual exploitation.

This form of discrimination manifests across both the origin and destination phases of trafficking, unfolding in three distinct manners. Primarily, disability increases the vulnerability of victims directly, impacting the individuals themselves, and indirectly influencing the circumstances of their parents, often the father. On the destination side, akin to the dynamics of poverty, disability may serve as an underlying factor motivating some individuals to purchase a child. This multifaceted impact of disability not only exacerbates the risks associated with trafficking but also highlights the complex interplay between various forms of disadvantage and exploitation.

Box 14 Case of Tan Tao and Yu Haiyu, M1, 2017-AH-10-Final Criminal Trial-No. 15
2017-AH-10-Final Criminal Trial-No. 15 [(2017)皖10刑终15号]

Date: 8 March 2017.

Before: Intermediate People's Court of Huangshan City, Anhui Province.

Public Prosecution Agency: People's Procuratorate of Tunxi District, Huangshan City, Anhui Province.

Appellant (original trial defendant):

Tan Tao (Male, born on 17 April 1985. Residence: Linquan County, Anhui Province).

Yu Haiyu (Female, born on 28 March 1975. Residence: Shizhu Tujia Autonomous County, Chongqing City).

Case summary:

In August 2014, the defendant *Tan Tao* sold an abandoned disabled boy he had found for 10,000 yuan at a hotel in Fu'an City, Fujian Province, to the defendant *Yu Haiyu*. Later, *Yu Haiyu* and her husband *Wang X* took the disabled boy to beg across the country. On 24 June 2016, *Wang X* was reported by the public while begging with the disabled boy at the Fushang Market in Tunxi District, Huangshan City, and the police subsequently arrested *Yu Haiyu*. On 19 July 2016, the defendant *Tan Tao* was arrested by the public security organs.

Generally, due to pervasive discrimination, children with disabilities face a lower risk of being trafficked compared to the likelihood of being abandoned or subjected to maltreatment by their families. Nonetheless, notable exceptions have been documented. Although not a predominant theme in this research, instances have been reported where children with disabilities were trafficked for the purpose of begging on the streets. This study identifies a singular case of such a pattern. As elucidated in Box 14, children with physical, often visible, disabilities are exploited by traffickers to elicit sympathy from the public and thus generate profit. In the late 1990s and early 2000s, the presence of disabled children begging on the streets was markedly more common. However, they conspicuously vanished following an anti-trafficking social initiative in 2011, during which the public was encouraged to photograph begging children and post these images on social media, with the aim of identifying them as potential victims of trafficking.[1]

Children, particularly teenagers with intellectual disabilities, face heightened risks of physical and sexual exploitation. A prevalent manifestation of how discrimination against individuals with disabilities serves as a causative factor for child trafficking

---

[1] The initiative "#To rescue begging children by taking photos#" (#随手拍照解救乞讨儿童#) was launched on the Chinese social media platform Weibo.

involves young girls with mental disabilities being trafficked to serve as a "wife" to a man. In such circumstances, the individuals with disabilities are directly victimised. Their intellectual challenges make them prime targets for traffickers, who exploit their limited capacity for self-defence. The Case of Huang A, detailed in Box 15, represents a typical scenario with a relatively positive outcome. The victim, Mei, who has intellectual disabilities, was enticed away while playing in a park and subsequently sold to a family with the intention of making her a bride. Fortunately, she was rescued before any harm could befall her. Additionally, there have been reports, such as those by BBC News in 2007, of boys and men with intellectual disabilities being forced into slave labour in illegal brick kilns (BBC News 2007). However, such cases have not been identified in the judgments reviewed for this study, likely because the majority of forced labour victims are over the age of fourteen and, therefore, not classified as children under Chinese anti-trafficking laws and regulations.

Box 15 Case of Huang A, M1, 2016-AN-YQ-Preliminary Criminal Trial-No. 00150
2016-AN-YQ-Preliminary Criminal Trial-No. 00150 [(2014)皖刑初字第00150号]

Date: 28 February 2014.

Before: People's Court of Yongqiao District, Suzhou City, Anhui Province.

Public Prosecution Agency: People's Procuratorate of Yongqiao District, Suzhou City, Anhui Province.

Defendant:

Huang A (Male).

Case summary:

On the afternoon of 18 May 2013, in the Dongxianqiao Riverside Park of the Yongqiao District in Suzhou City, *Xu* lured away the victim *Mei* (female, born on 10 September 1999), who was playing in the park following her grandfather, *Mei A*. The next day, *Xu* took *Mei* to the home of *Huang A* in the same district, to be the bride for *Huang A*'s son, *Huang Wei*. The defendant *Huang A* paid *Xu* a gratuity of 200 yuan. The case was reported by the *Mei A*.

On 25 May 2013, the defendant *Huang A* was arrested, and on the same day, the victim *Mei* was rescued by the public security organs.

The victim *Mei* has certain level of developmental intellectual delays.

Box 16 Case of Song, M2, Case 2016-SD-1403-Preliminary Criminal Trial-No. 136

2016-SD-1403-Preliminary Criminal Trial-No. 136 [(2016) 鲁1403刑初136号]

Date: 28 February 2017.

Before: People's Court of Lingcheng District, Dezhou City, Shandong Province.

Public Prosecution Agency: People's Procuratorate of Lingcheng District, Dezhou City, Shandong Province.

Defendant:

Song (Male, born in March 1960. Residence: Lingcheng District, Dezhou City, Shandong Provincc).

Case summary:

The defendant, *Song*, lived with a woman diagnosed with intellectual disability. Between 2008 and 2016, he trafficked all five of their newborn children to different purchasers.

1. In Autumn 2008, after his cohabitant gave birth to a baby boy, *Song* sold him for 10,000 yuan.
2. In 2010, upon request from another buyer, *Song* sold a second baby boy born on 21 May 2010 by the same woman, for the same amount of 10,000 yuan.
3. By March 2011, anticipating another child, *Song* had already arranged a buyer. Following the birth of another boy in September 2011, he repeated the sale for 10,000 yuan.
4. In summer 2014, with his cohabitant pregnant again, *Song* secured a buyer in advance. The birth of a girl on 29 November 2014 led to her being sold for 18,200 yuan.
5. In late 2015, a broker approached *Song* about purchasing his next child. In March 2016, another girl was born and sold for 24,000 yuan.

Forensic psychiatric evaluation revealed that the woman living with *Song* is severely intellectually disabled and lacks the capability to defend herself sexually. The defendant *Song* also suffers from mild intellectual disability and, at the time of the crimes, was considered to have limited criminal responsibility.

Discrimination against individuals with disabilities indirectly affects children, particularly when those children's parents, who may have intellectual disabilities, are incapable of adequately protecting them. This is often the case with mothers or both parents who suffer from intellectual deficiencies. In the Case of Song (referenced in Box 16), a man trafficked five children he had with a woman he had taken from the street, who was diagnosed with severe intellectual disability. An examination of the birth dates of these children reveals that the woman was essentially used as a means for producing offspring, with minimal recovery time between each childbirth. Forensic evaluations confirmed that the perpetrator himself had mild intellectual disability, attributing to him limited criminal responsibility. The woman, having lived with the perpetrator since 2000, was found to have no ability to defend herself sexually or to protect her children, highlighting the compounded vulnerabilities faced by women and families affected by intellectual disabilities and the exploitative situations they may endure. Song's case is not an isolated incident; it reflects a broader issue where women with mental illnesses are sold to or randomly picked up from the streets by men, subsequently becoming their "wives" and bearing children with them.

Similar to how poverty acts as both a driving and attracting force in child trafficking within China, discrimination against individuals with disabilities also plays a role in fostering demand for children. This demand arises because disabilities can impede one's ability to marry or legally adopt a child. The victims in such cases may be young girls trafficked to become brides or infants trafficked for illegal adoption. Typically, the direct purchasers in these scenarios are family members—parents, siblings, or other relatives—of the individual with disabilities. Their objective is often to secure a caretaker for the family member with disabilities for the future.

In the Case of Lu A (referenced in Box 8), the defendant, Lu A, trafficked a 16-year-old Burmese girl to Yao, who sought a "wife" for his 24-year-old son with intellectual disabilities. Yao recounted that his son suffered a traumatic brain injury at the age of five, which resulted in a disability preventing him from finding a partner, leading Yao to purchase a "wife" for him. Another instance is the Case of Lu (mentioned in Box 17), where the defendant, Lu, sold a male infant to Wang. Wang justified the purchase by stating it was for his son and daughter-in-law, both of whom were mentally disabled and unable to conceive, underscoring the complex interplay of disability discrimination and the demand within the child trafficking spectrum.

Box 17 Case of Lu, M3, 2017-SD-1724-Preliminary Criminal Trial-No. 94 2017-SD-1724-Preliminary Criminal Trial-No. 94 [(2017)鲁1724刑初94号]

Date: 17 April 2017.

Before: People's Court of Juye County, Shandong Province.

Public Prosecution Agency: People's Procuratorate of Juye County, Shandong Province.

Defendant:

Lu (Male, born on 7 July 1958. Residence: Juye County, Shandong Province).

Case summary:

The defendant *Lu* intermediated and assisted in the sale of a child for 74,000 yuan (9250 euros) outside a hospital.

The buyer, *Wang*, was the father of an intellectually disabled person, whose wife was also mentally ill. As he stated in the testimony, he bought the child for his son and daughter-in-law, who were infertile.

In conclusion, discrimination against individuals with disabilities manifests in multiple facets within the context of child trafficking. On the one hand, there is scant demand for infants with disabilities, as the majority of buyers seek a healthy child. On the other hand, when intertwined with other elements such as poverty, gender-based violence, and inadequate social protection, disability discrimination becomes a significant causative factor in child trafficking. Disabilities heighten the risk of trafficking for older female children and for children born to mothers with intellectual challenges. Furthermore, discrimination also stimulates demand among buyers who themselves have disabilities, underscoring the multifaceted impact of disability discrimination on both the supply and demand sides of child trafficking.

(3) *Other Statuses*

Family serves as the primary sanctuary for a child's protection, thereby making the marital status of parents a direct influence on a child's vulnerability to trafficking. In Chinese society, single mothers face widespread discrimination, and children born out of wedlock experience discrimination not only within the family but also in societal and legal contexts (refer to Box 6 above). It is common for the parents and/or other relatives of a single mother to either coerce or persuade her into terminating her pregnancy. Moreover, it is not uncommon for the parents and/or relatives of a single mother to sell her child, particularly in cases involving young, unmarried women or girls. Additionally, the disintegration of families due to divorce, widowhood, or other factors further compounds children's susceptibility to trafficking.

The birth control policy and its accompanying regulations severely aggravate the situation for children born outside of marriage. This policy greatly obstructs the childbirth registration process (Li et al. 2010), tying it to the parents' official residence, the issuance of a medical birth certificate, and a birth permit from the Population and Family Planning department. Women or unmarried couples face a plethora of difficulties when having a child outside the sanctioned bounds of marriage. The absence of legal marriage registration complicates the acquisition of a birth permit, which can result in hospital refusals. This, in turn, leads to a significant increase in the costs associated with childbirth, far exceeding those of a normal delivery. Additionally, up until 1997, children of unmarried couples were denied birth registration, a fundamental right that influences other critical human rights, including the right to obtain a nationality and the right to education. Among 835 victims whose parents' marital status was detailed in the judgments, an alarming one-third were born outside of wedlock, with an additional 9% being children of divorced parents. These obstacles markedly amplify the likelihood of children becoming victims of trafficking at the hands of their own family members or relatives.

C. Inadequate Protection of the Rights of the Child

Poverty, inequality, and various forms of discrimination are recognised as structural factors contributing to child trafficking. These issues are deeply embedded within a broad societal framework, impacting a wide range of individuals. Addressing these challenges requires policymakers to enact systematic reforms and commit to long-term efforts. However, the reality frequently demonstrates that the vulnerability of children from disadvantaged groups is exacerbated by policies, legislation, and practices that may contravene international human rights principles. This vulnerability is further compounded when their legitimate rights and necessary protections are neglected, ignored, or outright violated.

In the context of child trafficking, a fundamental principle is that children deserve special care and assistance, with their best interests being of paramount importance in all decisions affecting them. Despite this, there are innumerable instances where the rights and welfare of children are overlooked by those in positions of responsibility. This neglect facilitates the mechanisms of child trafficking, thereby amplifying the risks faced by children, especially those from marginalised communities. The gap between the principles enshrined in international frameworks and their implementation highlights a critical area for improvement in safeguarding the rights and well-being of children.

(1) Family Planning Policy

Implemented rigorously since the late 1970s and only recently relaxed, this contentious family planning policy was designed to manage China's population growth. Up until 2015, the policy predominantly restricted urban families to a single child, though exceptions were made for ethnic minorities, rural families, and families with children with disabilities, allowing them two or three children. Violation of this policy resulted in harsh penalties, such as substantial fines, termination of employment for both parents if they held public positions or were employed by state-owned enterprises, denial of household registration for the child, consequently leading to a lack of access to ration coupons, educational opportunities, and other social benefits and rights (Whyte et al. 2015, p. 150; Feng et al. 2013). The "one-child policy" has faced international criticism for violating human rights and its adverse outcomes, such as sex-selective abortions, female infanticide, and the abandonment of children (Feng et al. 2013).

The family planning policy in China considerably influences other statutes and regulations. Notably, the Criminal Law (Article 261), the Civil Code (Article 26), and the Law on the Protection of Minors explicitly prohibit parents from abandoning their offspring or neglecting their duty of care. Moreover, the Adoption Law, which the Civil Code superseded in 2021, asserted that "adoption must not contravene laws and regulations concerning family planning" (Article 3) and stipulated that "individuals who have placed a child for adoption are prohibited from having more children in breach of family planning regulations, on the pretext of having placed their child for adoption" (Article 19). Currently, the Civil Code (Article 1100) has amended this stipulation in line with the revised family planning policy, dictating that "adopters without offspring may adopt two children; those with offspring are permitted to adopt only one additional child."

While these regulations aim to safeguard children against abandonment, they also, paradoxically, may place some children at increased risk of mistreatment or neglect. Notably, the stringent regulations governing the legal process of transferring a child to social welfare institutions force some parents facing difficulties in child-rearing into a corner, pushing them towards illicit solutions such as infanticide, abandonment, or the sale of the child. This legal and regulatory framework, while designed to uphold family planning policies, inadvertently creates conditions that may facilitate child trafficking by limiting legal and safe options for parents in distress. The intertwining of the family planning policy with child protection laws creates a complex legal landscape where the intended protective measures can have unintended negative consequences on the well-being of children, especially those from families struggling to navigate the strictures of family planning regulations (Cao 2014, p. 165).

The strict enforcement of the "one-child policy" has undeniably shaped the landscape of child trafficking in China, with a substantial portion of the cases analysed in this study occurring under its regime. The birth control policy has profoundly influenced child trafficking dynamics, though assessing whether it has amplified the crime by boosting demand or reduced it by limiting potential victims remains complicated.

Box 18 Case of Wang and Yang, M3, 2016-YN-2628-Preliminary Criminal Trial-No. 83
2016-YN-2628-Preliminary Criminal Trial-No. 83 [(2016)云2628刑初83号]

Date: 1 July 2016.

Before: People's Court of Funing County, Yunnan Province.

Public Prosecution Agency: People's Procuratorate of Funing County, Yunnan Province.

Defendants:

Wang (Male, born on 3 July 1977. Residence: Funing County, Yunnan Province).

Yang (Female, born on 14 September 1973. Residence: Funing County, Yunnan Province).

Case summary:

In early 2015, specifically during the first lunar month (approximately February and March), while working in Ningde, Fujian Province, the defendants *Wang* and *Yang* encountered *Zhong* (accused in Fujian Province) on the street. Observing that *Yang* was pregnant, *Zhong* suggested that if they were unable to support the baby, they could give it to someone else. *Wang* took *Zhong*'s phone number following this encounter. Several months later, during the third and fourth lunar months of 2015 (around May and June), *Yang* gave birth to a baby boy. Subsequently, *Wang* reached out to *Zhong*, and on 15 June 2015, in a hotel in Nan'an, Fujian, they sold their son to a local couple for 100,000 yuan through *Zhong*'s mediation.

Wang's defence counsel argued that while Wang's actions constituted the crime of "abduction and sale of children", mitigating factors should be taken into account. Among these factors, the defence highlighted that the child was born in violation of the child control policy, adding that financial difficulties made it impossible for the family to support the child. Yang's defence counsel also cited similar mitigating factors, adding that Yang had two other children and elderly parents at home who required care and attention.

It's evident that the birth control policy has, in certain instances, acted as a catalyst for trafficking. On the one side, the policy has indeed escalated the demand for male offspring. The punitive measures associated with the policy have driven individuals, particularly those with one or two daughters but desiring a son, to circumvent high penalties or job losses. Legal adoption, though a potential avenue, becomes unfeasible for those with existing children due to restrictive birth control and adoption laws. This has led to some resorting to purchasing children from traffickers under the guise of "adoption". On the other side, the birth control policy also has influenced some parents' decisions to sell their children, often justified by the inability to afford fines for policy violations, as seen in cases highlighted in Case of Wang and Yang in Box 18.

However, the extent to which the birth control policy truly motivates these individuals to sell their children warrants deeper contemplation. There's a possibility that the policy and its sanctions serve as mere pretexts for profiting from the sale of children. Notably, families involved in these cases, having multiple children, have likely already faced sanctions, indicating a pre-existing willingness to contravene the policy. Given its three-decade-long enforcement, these families had ample opportunity to adhere to the regulations. Furthermore, if financial hardship were the true concern, families could opt for non-profit civil adoption, which is not prohibited by law, instead of seeking monetary compensation through trafficking.

Furthermore, what cannot be observed from the studied cases is the impact of family planning policies on reducing the number of children sold due to family poverty. It is clear that from 1980 to 2015, the majority of Chinese families adhered to the birth control policy, generally having only one or two children. Without this policy, it is plausible that a greater number of families would face economic hardships severe enough to consider selling their children, thus potentially increasing the supply of children vulnerable to trafficking. Additionally, the policy indirectly contributes to the prevention of child trafficking by enabling a considerable number of women to transition from family obligations to the workforce. This shift towards employment not only fosters independence among women but also enhances their ability to safeguard themselves and their children from exploitation.

In conclusion, the impact of the birth-control policy on child trafficking in China is multifaceted and complex. Although the strict enforcement of the "one-child policy" between 1980 and 2015 has undeniably influenced the dynamics of child trafficking, determining its comprehensive impact remains challenging. On the one hand, the policy has indirectly fostered demand for male children among families desiring sons without facing punitive measures, leading to increased interactions with traffickers. On the other hand, it has potentially reduced the number of children vulnerable to trafficking by limiting family sizes and alleviating the economic pressures that might compel families to sell their children. Moreover, by encouraging smaller family units, the policy inadvertently contributed to women's economic empowerment and independence, enhancing their ability to protect themselves and their offspring from exploitation. Therefore, while the birth control policy has been criticised for its human rights implications, it also appears to have had indirect benefits in terms of reducing the pool of children at risk of trafficking and empowering women within the societal and familial context.

(2) *Child Protection System*

The State bears the fundamental responsibility to furnish special care, protection, and assistance to children, prioritising their best interests. Under international human rights law, it is the State's duty to shield children from all manners of violence.[2] An effective child protection system encompasses laws, policies, regulations, and services spanning various social sectors, designed both to prevent vulnerabilities in children and their families and to offer robust protection for victims of violence, abuse, exploitation, and neglect (Man et al. 2017; UNICEF 2008). Beyond essential components such as a designated agency for child protection, a mandatory reporting system, a defined procedure for handling child abuse cases, and provisions for alternative out-of-home care, a comprehensive approach to child protection also involves preventative strategies aimed at supporting and fortifying families. This helps to mitigate social exclusion and diminishes the risks of violence and exploitation.

It has been noted that there is a lack of a comprehensive child protection system in China. Despite the existence of several pieces of legislation aimed at safeguarding children's rights, such as the Law on the Protection of Minors (1991), the Criminal Law, and the Domestic Violence Act (2016), there is a notable gap in the form of a unified, directly applicable national child protection act. Furthermore, China lacks a designated agency responsible for child protection, with the duty dispersed among various entities, including civil affairs departments, Working Committees on Women and Children, and public security departments. The introduction of a compulsory reporting system, a recent development through the Domestic Violence Act, mandates that staff at institutions frequently in contact with children and their families—such as schools, kindergartens, medical institutions, and social welfare

[2] UN Committee on the Rights of the Child (CRC), (2011) General comment No. 13 (2011): The right of the child to freedom from all forms of violence, 18 April 2011, CRC/C/GC/13, para. 32.

organisations—must promptly report suspected cases of domestic violence to local public security authorities.[3] However, the effectiveness of this reporting system has been subject to critique by researchers (Man et al. 2017; Zhao et al. 2017).

Given that the vast majority of victims in this study were infants, the shortcomings of child protection within medical institutions emerged more starkly than in other settings, such as schools. Medical personnel, especially those in gynaecology, paediatrics, and obstetrics, often interact directly with children and their families and are ideally positioned to offer protection. Yet, there was a notable failure to identify children at risk of trafficking at an early stage. In numerous instances of parental sale of children and organised child trafficking, hospitals or medical institutions were implicated (refer to Box 3). A prevalent scenario involved traffickers and buyers taking infant or young child victims to medical institutions for examinations. Some infants were even sold directly from hospital wards shortly after birth. In these situations, medical professionals had opportunities to observe or become aware of indicators of trafficking and had the responsibility to alert the authorities; however, none of the cases reviewed in this study were reported by medical staff. This oversight highlights a significant gap in the involvement of medical workers within child protection networks.

Alarmingly, there were situations where medical personnel actively participated in the trafficking network. For example, in the Case of Fan (highlighted in Box 5), healthcare workers were reported to have supplied intermediaries with details about newborns and their families. Moreover, some medical professionals went beyond mere facilitation to profit from these illicit activities. In the Case of Wang Chaoyun and others (mentioned in Box 19), medical worker Miao and her father-in-law earned 11,000 yuan for assisting the Wangs in selling their newborn. Additionally, there were instances where healthcare workers aided traffickers in creating fraudulent birth certificates. Some medical professionals admitted during their testimonies to witnessing child trafficking transactions within their wards and failing to report them to the authorities. These actions muddle the ethical and professional duties expected of healthcare providers in such critical scenarios, highlighting a pressing need for more stringent oversight and accountability within medical institutions.

Box 19 Case of Wang Chaoyun and others, M2, 2014-AH-DS-Preliminary Criminal Trial-No. 00158

2014-AH-DS-Preliminary Criminal Trial-No. 00158 [(2014)初刑初字第00158号]

Date: 26 August 2014.

Before: People's Court of Dangshan County, Anhui Province.

Public Prosecution Agency: People's Procuratorate of Dangshan County, Anhui Province.

[3] Article 14 of Anti-domestic Violence Law of the People's Republic of China.

Defendants:

Wang Chaoyun (Male, born on 25 October 1982. Residence: Dangshan County, Anhui Province).

Wang X (Female, born on 22 November 1988. Residence: Dangshan County, Anhui Province).

Miao (Female, born on 8 October 1980. Residence: Yucheng County, Henan Province).

Liu A (Female, born on 6 January 1974. Residence: Dangshan County, Anhui Province).

Liu B (Male, born on 10 August 1978. Residence: Dangshan County, Anhui Province).

Case summary:

In May 2008, the defendant, *Wang X*, gave birth to a baby boy at the Zhangji Health Clinic's Xiaqiaoji Branch in Yucheng County, Henan Province. The defendants, *Wang Chaoyun* and his wife *Wang X*, believing their family life to be difficult, decided to give the child up for adoption. Upon learning of this, a staff member of the health clinic, *Miao*, contacted the defendant *Liu A*. Previously, *Liu A*, due to his brother *Liu B*'s lack of children, had entrusted *Miao* to help adopt a child. After learning of this situation, *Liu B* and *Liu A* drove to *Miao*'s home to discuss the matter and subsequently bought the baby boy for 59,000 yuan for adoption, of which the defendants *Wang Chaoyun* and *Wang X* received 48,000 yuan, and the defendant *Miao* and his father-in-law *Zhao* (deceased) received 11,000 yuan. More than ten days later, *Wang Chaoyun*'s brother-in-law, *Zou Moujia*, learned of this and, using the pretext of wanting the child back, took 3800 yuan from *Zhao*.

(3) Other Relevant Social Protection Frameworks

Beyond focusing solely on child-centric protection systems, it is imperative to recognise that safeguarding frameworks for women and individuals with disabilities significantly influence child welfare. It has consistently been documented that, women, especially those living with disabilities, often do not receive the requisite or adequate protection. Instances such as the Case of Song (see Box 16), where mentally disabled women were subjected to sexual exploitation and their offspring sold over decades, highlight how the lack of comprehensive social welfare institutions can indirectly enable such egregious crimes. Moreover, should persons with disabilities be fully integrated into society with their rights unequivocally protected, they might encounter less discrimination and economic hardship, thereby reducing the likelihood of resorting to the illegal market to procure a spouse or child.

Furthermore, numerous instances have underscored the dire circumstances faced by mothers subjected to domestic violence, who lack efficacious support or protective measures. Bereft of accessible resources for assistance and safeguarding, these women are powerless to protect themselves and their children, thereby rendering both themselves and their progeny susceptible to exploitation by traffickers. This highlights the critical need for an inclusive rights protection system that not only focuses on children but also addresses the vulnerabilities of other at-risk groups, such as women and individuals with disabilities, to effectively prevent exploitation and break the cycle of abuse.

2 Human Rights Abuses During the Trafficking Cycle

Trafficking and the sale of children are recognised as intrinsic and heinous breaches of children's rights, not only under international human rights treaties but also within the Chinese legal framework. For instance, in the judgement of the Case of Zhang (referenced in Box 20), the judiciary unequivocally declared that, even though the sale of the child was not consummated, the perpetrator's actions amounted to a violation of the victim's liberty and caused significant harm to the child's physical and mental well-being.

Box 20 Case of Zhang, M2, 2016-SD-0181-Preliminary Criminal Trial-No. 410
2016-SD-0181-Preliminary Criminal Trial-No. 410 [(2016)鲁0181刑初410号]

Date: 23 November 2016.

Before: People's Court of Zhangqiu City, Shandong Province.

Public Prosecution Agency: People's Procuratorate of Zhangqiu City, Shandong Province.

Defendant:

Zhang (Female, born on 28 November 1988. Residence: Shandong Province).

Case summary:

On 16 June 2016, defendant *Zhang* attempted to sell her 6-year-old daughter for 80,000 yuan. Following a divorce from the child's father, the daughter had been residing with her father and stepmother until just a few days prior to the incident. Subsequently, the child's father transferred her care to *Zhang*. *Zhang*, claiming an unwillingness to care for her daughter, approached the owner of a clothing store to enquire if she was interested in purchasing a child. The store owner immediately contacted the police upon being offered a price and after an arrangement was made to sell the child.

The infringement of human rights during the trafficking process manifests in both overt and covert forms. Trafficking in persons is a complex and often extended process, rather than a singular occurrence. This process may unfold over days, months, years, or even decades. From the perspective of the victim, the ordeal of child trafficking commences with the initial illicit act perpetrated against the child and/or their family and persists until the victim has been liberated from the control and exploitation of the perpetrators. The violation of human rights is not confined to sexual or labour exploitation. The dignity and fundamental human rights of the child are compromised at every stage of the trafficking process. This includes the right to life, liberty, and security of person; the right of the child to maintain their identity; the right of the child not to be arbitrarily separated from their parents; the right to protection from violence and exploitation; the right to freedom from slavery; among others. Each of these rights is critical and may be jeopardised at any point during the trafficking ordeal, underscoring the pervasive human rights violations that characterise scenarios of child trafficking.

Whilst the primary victims are indeed the trafficked children or infants, it is evident that, in many instances, children are not the sole victims. In certain cases, the victims also encompass their parents, particularly their mothers. The perpetrators are predominantly individuals. Although our research has not pinpointed specific public organs directly or indirectly involved, the negligence of certain officials and systemic failure of providing protection has undeniably facilitated criminal endeavours.

A. Right to Be Free from Enslavement

> No one shall be held in slavery or servitude; slavery and the slave trade shall be prohibited in all their forms.
>
> —Article 4, Universal Declaration of Human Rights

In instances of human trafficking, particularly those involving victims trafficked for physical or sexual exploitation, the treatment they endure constitutes a form of enslavement. For example, in the case of Tan Tao and Yu Haiyu (highlighted in Box 14), victims trafficked for street begging were subjected to constant surveillance by their traffickers. These individuals not only appropriated all the money earned through begging but were also capable of administering corporal punishment if the victims either communicated with others or failed to collect a sufficient amount of money. A similar pattern of enslavement is observed in cases where children are trafficked for the purpose of engaging in unlawful activities, such as theft.

This pattern of enslavement-like treatment extends to forced marriages and sexual exploitation. Victims trafficked for these purposes not only suffer sexual violence within the confines of the buyer's home—where they are effectively enslaved—but also experience sexual violence throughout the trafficking journey. Typically, these women are subjected to rape, coerced into pregnancy, and exploited as means for reproduction. The distressing narrative presented in the Case of Wang X and Fan Qilong, as outlined in Box 21, serves as a poignant illustration of the grim realities faced by women and teenage girls who fall victim to trafficking for forced marriage. This case typifies the severe abuses that occur within these contexts, where victims are sold to remote villages, confined, and subjected to repeated violations by the individual who has acquired them under the pretence of "marriage". The extended period of captivity, often lasting until the victim bears one or two children for their buyer, highlights the deeply entrenched system of oppression and control exerted over these individuals. The complicity of the buyer's family members, neighbours, and even local authorities in maintaining this enslavement underscores the complex and multifaceted challenges in combating such human rights violations. The victim's marginal chance of escape, exacerbated by the remoteness of the village and the potential for betrayal by those she might turn to for help, paints a harrowing picture of entrapment and despair. The conditional "liberty" afforded to the victim following childbirth, serving as a stratagem to bind her to the purchaser's domicile. Invariably, the buyer has no apprehension regarding her potential escape, for he has already secured the child, and her fundamental value—her fertility—has been exploited.

Box 21 Case of Wang X and Fan Qilong, M1, 2017-GZ-04-Final Criminal Trial-No. 127
2017-GZ-04-Final Criminal Trial-No. 127 [(2017)黔04刑终127号]

Date: 30 September 2017.

Before: Intermediate People's Court of Anshun, Guizhou Province.

Public Prosecution Agency: People's Procuratorate of Xixiu District, Anshun City.

Appellant (original trial defendant):

Wang X (Male, born on 5 July 1991. Residence: Zhijin County, Guizhou Province).

Fan Qilong (Male, born on 5 March 1972. Residence: Zhijin County, Guizhou Province).

Case summary:

In May 2013, Defendant *Wang X* met the runaway victim *Liu* (born on 1 March 2001, 12 years old) at the Nanma Avenue Square in the Anshun Economic and Technological Development Zone, and then *Wang X* brought *Liu* to a hostel within Wangjiashan, Xixiu District, Anshun City, where *Wang X* sexually abused *Liu*.

Subsequently, the defendant *Wang X* took *Liu* to Heitu Township, Zhijin County, Guizhou Province, and sold *Liu* to *Fan X Kai* (prosecuted in a separate case) for 16,000 yuan. Subsequently, *Wang X* and *Fan X Kai* took *Liu* to Haining City, Zhejiang Province, and handed her over to *Fan X Kai*'s son, the defendant *Fan Qilong*. After *Fan Qilong* paid *Wang X* 12,000 yuan, *Fan Qilong* began cohabiting with *Liu*, who was under the age of fourteen.

On 11 September 2014, *Liu* (then 13 years old) gave birth to a son, *Fan XX*. Forensic identification confirmed that the defendant *Fan Qilong* and the victim *Liu* are the biological parents of *Fan XX*.

On 2 March 2016, upon learning of the above circumstances, the parents of *Liu* reported the crime to the public security authorities. On 6 April 2016, public security police arrested the defendant *Wang X* in the Renbin Jiahuan Green Energy Oil Factory, Xincheng Town, Xiuzhou District, Jiaxing City, Zhejiang Province. On 14 April 2016, the public security police arrested the defendant *Fan Qilong* at the victim *Liu*'s home in Cuilu Sunshine Community, Anshun Economic and Technological Development Zone.

The enslavement may happen to the victim's mother, during and right before the trafficking. In the preceding section, we explored instances where the crime of child trafficking stemmed from inadequate protection for vulnerable women, leading to sexual abuse. This issue is particularly acute for women with mental disabilities, who may be exploited by the men they live with. An illustrative example is the Case of Song (referenced in Box 16), where a woman with intellectual disability had all five of her children sold by their biological father in 8 years. In scenarios concerning the trafficking of children born from pre-arranged pregnancies, the women involved typically originate from impoverished backgrounds. They are recruited and then relocated to areas under the dominion of traffickers. These women are escorted to hospitals or clinics with the sole intent of giving birth, after which their newborns are promptly sold. Moreover, these women are deprived of vital antenatal care. An illustrative case is that of Aojierzi and Mamesezu (referenced in Box 22), which entailed the orchestration of five pregnant women, culminating in the immediate sale of three children post-birth. The defendants asserted that the health condition of each child was authenticated through medical examinations before any sale. Within this cohort, one girl was diagnosed with a sexually transmitted disease. Additionally, a witness claimed he endeavoured to aid the defendant Aojierzi in finding purchasers for two infants; yet, these efforts were thwarted as both infants were diagnosed with syphilis. All these women hailed from the same locality, the traffickers' hometown, suggesting that this form of trafficking had burgeoned into an illicit industry within that region. It has become an accepted reality among the community, including the women and their spouses, that their fertility could be commodified for financial gain. To conclude, although there is no concrete evidence to suggest these women were compelled into pregnancy or to sell their offspring, the exploitative manipulation of their reproductive capabilities by traffickers is evident.

Box 22 Case of Aojierzi and Mamesezu, M4, 2017-SC-3429-Preliminary Criminal Trial-No. 134
2017-SC-3429-Preliminary Criminal Trial-No. 134 [(2017)川3429刑初134号]

Date: 6 December 2017.

Before: People's Court of Butuo County, Sichuan Province.

Public Prosecution Agency: People's Procuratorate of Butuo County, Sichuan Province.

Defendant:

Aojierzi (Male, born on 12 February 1980, of the Yi ethnicity. Residence: Butuo County, Sichuan Province).

Mamesezu (Female, born on 8 November 1976, of the Yi ethnicity. Residence: Puge County, Sichuan Province).

Case summary:

After the defendant *Aojierzi* and his wife rented a house in Pingyi, Shandong, they contacted pregnant women from Liangshan, Sichuan Province by phone. After agreeing on a price, *Aojierzi* would travel to Chengdu and other places to bring these pregnant women to their rented house to await childbirth. Once the babies were born, *Aojierzi* and his wife would arrange for the sale of the infants and earn a broker's fee from these transactions.

In March 2017, a pregnant woman from Butuo County arrived in Pingyi County, Shandong, and stayed in the house rented by *Aojierzi* and his wife. A few days later, one of the pregnant women gave birth to a male infant, who was sold for 65,000 yuan, with a share of 14,800 yuan going to them. About a week later, another pregnant woman gave birth to a female infant, sold for 48,000 yuan, from which they received 13,800 yuan. The last female infant, who was ill, was sold for 32,000 yuan, earning them 12,000 yuan; the sale was facilitated by the defendant *Mamesezu*, who made a profit of 2000 yuan from the transaction. The pregnant women *Hu X* and *Su X*, who were brought in by *Aojierzi*, had not yet given birth when they were arrested alongside *Aojierzi* and *Mamesezu* by the public security authorities on the night of 16 May 2017.

B. Right to Life and Security of Person

Everyone has the right to life, liberty and security of person.

—Article 3, Universal Declaration of Human Rights

The infringement of the right to life and security of person is frequently linked with child trafficking. This association is particularly pronounced in instances of abduction and sale of children, wherein the child victims are forcibly separated from their parents or legal guardians through abduction, physical violence, coercion, deception, abuse of authority, or other violent methods. The perpetration of violence is not confined solely to the child victim. On occasions, the family members of the child, or both the child and their family members, are subjected to violence, as exemplified in the Case of Li Lianggui and others (referenced in Box 23). In this case, the defendant Chen Minggao, along with seven accomplices, invaded the victim's home at night, attacked and restrained three adults present, and kidnapped their two children. This instance serves as a quintessential illustration of child trafficking executed through acts of violence against the family members of the child.

Certainly, the children who are trafficked are not the sole victims whose personal security is compromised. Instances have been recorded where child trafficking ensued as a by-product of women trafficking. In such scenarios, the child, either abducted or transported alongside their mother, was subsequently sold separately, or the child was born to a victim of trafficking who was coerced into pregnancy. An illustrative case of this is the Case of Lu, detailed in Box 8, wherein the child involved was the daughter of a victim of cross-border trafficking of women.

Box 23 Case of Li Lianggui and others, M1, 2016-GD-19-Final Criminal Trial-No. 85
2016-GD-19-Final Criminal Trial-No. 85 [(2016)粤19刑终第85号]

Date: 3 September 2016.

Before: Intermediate People's Court of Dongguan, Guangdong Province.

Public Prosecution Agency: People's Procuratorate of the Second Urban District of Dongguan City, Guangdong Province.

Defendants:

Li Lianggui (Male, born on 15 February 1966. Residence: Sichuan Province).

Chen Minggao (Male, born on 11 May 1974. Residence: Chongqing Municipality).

Zhou Jianxin (Male, born on 19 March 1965. Residence: Sichuan Province).

Jiang Shiyou (Male, born on 9 September 1966. Residence: Sichuan Province).

Jiang Banggen (Male, born on 17 October 1950. Residence: Sichuan Province).

Case summary:

On the 5th of September 1995, five defendants, along with three others charged separately, forcibly entered the residence of the *Chen* and *Li* families. The intruders assaulted the family members, restraining them before abducting two children, *Chen A* and *Li A*, both males, and subsequently selling them to distinct locations. *Chen A*, at the tender age of nine months, was sold for 10,000 yuan.

Efforts to trace *Chen A* revealed that his name had been altered by the individuals who purchased him, ostensibly his "adoptive parents". *Chen A* conveyed his decision not to reunite with his biological parents, although he expressed a desire to maintain contact with them. As for *Li A*, detailed information about his whereabouts remained elusive at the time the defendants were prosecuted, leaving him unaccounted for.

Even in circumstances where trafficking occurs without overt violence, the health and safety of the victim remain jeopardised at every stage of the trafficking process. For example, during transportation, it is commonplace for traffickers to administer sleeping pills to children or infants to keep them quiet. In some instances, traffickers have been known to conceal newborn babies in plastic bags or travel bags to evade detection by police checks and surveillance cameras, as highlighted in the Case of Yang ZH and Yang YH (detailed in Box 24). A tragic outcome of such practices is that some victims perish during the trafficking process due to inadequate care. Furthermore, victims of child trafficking often find themselves ensnared in conditions akin to slavery upon being trafficked into the sex industry, coerced into marriages, or subjected to forced labour. Reports have also surfaced of victims enduring torture and being compelled into performing strenuous labour, engaging in street begging, and pickpocketing. These reprehensible acts underscore the grave risks to the well-being and security of individuals ensnared in trafficking, even absent physical violence during the initial act of trafficking.

Box 24 Case of Yang ZH and Yang YH, M3, 2014-YN-FN-Preliminary Criminal Trial-No. 183
2014-YN-FN-Preliminary Criminal Trial-No. 183 [(2014)富刑初字第 183 号]

Date: 11 December 2014.

Before: People's Court of Funing County, Yunnan Province.

Public Prosecution Agency: People's Procuratorate of Funing County, Yunnan Province.

Defendants:

Yang ZH (Male, born on 13 September 1979. Residence: Yunnan Province).

Yang YH (Male, born on 10 November 1969. Residence: Guangdong Province).

Case summary:

On 16 April 2014, the defendant *Yang YH* bought a newborn girl from an unidentified man with the price of 5500 yuan (687.50 euros). He then sold the child to *Yang ZH* for 7500 yuan (937.50 euros). When *Yang ZH* and his father-in-law were transporting the child to their home, they were seized by patrol policemen, and the child was found in a travel bag.

C. **Human Dignity**

All human beings are born free and equal in dignity and rights.

—Article 1, Universal Declaration of Human Rights

Even in the absence of explicit or implicit exploitation, the violation of human dignity is unmistakably evident throughout the process of child trafficking. As delineated within the Chinese legal framework, the act constituting child trafficking is the "sale", highlighting its core essence as the commodification of children. This commodification profoundly deprives children of their inherent human dignity and rights, reducing them to mere commodities in transactions. The engagement of offenders, including traffickers, parents selling their offspring, and purchasers, in this clandestine trade of children, fundamentally annihilates the victims' humanity and strips them of the fundamental human rights innate to every individual. Children, infants, and even foetuses, likened to mundane commodities, are affixed with price tags that fluctuate based on gender, age, health status, physical attributes, and weight. Boys, perceived as more valuable, command higher prices, and any detectable imperfections, such as a mole or a birthmark, become subjects of bargaining, exacerbating the dehumanisation of the victims. Moreover, this commodification of children is reflected in the attitudes of the perpetrators, notably in instances of parental sales. Despite claims of desiring a more prosperous future for their children, the act of exchanging them for considerable sums of money uncovers the real intent: to monetise their progeny. Evidently, to middlemen and traffickers operating within organised criminal networks, children and infants are merely commodities. As evidenced in the colloquial terminology of traffickers in Yunnan Province, male children are referred to as "big goods" (as documented in Case of Ma HF and others in Box 25), and female children as "small goods" (detailed in Case of Cui YS and others in Box 26).

Similarly, despite many purchasers ostensibly seeking a child for adoption rather than exploitation, their underlying motivation frequently belies a disregard for the child's welfare. The most commonly cited justifications for purchasing a child, as identified in this research, include childlessness, the absence of a male heir, or the desire to complete the familial unit with both a son and a daughter. What emerges is a stark prioritisation of the buyer's needs over the intrinsic rights and interests of the child, who is reduced to a mere instrument for fulfilling personal desires and achieving an idealised "perfect family".

Notably, in this research we did not identify cases where trafficked children were coerced into the sex industry and forced labour. This absence of examples probably is attributable to such instances not being prosecuted under the crime of trafficking in persons, but rather under related offences such as forced prostitution and forced labour. Another possible reason is the age limit set in anti-trafficking regulations, as most of the victims who are more "welcomed" by the above-mentioned industries are older children and young adults.

Box 25 Case of Ma HF and others, M3, 2013-SD-PY-Preliminary Criminal Trial-No. 458
2013-SD-PY-Preliminary Criminal Trial-No. 458 [(2015)平刑初字第458号]

Date: 31 October 2016.

Before: People's Court of Pingyi County, Shandong Province.

Public Prosecution Agency: People's Procuratorate of Pingyi County, Shandong Province.

Defendants:

Ma HF (Female. Residence: Shandong Province).

Jike SR (Male. Residence: Sichuan Province).

Han JZ (Male. Residence: Heilongjiang Province).

Zhao LR (Female. Residence: Shandong Province).

Hu FX (Male. Residence: Shandong Province).

Li GK (Male. Residence: Shandong Province).

Wang XY (Female. Residence: Shandong Province).

Zhang ZC (Male. Residence: Shandong Province).

Case summary:

Between 2010 and August 2014, the defendants *Ma HF* and *Jike SR* were implicated in nine instances of child trafficking within Shandong Province, facilitated by the introductions from *Han JZ*, *Zhao LR*, *Hu FX*, *Li GK*, *Wang XY*, and *Zhang ZC*. *Ma HF* and *Jike SR* participated in all nine cases; *Han JZ*, *Zhao LR*, and *Hu FX* were involved in three cases each; *Li GK* took part in two cases; while *Wang XY* and *Zhang YC* each contributed to one case. An accomplice's testimony revealed that in their communications, the term "big goods (大货)" was used to denote "boys or male infants".

1. One day in October 2010, *Ma HF* and *Jike SR*, through *Hu FX*, sold a new-born boy to a buyer for 45,000 yuan. Eight months later, the buyer found that the child was infected with HIV/AIDS and then returned him to *Ma HF* and *Jike SR*.

2. On 17 May 2014, *Ma HF* and *Jike SR*, through *Li GK*, sold a new-born boy to a buyer for 40,000 yuan. *Li GK* was paid for 200 yuan.
3. On 11 July 2014, *Ma HF* and *Jike SR*, through *Han JZ* and *Zhao LR*, sold a new-born girl to a buyer for 40,000 yuan. On the next day, the girl was returned to *Jike SR* because the girl was found unhealthy after a medical examination.
4. On 15 August 2014, *Ma HF* and *Jike SR*, through *Han JZ* and *Zhao LR*, sold a new-born girl to a buyer for 53,000 yuan. After several days, the girl was returned to *Jike SR* because the girl was found unhealthy after a medical examination.
5. On 16 August 2014, *Ma HF* and *Jike SR*, through *Han JZ* and *Zhao LR*, sold a new-born boy to a buyer for 78,000 yuan. On the next day, the boy was returned to *Jike SR* because the boy was found unhealthy after a medical examination.
6. On 17 August 2014, *Ma HF* and *Jike SR*, through *Hu FX*, planned to sell a boy for 50,000 yuan. The trade was cancelled because the two parties failed to make an agreement on the price.
7. On 19 August 2014, *Ma HF* and *Jike SR*, through *Wang XY*, sold a new-born boy for 68,700 yuan (8587.50 euros), of which 2000 yuan was given to *Ma HF* and 6500 was given to *Wang XY*.
8. On 24 August 2014, *Ma HF* and *Jike SR*, through *Li GK*, sold a new-born boy for 35,000 yuan, of which was given 5000 yuan to *Ma HF* and 600 yuan was given to *Li GK*.
9. On 31 August 2014, *Ma HF* and *Jike SR*, through *Zhang YC*, sold a new-born boy for 65,000 yuan, of which 5000 yuan was given to *Ma HF* and 5000 yuan was given to *Zhang YC*.

Box 26 Case of Cui YS and others, M3, 2013-SD-DM-Preliminary Criminal Trial-No. 132

2013-SD-DM-Preliminary Criminal Trial-No. 132 [(2013)东刑一初字第132号]

Date: 19 December 2013.

Before: People's Court of Dongming County, Shandong Province.

Public Prosecution Agency: People's Procuratorate of Dongming County, Shandong Province.

Defendants:

Cui YS (Male, born on 25 April 1968. Residence: Shandong Province).

Shi ZSQ (Male, born on 13 May 1981. Residence: Sichuan Province).

Bi TZE (Male, born on 21 July 1985. Residence: Sichuan Province).

Li SL (Male, born on 7 April 1969. Residence: Shandong Province).

Bian XX (Male, born on 10 May 1947. Residence: Shandong Province).

Chen XY (Female, born on 1 February 1967. Residence: Shandong Province).

Sun XX (Male, born on 16 October 1962. Residence: Shandong Province).

Sun XA (Female, born on 10 November 1965. Residence: Shandong Province).

Wang XX (Male, born on 19 December 1965. Residence: Shandong Province).

Wang XA (Female, born on 23 August 1988. Residence: Shandong Province).

Li XX (Male, born on 17 April 1968. Residence: Shandong Province).

Case summary:

1. One day in October 2010, the defendant *Cui YS* sold a male infant to the defendant *Sun XA* for 45,000 yuan.
2. On 16 February 2013, the defendant *Cui YS* sold a female infant to a buyer (accused separately) for 48,500 yuan.
3. One day in February or March 2012, the defendant *Cui YS* sold a male infant to the defendant *Sun XA* for 52,000 yuan.
4. On 10 March 2013, the defendants *Cui YS*, *Li SL*, *Shi ZSQ*, *Bi TZE*, and *Bian XX*, sold a female infant to a buyer (accused separately) for 46,000 yuan.
5. On 14 March 2013, the defendants *Cui YS*, *Li SL*, *Chen XY*, *Shi ZSQ*, *Bi TZE*, *Bian XX*, *Li XX* and *Wang XX* sold a female infant to the defendant *Wang XA* for 33,000 yuan.

The defendant *Cui YS* was identified as the chief intermediary within this child trafficking network. Defendants *Shi ZSQ* and *Bi TZE* functioned as middlemen who maintained direct liaisons with the parents selling the trafficked children and supplied these children to *Cui YS*. Defendants *Li SL*, *Chen XY*, *Sun XX*, and *Bian XX* were in contact with purchasers, who acquired children for unlawful adoption purposes. *Cui YS* procured children from various sources, including *Shi ZSQ* and *Bi TZE*, and subsequently resold them to buyers via *Li SL*, *Chen XY*, *Sun XX*, and *Bian XX*. According to the testimony of defendant *Shi ZSQ*, in their communications, the term "small goods (小货)" was employed to denote "girls or female infants", while "goods" referred to "child or children". Before finalising the transaction, the buyers and involved traffickers invariably arranged for the child to undergo a health examination at a hospital.

D. Rights of the Child

Owing to their physical and mental immaturity, children necessitate special safeguards and protection. The overriding principle must always be the child's best interests.[4] Nonetheless, this fundamental right of the child is grievously infringed upon during the trafficking process. In certain instances of parental sale, parents may have intentions of placing their children with economically wealthier families, hoping these families will treat their children well. However, in the majority of such cases, the children's well-being and safety are not the primary concerns. Predominantly, in scenarios of parental sale, organised child trafficking, and pre-arranged trafficking, parents sell their offspring to a stranger or a trafficker with no consideration for the child's future welfare, egregiously ignoring the potential risks of exploitation and abuse. Traffickers exhibit no regard for the child's protection, nor do they take into account whether the buyer will provide a nurturing environment that supports the child's physical, mental, and moral growth. Their singular aim is to derive profit from the sale of the child.

According to Article 9 of the Convention on the Rights of the Child (CRC), "a child shall not be separated from his or her parents against their will". In scenarios involving the "abduction and sale of children", the child is involuntarily separated from their parents, constituting a direct violation of this stipulation. Such acts, perpetrated by either strangers or relatives of the victims, not only infringe upon the rights granted to both the child and their parents under the CRC but also deprive parents of their rights over their children, such as the right to provide guidance and direction in the exercising of the child's rights. Regrettably, the breach of this right and the resultant trauma are often irreparable.

For example, in Case of Li Lianggui and others (outlined in Box 23), two children were abducted and sold by eight traffickers in 1995. Twenty years later, the police located one of the victims, while the other remains unaccounted for. Upon reunion, the found victim, having grown accustomed to his life away from his biological family, opted to maintain contact with his parents but declined to return to his original family. Annually, similar heartbreaking stories emerge, highlighting the enduring anguish of parents who spend their lives searching for their abducted children, many of whom never experience the joy of reunion. These parents are thus robbed of the opportunity and right to nurture, educate, or protect their children.

Child trafficking, particularly the trafficking of infants for illicit adoption, constitutes a grave violation of "the right of the child to preserve his or her identity, including nationality, name, and family relations as recognised by law".[5] By severing children from their original families and transferring them to new guardians, the intrinsic connection between the child and their biological relatives is disrupted. The purchasers, driven by the fear of losing the child they have acquired, often opt to

---

[4] CRC, at Article 3.1, and UN Committee on the Rights of the Child, (2013) *General comment No. 14 (2013) on the right of the child to have his or her best interests taken as a primary consideration (art. 3, para. 1)*, 29 May 2013, CRC/C/GC/14.

[5] CRC, Article 8. See also European Court of Human Rights Case of Godelli V. Italy.

conceal the child's true identity. Nonetheless, when the truth about the child's origins emerges, typically disclosed by neighbours or other family members, the child invariably expresses a strong desire to locate his or her biological parents—a pursuit that is frequently not supported by the adoptive parents.

On the platform of *Bao Bei Hui Jia*, detailed further in the subsequent chapter, there are myriad postings by individuals, now adults, who were victims of child trafficking, earnestly searching for their biological parents. The scant information they possess often consists of hearsay from neighbours or relatives, fragmented memories of the incident, familiar dialects, traditional foods, landscapes of their birthplace, or nicknames by which they were once called. Their quest is a search for their authentic identities and to re-establish a fundamental connection with their original families—a right that is unequivocally theirs to claim.

In addition, being trafficked to a loving adoptive family does not ensure the safeguarding of some fundamental rights. Under Chinese regulations, children lacking medical birth certificates were ineligible for registration in the Household Registration system until 2015, when the State Council promulgated the *Opinions concerning the Issue of Solving the Problem of Household Registration for Persons without Registered Residence*.[6] This provision allowed individuals without a registered domicile, encompassing victims of child trafficking and those adopted outside legal procedures, to acquire legal status as Chinese citizens. Nevertheless, individuals who had engaged in the illegal adoption of children remained unable to legally register the child in their household, as this contravened criminal law. Absence of a registered domicile precludes a child from accessing social welfare benefits, including health insurance and complimentary education. Furthermore, without a registered domicile, an individual cannot obtain the Resident Identity Card, indispensable for engaging in various societal activities such as sitting for the college entrance examination, opening a bank account, lawful employment, participating in elections, marriage registration, or travelling via public transport, including trains and planes. Consequently, victims of child trafficking may endure various infringements of their basic human rights, encompassing political, civil, economic, and social rights, notwithstanding the absence of exploitation by the purchasers.

Furthermore, the rights of children to be registered immediately after birth, to be given a name, and to acquire a nationality are frequently infringed upon. As highlighted earlier, numerous victims of parental child sale and organised child trafficking are born "illegally". Such births may go unregistered within the healthcare system. A more comprehensive discussion on this matter will be provided in the subsequent sub-paragraph.

[6] The State Council, (2015) 国务院办公厅关于解决无户口人员登记户口问题的意见[Opinions concerning the Issue of Solving the Problem of Household Registration for Persons without Registered Residence], No. 96 [2015] of the State Council, issued and entered in force on 31 December 2015, retrieved from http://www.gov.cn/zhengce/content/2016-01/14/content_10595.htm.

3 Human Rights Challenges After the Trafficking Cycle and Rescue

The association between child trafficking and human rights extends well beyond the act of trafficking itself. Victims, and at times their legal guardians, are bearers of a plethora of fundamental human rights intricately linked to child trafficking and associated offences. The matters of import encompass, but are not confined to, the care of the victims subsequent to their rescue, their safe repatriation to their families, healthcare provision, assistance to the child victim, and the right to reparation.

These rights are essential for the rehabilitation and reintegration of trafficking victims into society. Proper care after rescue involves ensuring that victims receive psychological support to help them recover from the trauma of trafficking. The safe return to their families requires careful assessment and planning to ensure that the environment they are returning to is secure and supportive. Healthcare and assistance are pivotal in addressing the immediate and long-term physical and psychological needs of the child victim. Lastly, the right to remedy acknowledges the harm suffered by the victims and seeks to provide compensation, rehabilitation, and measures to prevent future occurrences.

Addressing these concerns requires a coordinated effort from governments, non-governmental organisations, and the international community to ensure that the rights of trafficking victims are fully realised and protected.

A. The Care of the Victims After Rescue

The primary concern in the aftermath of a rescue operation is the child's appropriate resettlement and potential reunification with their family. Upon rescue, the child may temporarily come under the guardianship of the police, a period during which they are entitled to special protection and assistance from the State, as delineated in Article 20 of the Convention on the Rights of the Child (CRC). The State bears the responsibility to implement necessary actions to enable the child's return to their original family, ensuring that such measures prioritise the child's best interests.

A plethora of issues related to child protection post-rescue operation necessitates attention. These include assessing the child's physical and psychological health to address any immediate needs, determining the child's best interests for short and long-term well-being, and identifying and securing a safe and supportive environment for their reintegration. The complexities of reintegrating a child with their family often involve legal, social, and psychological considerations, including the potential for re-trafficking or the risk of not being accepted back into their family or community. Moreover, the process must be handled with sensitivity and care to ensure the child's rights are upheld throughout. This includes, but is not limited to, the right to be heard and to have their views taken into consideration, the right to privacy, and the right to be protected from further harm. Implementing these measures requires a coordinated approach involving various stakeholders, including social services, legal authorities, child protection agencies, and non-governmental organisations, to ensure a holistic and child-centred approach to resettlement and reintegration.

However, the revelations from judicial decisions highlight a troubling scenario regarding the lack of clear regulations or guidelines for the immediate protection and resettlement of child trafficking victims. This gap in policy creates considerable challenges in ensuring the welfare and security of these vulnerable individuals. The *Notice of the Ministry of Civil Affairs and Ministry of Public Security on Carrying out Works of Adoption of the Rescued Child Victims of Child Trafficking Who cannot Find a Biological Parent*[7] issued in 2015 does make provisions for the return of children to their identified parents and suggests that those without identifiable parents be cared for by social welfare or child assistance and protection agencies. However, this directive does not sufficiently address the nuances of immediate custody following a rescue operation, nor does it provide detailed guidance on the timing and nature of interventions by child protection agencies.

A particularly thorny issue arises regarding whether children should be returned to their parents if these parents were the ones who originally sold the child. The 2015 Notice mandates the return of rescued children to their parents if found, without addressing situations where the parents are implicated as offenders in the child's trafficking. Data highlighted in Table 3.4 indicate that at least 32 children were returned to their parent(s), who had initially sold them, after rescue. Although the numbers might not be substantial, they underscore a significant loophole in China's child protection framework. In instances where parent(s) who sold their child express a lack of desire or capacity to care for the child upon rescue, the practice has often been to return the child to them or place the child with other family members, such as grandparents, uncles, and aunts. This practice has been confirmed by judges of the Intermediate People's Court of Guangzhou during an anonymous interview (referenced in Appendix C).

These circumstances reveal critical gaps in the system, highlighting the need for a more nuanced approach that considers the safety and best interests of the child above all. Ensuring that the child's welfare is the primary consideration necessitates revising existing policies to address these shortcomings explicitly. This might include establishing clearer guidelines for immediate care post-rescue, creating robust mechanisms for assessing the suitability of biological parents or relatives to care for the child, and providing alternative care solutions that prioritise the child's needs and rights.

The decision to return children to the buyer's family post-rescue is driven by two primary factors: the inadequate capacity of local welfare agencies to accommodate all victims, particularly in rural areas, and the emotional attachment that some children develop towards their buyers. The data presented in the preceding chapter indicates that a significant proportion of the victims rescued over the last decade were infants, often rescued in groups during the same operation. The limited resources and facilities

---

[7] The State Council, (2015) 民政部、公安部关于开展查找不到生父母的打拐解救儿童收养工作的通知 [Notice of the Ministry of Civil Affairs and the Ministry of Public Security on Carrying out Works of Adoption of the Rescued Child Victims of Child Trafficking Who Cannot Find a Biological Parents], No. 159 [2015] of the Ministry of Civil Affairs, issued and entered in force on 20 August 2015, retrieved from http://www.gov.cn/xinwen/2015-09/18/content_2934413.htm.

of welfare agencies, especially in less urbanised areas, pose a challenge in providing care for multiple victims simultaneously.

Additionally, the rationale frequently cited by police for placing rescued children back with the buyer's family is the strong emotional bond that develops, particularly when the child was sold to the buyer's family as an infant and has since been cared for by them over a prolonged period. This scenario presents a complex dilemma for law enforcement and child protection agencies: on the one hand, some buyers may offer a more nurturing environment for the child's development compared to welfare institutions, and forcibly removing the child from a familiar setting could result in significant psychological trauma; on the other hand, legally and ethically, fostering the child with the buyer's family is contentious and potentially places the child at risk.

While the challenges faced by local welfare agencies in accommodating multiple children and infants are understandable, and the potential for trauma during rescue operations is acknowledged, allowing victims to remain with individuals who have engaged in criminal activities related to child trafficking is indefensible. It is difficult to argue that such arrangements align with legal standards or the principle of prioritising the child's best interests, nor is it convincing to claim that government resources are insufficient to provide a safe environment for these children.

In conclusion, the absence of a comprehensive child protection system and a dedicated agency equipped to intervene promptly in situations where a child is at risk of abuse or violence has led to the exposure of some rescued child trafficking victims to the danger of secondary victimisation. This underscores the urgent need for systemic reforms to ensure the protection and well-being of vulnerable children, prioritising their safety, psychological health, and legal rights above all considerations.

B. **Alternative Care**

It is widely acknowledged that for a child's personality to develop fully and harmoniously, growing up in a family environment is indispensable. Children who are temporarily or permanently bereft of this environment are entitled to special protection and assistance from the State, which is also tasked with ensuring alternative care arrangements, including foster care, adoption, or placement in institutions specifically designed for child care.[8]

In cases where a child is rescued from child trafficking and their parents cannot be timely identified, the child is typically placed in local welfare agencies or child assistance and protection agencies.[9] A significant number of these victims end up in welfare institutions—some are fortunate to be reunited with their biological parents, while others never experience such reunion. According to Article 4 of the *Adoption Law of the People's Republic of China*, adoption is restricted to children under

[8] CRC, Preamble and Article 20.

[9] The State Council, (2015) 民政部、公安部关于开展查找不到生父母的打拐解救儿童收养工作的通知 [Notice of the Ministry of Civil Affairs and the Ministry of Public Security on Carrying out Works of Adoption of the Rescued Child Victims of Child Trafficking Who Cannot Find a Biological Parents], No. 159 [2015] of the Ministry of Civil Affairs, issued and entered in force on 20 August 2015, retrieved from http://www.gov.cn/xinwen/2015-09/18/content_2934413.htm.

14 years of age who are orphans, abandoned infants or children whose parents cannot be identified, and children whose parents are unable to care for them due to significant hardships. However, children rescued from trafficking, whose parents cannot be found, do not fit any of these categories since they cannot be conclusively considered orphans or abandoned; their parents might be actively searching for them. Thus, their biological parents retain legal guardianship, leaving these children ineligible for adoption or foster care. While welfare institutions serve as qualified caretakers, the deprivation of a familial environment remains a significant concern, particularly following the surge in children placed in such institutions after the crackdowns initiated in 2011. The need to provide these children with a family setting has been a topic of discussion among experts and the media.

This situation began to shift in September 2015 with the issuance of the *Notice of the Ministry of Civil Affairs and Ministry of Public Security on Carrying out Works of Adoption of the Rescued Child Victims of Child Trafficking Who Cannot Find a Biological Parent*. This notice outlined that children, in the absence of identifiable biological parents or guardians, should be cared for by social welfare or child protection institutions, which assume temporary guardianship. Concurrently, public security organs are required to collect blood samples from rescued children to be entered into a national anti-human trafficking DNA database for potential matching with parents searching for their missing children. If no biological parents or relatives are matched within a month, the institution is directed to seek families for these children through public announcements. If, after an additional month, no family connections are established, the child is then permanently placed within the welfare institution, becoming eligible for adoption after a year's wait. Notably, even if a child trafficking victim is legally adopted, the adoptive relationship can be dissolved if the biological parents assert guardianship—unless it is proven that they were involved in selling or abandoning the child, in which case the adoption remains irrevocable.

This approach represents a structured attempt to balance the urgent need for a protective and family environment for these children while navigating the complexities of legal guardianship and the potential for family reunification.

C. **Health Care and Assistance to Victims of Trafficking**

The right to health and access to healthcare services are indeed fundamental human rights for every child.[10] As defined by the World Health Organization (WHO), health encompasses complete physical, mental, and social well-being, beyond the mere absence of disease or infirmity. It emphasises that enjoying the highest attainable standard of health is a fundamental right of every human being, irrespective of race, religion, political belief, economic, or social condition. In light of this, states are obligated to undertake appropriate measures to facilitate the social, physical, and psychological recovery of victims of child trafficking, which includes providing medical and psychological assistance among other forms of support.[11]

---

[10] CRC, Article 24.

[11] CRC-OPSC Article 9.3, and Palermo Protocol Article 6.3.

The health of children who have been trafficked is jeopardised at every stage of the trafficking cycle—starting from before the departure, during transit, upon arrival at the destination, throughout any period of detention and exploitation, and extending into the post-rescue and reintegration phases. The associated health consequences span a wide range, including physical health problems like injuries and damage to reproductive and sexual health, as well as mental health issues such as symptoms of post-traumatic stress disorder (PTSD). Given that these abuses and traumas occur during crucial developmental periods, the impact on children and adolescents can be particularly profound, affecting their physical, psychological, and social development.

Research identifies physical health problems occurring across three main stages: initially, children and their guardians may suffer harm during violent abduction incidents; subsequently, during the transition phase, victims face challenges such as inadequate diet and hygiene, neglect, and substance abuse; finally, in the destination, detention, and exploitation phase, victims may endure imprisonment, inhumane living conditions. In cases of girls trafficked for forced marriage, they may endure physical and sexual violence. These conditions further expose them to risks like unsafe sexual practices, unwanted pregnancies, and perilous childbirth environments. In cases of children trafficked specifically for forced labour, begging, or engaging in criminal activities, trafficking victims often suffer from injuries resulting from torture, cruel, inhuman or degrading treatment, or punishment, and from working under harsh or hazardous conditions for extended periods. These findings highlight the critical need for comprehensive healthcare interventions that address the diverse and complex health issues faced by trafficked children, ensuring their right to health is upheld throughout their recovery and beyond.

The trauma associated with child trafficking can indeed precipitate a multitude of persistent psychological challenges. These challenges can encompass a wide array of issues such as anxiety, depression, hostility, impaired social skills, difficulties in fostering trust and forming meaningful relationships, manifestations of sexualised behaviour, as well as feelings of guilt, shame, and PTSD. Such psychological harm can be inflicted at any point within the trafficking continuum—from the initial pre-capture phase, through the period of exploitation, and extending into the post-rescue phase.

One of the primary sources of psychological distress stems from the physical harm and sexual abuse endured by the child. These experiences can lead to a range of adverse emotional outcomes, including depression, social isolation, and PTSD. Moreover, the emotional trauma associated with child trafficking is not limited to the direct consequences of physical and sexual abuse. The process of separation and removal from their homes, families, including the "adoptive families" and communities also constitutes a significant source of emotional trauma. This sense of loss and disconnection can exacerbate the child's psychological challenges, hindering their ability to recover and reintegrate into society.

In instances where children were trafficked for illegal adoption and treated well by adoptive families, the separation from these families during rescue can be traumatising. This is compounded by the difficulty some victims face in reconnecting with their biological parents or being rejected upon attempting to return home, leaving them with a lingering sense of uncertainty about their origins and identity.

The psychological ramifications extend to the parents and families of trafficked children, who suffer from guilt, depression, and PTSD, with their anguish persisting long after the children's rescue. The severity of these emotional issues escalates when children have been subjected to physical, emotional, or sexual abuse or torture.

The existing framework for supporting victims of child trafficking, particularly in terms of psychological care, reveals significant deficiencies despite the acknowledged need. The *China National Plan of Action on Combating Trafficking in Women and Children (2013–2020)* does indeed call for the provision of basic medical, physiological, and psychological services for trafficking victims. Yet, the implementation falls short, with a notable lack of professional psychological support structures or institutions dedicated to the rehabilitation of rescued children. This gap is further highlighted by the *Measures for the Administration of Child Welfare Organizations*,[12] which, since coming into effect on 1 January 2019, fails to specifically mandate or even mention the provision of psychological assistance.

Responsibility for the medical and psychological well-being of trafficking victims primarily lies with local governments or relevant institutions. This responsibility ostensibly transitions to the biological parents once they reclaim custody of their child. However, this transition does not guarantee the provision of necessary psychological care, as evidenced by the limited availability of intervention programs, a concern highlighted by volunteers from BBHJ. This situation underscores a critical gap in care for trafficking victims, leaving them and their families without adequate support for the complex and enduring psychological impacts of their experiences.

This gap in care underscores the need for a more robust and accessible framework for psychological support, highlighting the importance of establishing dedicated services and programs to address the complex and long-lasting emotional and mental health needs of both trafficking victims and their families.

D. **Right to Remedy**

Child trafficking constitutes a severe violation of human rights, thus entitling the victims and their legal guardians to monetary compensation. This compensation should be commensurate with the extent of material losses and moral suffering endured due to the trafficking. The entitlement to remedies, including access to compensation, is a fundamental human right enshrined in international human rights frameworks such as the Basic Principles and Guidelines on the Right to a Remedy and Reparation for Victims of Gross Violations of International Human Rights, the Universal Declaration of Human Rights (Article 8), and the International Covenant on Civil and Political Rights (ICCPR) (Article 2). Furthermore, trafficking-specific legal instruments within human rights treaties and international criminal law underscore the obligation of States to provide remedies to trafficking victims. This includes the

[12] Ministry of Civil Affairs, (2019) 儿童福利机构管理办法 [Measures for the Administration of Child Welfare Organizations], Order No. 63 of the Ministry of Civil Affairs, issued on 30 October 2018, entered in force on 1st January 2019, retrieved from http://www.gov.cn/xinwen/2019-01/25/content_5361171.htm#1.

confiscation of assets from those involved in trafficking, using these assets to support and compensate victims, and the establishment of a compensation fund for victims (OHCHR 2010).

China's establishment of a state judicial assistance system through the *Opinions on Establishing and Improving a System of State Judicial Relief (for Trial Implementation)*,[13] and its judicial interpretation[14] by the Supreme People's Court in 2016 marks a significant step in providing economic assistance to victims of crime who struggle to secure financial compensation. In 2015, this system facilitated payments totalling 1.67 billion Yuan to 71,700 victims and their families. However, there is an absence of explicit information regarding the provision of judicial assistance specifically to victims of child trafficking or their families. Additionally, this judicial assistance is only accessible to victims facing life hardships, without a dedicated fund for addressing the material and psychological damages resulting from child trafficking or human trafficking offences.

The scarcity of financial compensation for trafficking victims and their families in China is notable. Among all reviewed judicial decisions, fewer than ten cases included civil claims for economic compensation linked to the criminal procedure, all of which were dismissed. There is a lack of judicial decisions mandating financial compensation in other cases. Therefore, monetary compensation tends to be the outcome of private agreements between the defendant and the victim or the victim's family, contingent upon the defendant's ability to pay.

This scenario highlights a significant gap in the provision of adequate compensation for trafficking victims, underscoring the need for a more systematic approach that ensures victims and their families receive just reparation for the injustices and harms they have endured.

4 Conclusion

This chapter has elucidated the intricate relationship between human rights issues and child trafficking in China through anecdotal evidence derived from case law. It reveals that human rights violations and issues are not only the catalysts and repercussions of crimes related to child trafficking but also persist following the victims' rescue.

[13] Committee of Political and Legal Affairs of the Central Committee of the Communist Party of China (CPC), Ministry of Finance, the Supreme People's Court, the Supreme People's Procuratorate, the Ministry of Public Security and the Ministry of Justice, (2014) 关于建立完善国家司法救助制度的意见(试行) [Opinions on Establishing and Improving a System of State Judicial Relief (for Trial Implementation)], No. 3 [2014] of the CPC, issued and entered in force on 17 January 2014, retrieved from https://www.spp.gov.cn/spp/zdgz/201512/t20151208_109020.shtml.

[14] Supreme People's Court, (2016) 最高人民法院关于加强和规范人民法院国家司法救助工作的意见 [Opinions of the Supreme People's Court on Strengthening and Regulating the State Judicial Relief Work of the People's Courts], No. 16 [2016] of the Supreme People's Court, issued and entered in force on 1st July 2016, retrieved from http://www.court.gov.cn/fabu-xiangqing-23171.html.

Like other regions, the underlying causes of child trafficking in China are predominantly poverty and discrimination. The study uncovers a less acknowledged manner in which poverty promotes child trafficking: it not only heightens the susceptibility of children from economically disadvantaged families but also fuels the demand for trafficked children. Discrimination likewise propels child trafficking in various ways; gender-based discrimination, for example, predisposes girls to being sold or trafficked for sexual exploitation, while boys, due to high demand influenced by societal preferences, are also vulnerable. Paradoxically, the preference for boys can render them economic liabilities, driving some parents to sell their sons.

Children of mentally disabled women, or those with disabilities themselves, are particularly vulnerable to trafficking, as discrimination against persons with disabilities exacerbates this issue, impacting both the supply and demand sides of trafficking. Discrimination against children born out of wedlock further increases their susceptibility to trafficking. The birth control policy interplays with poverty and discrimination, contributing to the complexity of the issue. Fines imposed on children born in violation of this policy exacerbate their vulnerability. Additionally, the family planning policy fuels child trafficking by creating discrepancies between the child adoption system and the populace's needs, leading parents to resort to illegal measures like infanticide, abandonment, or selling their children due to the stringent legal procedures associated with relinquishing a child to social welfare institutions.

The chapter also highlights that child trafficking infringes upon fundamental human rights, such as the right to life, liberty, security, and freedom from torture and enslavement. Furthermore, the commodification inherent in child trafficking assaults the dignity and inherent rights of the child, violating their rights to identity, family unity, immediate registration after birth, and nationality. Post-rescue, new human rights challenges emerge, including issues related to victim care, family reintegration, healthcare, assistance, and the right to remedy. Despite victims' entitlement to special protection and assistance from the State, there is a glaring absence of clear regulations or guidelines on their immediate protection and resettlement. The practice of returning child victims to their original families, including those who were the perpetrators of the child's sale, contests the principle of the child's best interest. Furthermore, victims' entitlement to physical and mental health assistance highlights the dire need for comprehensive support from the State. Yet, evidence suggests a significant gap in fulfilling the right to remedy for victims of child trafficking in China, with no established fund for addressing the material losses and psychological damages suffered by victims.

In conclusion, while efforts have been made to combat child trafficking and its repercussions in China, substantial gaps in policy, implementation, and support systems remain, underscoring the need for more robust, victim-centered approaches that safeguard and promote the human rights of trafficking victims.

References

Bales, Kevin. 2007. 'What Predicts Human Trafficking?' *International Journal of Comparative and Applied Criminal Justice* 31 (2): 269–279. https://doi.org/10.1080/01924036.2007.9678771.

BBC News. 2007. 'China "Will Catch Slave Owners"', June 16. http://news.bbc.co.uk/2/hi/asia-pacific/6759399.stm.

Cameron, Sally, and Edward Newman. 2008. *Trafficking in Humans: Social, Cultural and Political Dimensions*. Tokyo: United Nations University Press.

Cao, Xianyu. 2014. 'Research on the Parentage Law under the Principle of the Best Interests of the Child [儿童最大利益原则下的亲子法研究]'. Southwest University of Political Science and Law (China).

Cheng, Jingwei. 2016. '中国GDP最高省份广东有179万贫困人口 誓言全线脱贫'.

Cohen, Jonathan. 2003. *Togo, Borderline Slavery: Child Trafficking in Togo*. Vol. 15. 8. Human Rights Watch.

Davis, Jamie, Neha Misra, Rebecca Surtees, and Anis Hamim. 2003. 'Factors That Lead to Trafficking'. In *Trafficking of Women and Children in Indonesia*, edited by Ruth Rosenberg. Jakarta: International Catholic Migration Commission and American Center for International Labor Solidarity.

ECOSOC. 2000. *Integration of the Human Rights of Women and the Gender Perspective – Report of the Special Rapporteur on Violence against Women, Its Causes and Consequences, Ms. Radhika Coomaraswamy, on Trafficking in Women, Women's Migration and Violence against Women, Submitted in Accordance with Commission on Human Rights Resolution 1997/44*. E/CN.4/2000/68.

Feng, Wang, Yong Cai, and Baochang Gu. 2013. 'Population, Policy, and Politics: How Will History Judge China's One-Child Policy?' *Population and Development Review* 38. Population Council: 115–129.

Gallagher, Anne T., and K. Skrivankova. 2015. 'Human Rights and Trafficking in Persons –15th Informal ASEM Seminar on Human Rights (Background Paper)'.

Kragten-Heerdink, Suzanne L. J., Corinne E. Dettmeijer-Vermeulen, and Dirk J. Korf. 2018. 'More Than Just "Pushing and Pulling": Conceptualizing Identified Human Trafficking in the Netherlands'. *Crime and Delinquency* 64(13): 1765–1789. https://doi.org/10.1177/0011128717728503.

Li, Shuzhuo, Yexia Zhang, and Marcus W. Feldman. 2010. 'Birth Registration in China: Practices, Problems and Policies'. *Population Research and Policy Review* 29 (3): 297–317. https://doi.org/10.1007/s11113-009-9141-x.

Man, Xiaoou, Richard P. Barth, Yue-e Li, and Zuobao Wang. 2017. 'Exploring the New Child Protection System in Mainland China: How Does It Work?' *Children and Youth Services Review* 76: 196–202. https://doi.org/10.1016/j.childyouth.2017.03.012.

OHCHR. 2010. Commentary on the Recommended Principles and Guidelines on Human Rights and Human Trafficking. New York and Geneva: United Nations Publication.

Shi, Lu. 2016. '山东贫困人口鲁西占8成 青烟等超国家贫困线 [Eighty percent of Shandong's poor population is in Western Shandong, surpassing the national poverty line in areas like Qingyan]'. http://f.china.com.cn/2016-07/08/content_38840760.htm.

Tavcer, Scharie. 2007. 'Causal Factors in the Crime of Trafficking of Women for the Purpose of Sexual Exploitation: An Exploration into Push and Pull Factors Relevant to Women Trafficked from Moldova to Western Europe'. Doctoral thesis, Germany: Albert Ludwig University of Freiburg. https://freidok.uni-freiburg.de/fedora/objects/freidok:4426/datastreams/FILE1/content.

UNICEF East Asia and Pacific Regional Office. 2009. *Child Trafficking in East and South-East Asia: Reversing the Trend*. Bangkok: UNICEF East Asia and Pacific Regional Office.

UNICEF. 2008. *UNICEF Child Protection Strategy*. Economic and Social Council.

Whyte, Martin King, Wang Feng, and Yong Cai. 2015. 'Challenging Myths about China's One-Child Policy'. *The China Journal*, no. 74: 144–159. https://doi.org/10.1086/681664.

Wu, Zhuochun, Kirsi Viisainen, and Elina Hemminki. 2006. 'Determinants of High Sex Ratio among Newborns: A Cohort Study from Rural Anhui Province, China'. *Reproductive Health Matters* 14 (27): 172–180. https://doi.org/10.1016/S0968-8080(06)27222-7.

Zhao, Fang, Juha Erkki Antero Hämäläinen, and Honglin L. Chen. 2017. 'Child Protection in China: Changing Policies and Reactions from the Field of Social Work'. *International Journal of Social Welfare* 26 (4): 329–339. https://doi.org/10.1111/ijsw.12268.

Chapter 5
China's National Policy and Practices in Combating Child Trafficking: Good Practices

Child trafficking has long been regarded as a malignancy afflicting society, undermining its stability. Consequently, China has a long history of combating this grievous crime. The nation's commitment has been significantly bolstered following its accession to the Palermo Protocol and the CRC-OPSC, under which it has undertaken various measures to criminalise and prevent activities associated with child trafficking and to facilitate, where feasible, the reunification of victims with their families of origin.

In accordance with international norms delineated by pertinent UN bodies, notably the OHCHR and the UNODC, human rights must be positioned at the heart of all initiatives aimed at preventing and eliminating trafficking. Such measures encompass legislation that not only criminalise trafficking and its related activities but also comprehensive national anti-trafficking strategies with a particular focus on crime prevention. Additionally, they include legislative and administrative measures designed to protect victims and bolster cooperative efforts with both civil society and global partners.

This chapter explores the suite of policies and programmes implemented by the Chinese government to combat child trafficking, especially in the wake of its accession to the aforementioned international conventions. An initial discussion on the National Plan of Action on Combating Trafficking in Children and Women sets the stage for a comprehensive examination of the measures China has embraced, guided by the "3Ps" mechanism—prosecution, protection, and prevention. Moreover, the pivotal role of civil society in the anti-trafficking crusade constitutes an essential component that will be thoroughly examined. The final section highlights the discrepancy between the actual needs and the governmental policies and efforts in tackling the issue of child trafficking.

L. Han, *Child Trafficking in China*, https://doi.org/10.1007/978-981-97-3717-8_5

1 National Plans of Action on Combating Trafficking in Children and Women

The State Council of China promulgated its inaugural National Plan of Action (NPA) on Combating Trafficking in Women and Children for the years 2008–2012 in December 2007. This was succeeded by the NPA for 2013–2020, unveiled in March 2013, and the most recent NPA covering the period 2021–2030, which was issued in April 2021. While it was only in the first NPA that the trafficking of women and children was explicitly acknowledged as a grave violation of human rights, inflicting considerable distress on both victims and their families, the latest NPA emphasises that "the effective protection of the fundamental human rights of citizens" stands as one of the primary guiding principles behind the anti-trafficking endeavours. As a regulatory framework, the NPA establishes the foundational operational structure for combating the trafficking of children and women, providing guidance across all facets pertinent to the issue.

Initially, the NPA (2008–2012) facilitated the establishment of an organisational and coordination mechanism. Under the auspices of the State Council, the Inter-ministerial Joint Conference System for Anti-Trafficking in Women and Children (IMCS) was formed. Chaired by the Ministry of Public Security (MPS), this comprehensive mechanism encompasses twenty-eight departments and agencies, including but not limited to the MPS, the Central Propaganda Department of the CCCPC, the Central Office for Comprehensive Management of Public Security,[1] and the Legislative Affairs Commission of the National People's Congress. Other notable members include the Ministry of Foreign Affairs, the National Development and Reform Commission, and the Ministry of Education, along with entities such as the Ministry of Civil Affairs, the Ministry of Justice, and the Ministry of Finance. The formation also includes the Ministry of Labour and Social Security, the Ministry of Railways, and the Ministry of Communications, alongside the Ministry of Agriculture, the Ministry of Commerce, and the Ministry of Culture. The health sector is represented by the Ministry of Health and the National Population and Family Planning Commission of China, with additional participation from the State Administration for Industry and Commerce, the Civil Aviation Administration of China, and the State Administration of Radio, Film and Television. The Office of Legislative Affairs of the State Council, the National Working Committee for Children and Women under the State Council, the State Council Leading Group Office of Poverty Alleviation and Development, the All-China Federation of Trade Unions, the Committee of the Communist Youth League, and the All-China Women's Federation are also integral to this multifaceted framework.[2] This elaborate structure aims to integrate all national sectors that interact with or affect children and their families

[1] The Central Office for Comprehensive Management of Public Security was abolished in the reform of party's and governmental institutions in 2018.

[2] The State Council (2007) 国务院办公厅关于印发中国反对拐卖人口行动计划(2008–2012年)的通知 [Notice of General Office of the State Council on the on Issuing China National Plan of Action on Combating Trafficking in Women and Children (2008–2012)], No. 69 [2007] of the State

in the execution of the NPA, overseeing its implementation and conducting periodic and final assessments.

Furthermore, the NPA (2008–2012) allocated specific action measures to each department. Although the initiatives outlined in the NPA did not explicitly adopt the "3Ps" mechanism, a framework commonly embraced by international and regional anti-trafficking agreements, the plan comprehensively addressed the three pivotal elements—prevention, prosecution, and protection—integral to combating human trafficking (see Chap. 2, 1.B). Beyond the overarching responsibilities of coordination, monitoring, and evaluation of the NPA, the IMCS was tasked with two particular functions related to its coordinating role. The first involved the exchange of best practices and information, the promotion of a working model that integrates prevention, combat, assistance, and rehabilitation efforts, alongside enhancements to the anti-trafficking infrastructure and rapid response capabilities. The second duty entailed orchestrating cooperation between regions of origin and destination, facilitated through the collection of bilateral letters of intent among provinces, autonomous regions, and province-level municipalities identified as principal sources or destinations of trafficking victims.

The NPA (2008–2012) also envisaged the establishment of a crime prevention mechanism necessitating multisectoral and multilevel collaboration.[3] Measures to prevent trafficking in children comprised: (1) enhancing public awareness, particularly among parents, guardians, and other custodians, about adhering to the Law on the Protection of Minors of the People's Republic of China, aiming to foster a nurturing family environment and education conducive to the healthy development of children (the Ministry of Justice as the lead agency, with the Ministry of Education, the Central Committee of the Communist Youth League, and the All-China Women's Federation as cooperating entities); (2) increasing the awareness of teachers and students regarding trafficking prevention and the enforcement of the Compulsory Education Law of the People's Republic of China, ensuring universal access to the 9-year compulsory education to deter premature societal entry (the Ministry of Education as the lead agency, with the Ministry of Civil Affairs and the Ministry of Culture as cooperating entities); (3) offering assistance and training to individuals, particularly women and children from socio-economically disadvantaged backgrounds, at risk of trafficking, and effectively utilising existing welfare systems to support and provide aftercare for homeless minors and abandoned infants (the Ministry of Civil Affairs as the lead agency, with the Ministry of Justice, the Ministry of Finance, and the Ministry of Health as cooperating entities); (4) spreading anti-trafficking awareness in key locations such as railway stations, bus terminals, ports, entertainment venues, and hotels (the Ministry of Railways, the Ministry of Transport, and the Civil Aviation Administration of China as lead agencies, with the Ministry of Public Security, the Ministry of Justice, the Central Committee of the

---

Council, issued and entered in force on 2 March 2013, retrieved from http://www.gov.cn/zwgk/2007-12/20/content_839479.htm.

[3] China National Plan of Action on Combating Trafficking in Women and Children (2008–2012), at III-1.

Communist Youth League, and the All-China Women's Federation as cooperating entities).

The National Plan of Action (2013–2020) has augmented its preventative strategies against child trafficking by including measures such as the imperative to thwart illegal child labour and the exploitation of individuals with mental disabilities in the workforce. Additional preventative strategies specifically targeting children comprise: the enhancement of pregnancy and birth regulation measures to diminish the incidence of unintended pregnancies and births outside the ambit of family planning policies, the prevention of school dropouts, the refinement of assistance and protection mechanisms for minors living on the streets, increasing awareness among children left behind by migrating parents about potential risks, reducing and actively combating the demand for children by controlling the birth sex ratio, regulating legal adoptions, prohibiting the issuance of fraudulent birth certificates, and instituting a system of mandatory reporting for healthcare professionals.

Compared to its predecessors, the latest National Plan of Action (2013–2020) has introduced a heightened focus on the significance of the internet and technology in the fight against trafficking. It focuses not only on preventing these tools from being exploited to facilitate trafficking-related offences but also on leveraging them as resources to counteract such crimes. Furthermore, this version recognises the pivotal role of educational and childcare facilities, such as schools and kindergartens. It mandates that personnel within these institutions swiftly report and cease any potential instances of child trafficking, whilst also urging parents and guardians to report any suspicious activities indicative of child trafficking crimes. This underscores a proactive approach towards safeguarding children under their care from the dangers associated with trafficking.

In terms of prosecution, the inaugural NPA (2008–2012) called for the enhancement of the capability and efficiency in identifying and detecting trafficking crimes against women and children. It outlined three key points specifically addressing child trafficking: (1) the adoption of a child-sensitive approach in all processes involving children; (2) the reduction of child demand through criminalisation and punishment of acts such as purchasing, enticing, and coercing victims into labour and sexual exploitation; (3) the development and improvement of a system for the collection and exchange of information regarding pertinent crimes. The MPS was designated as the lead agency for these measures, in collaboration with the Ministry of Civil Affairs and other departments.

The subsequent NPA (2013–2020) introduced more detailed requirements for prosecution measures. Initially, it mandated the continuation of special police operations against human trafficking crimes initiated after the first NPA. Furthermore, it called for the enhancement of the anti-trafficking mechanism for children and the effective implementation of an accountability system. The plan also emphasised the need for a quick response mechanism to incidents of child disappearance. Police are required to conduct exhaustive searches for children of unknown origins, collect DNA samples from suspected child trafficking victims, and integrate these into the national anti-trafficking DNA database for cross-referencing with samples from parents of missing children. Importantly, it forbids fostering of child trafficking victims within the family of the purchaser. Besides the MPS-led initiatives against trafficking, the NPA (2013–2020) underscored the necessity for stricter criminal penalties for those buying trafficked child victims, a responsibility assigned to the Legislative Affairs Commission of the Standing Committee of the National People's Congress. Finally, it incorporated the "non-punishment" principle for victims of trafficking who were deceived or coerced into participating in illegal or criminal activities—legal provisions should be enacted to reduce or absolve them from punishment.

The prosecution segment of the NPA (2021–2030) largely echoes the approaches of its forerunners, with the notable exception of an article mandating the establishment of definitive legal standards for the management of human trafficking cases. This includes uniform evidence evaluation and sentencing guidelines to guarantee consistency and fairness throughout the judicial proceedings.

In all three NPAs, the Ministry of Civil Affairs was primarily tasked with the protection of trafficking victims. The first NPA (2008–2012) called for the creation of support mechanisms for victims, offering necessary aid and services such as relief, social services, health recuperation, and vocational training. Additionally, it assigned the MPS the responsibilities of registering, managing, and safeguarding trafficking victims, including the establishment of victim archives and monitoring their living conditions. The plan also highlighted the importance of researching the physical and mental well-being of trafficking victims to provide more effective rehabilitation treatments. Furthermore, it encouraged civil society to engage in providing financial, service, and technical support for victim protection activities. While largely reiterating these measures, the second NPA (2013–2020) specified that the MPS and Ministry of Civil Affairs should develop protocols for the rescue, resettlement, recovery, and rehabilitation of victims. The NPA (2021–2030) appears to be a repetitive iteration of its predecessors, without introducing any novel measures in this regard.

Besides the "3Ps" (prosecution, protection, prevention), both NPAs emphasised departmental coordination, cooperation with civil society, and collaboration with international organisations. The establishment of the Inter-ministerial Joint Conference System for Anti-Trafficking in Women and Children underscored the commitment to organisational and coordination mechanisms. The plans reinforced the importance of departmental cooperation in each segment and stressed strengthening international partnerships in combating trafficking, involving entities such as the United Nations, the International Organization for Migration (IOM), UNICEF, the UNODC, other intergovernmental organisations, countries within the Greater Mekong Subregion (GMS), and international NGOs. Specific measures called for enhanced international police collaboration against trafficking-related crimes and international efforts in border control and capacity building to prevent human trafficking.

Despite the comprehensive measures outlined in China's National Plans of Action to address child trafficking, including crime prevention, offender prosecution, and victim protection, the implementation, monitoring, evaluation, and follow-up of these plans have encountered significant challenges. These challenges, related to policy gaps between the intended national policies and measures and the actual situation and needs on the ground, as well as discrepancies with international standards, will be explored in greater detail in subsequent sections.

2 "3Ps" Mechanism in Practice

Over the years, a range of anti-trafficking measures and actions have been put into practice, implementing the NPAs guidelines. These efforts, covering the prosecution, protection, and prevention, range from specialised police operations and the establishment of a DNA databank to the implementation of an Online Alert System and the application of new technologies like facial recognition. The impact of some of these concrete measures has been significant.

A. **Prosecution—Criminalisation and law enforcement**

Under the "3Ps" framework of action, prosecution constitutes the initial measure that China has adopted in response to crimes associated with trafficking. Efforts undertaken entail the imposition of stringent penalties and sanctions for trafficking-related offences, police operations aimed at the suppression of trafficking in children and women, and the reinforcement of national anti-trafficking legislation through the enhancement of the capabilities of criminal justice practitioners.

Following the issuance of the first National Plan of Action for 2008–2012, the initial step undertaken was a 4-year-long special police operation against trafficking in women and children, initiated by the Ministry of Public Security in April 2009. This operation, known as the National Public Security Organs' Special Action to Combat Trafficking in Children and Women (hereafter referred to as Police Anti-trafficking Actions), aimed to uncover a significant number of trafficking cases, rescue a considerable number of children and women, and restore areas where minors were organised to engage in illegal and criminal activities.[4] Local Public Security Departments were mandated to take immediate and proactive measures in several key areas: conducting surveys to identify and register suspected victims of trafficking; addressing and suppressing crimes related to forcing minors to beg or involving deaf adolescents in criminal activities; and dismantling criminal organisations and individuals responsible for these offences. A critical aspect of the working procedure was the appointment of a designated officer for each trafficking-related case, tasked with leading the investigation and follow-up until resolution. Emphasis was also placed on supporting street children and minors involved in criminal gangs, and on combating prostitution, especially the coercion and inducement of minors into such activities.

[4] Ministry of Public Security (2009) 公安部部署打击拐卖儿童妇女犯罪专项行动 [Ministry of Public Security deploys a special campaign against crimes of trafficking in children and women], *全国公安机关打击拐卖儿童、妇女犯罪专项行动 [National Public Security Organs' Special Action to Combat Trafficking in Children and Women]*, retrieved from http://www.mps.gov.cn/n2255079/n2255231/n2255233/c3579140/content.html, [accessed on 19/07/2018].

The special actions were quickly implemented at the provincial level, with the Public Security Department in eight provinces establishing provincial responses within approximately a month, in line with the national campaign's requirements.[5] For example, the Guangdong Province Public Security Department convened a meeting on the special action for combating trafficking in women and children, during which the significance of the initiative and the responsibilities of local public security organs were underscored, along with the strategies to be adopted moving forward. A key requirement was the formation of a joint investigation team within local public security organs in areas heavily affected by trafficking.[6] This team, comprised of a deputy police chief, criminal police officers, and members of the police technology team, was tasked with all aspects of combating trafficking in women and children. Their responsibilities included conducting surveys to identify suspected victims, gathering information on suspects and victims of trafficking-related crimes, developing and enhancing the DNA database, and fostering collaboration with other departments and civil society.[7]

For a brief period, the Police Anti-trafficking Actions appeared highly successful. By December 2009, for instance, police forces in Guangdong Province had uncovered 50 unresolved cases of child trafficking, collected 3654 blood samples, and identified 43 victims of child trafficking with the aid of the DNA database.[8] At the national level, by early August 2009, police had detected 1092 child trafficking cases, arrested 824 suspects, dismantled 525 criminal gangs, and rescued 1352 child victims of trafficking.[9] The total number of rescued trafficking victims, including women and children, had escalated to over 14,000 by mid-2010.[10] Nonetheless, the intensity

[5] Ibid.

[6] Ministry of Public Security (2010) 广东认真贯彻落实国家反拐行动计划 [Guangdong Province earnestly implements the NPA on Combating Trafficking in Women and Children], *全国公安机关打击拐卖儿童、妇女犯罪专项行动 [National Public Security Organs' Special Action to Combat Trafficking in Children and Women]*, retrieved from http://www.mps.gov.cn/n2255079/n2255231/n2255233/c3579508/content.html, [accessed on 19/07/2018].

[7] Ministry of Public Security (2009) 广东省公安厅动员部署打击拐卖儿童妇女犯罪专项行动 [Guangdong Provincial Public Security Department mobilized and deployed the Special Action to Combat Trafficking in Children and Women], *全国公安机关打击拐卖儿童、妇女犯罪专项行动 [National Public Security Organs' Special Action to Combat Trafficking in Children and Women]*, retrieved from http://www.mps.gov.cn/n2255079/n2255231/n2255233/c3579211/content.html, [accessed on 19/07/2018].

[8] Ministry of Public Security (2010) 广东认真贯彻落实国家反拐行动计划 [Guangdong Province earnestly implements the NPA on Combating Trafficking in Women and Children], *全国公安机关打击拐卖儿童、妇女犯罪专项行动 [National Public Security Organs' Special Action to Combat Trafficking in Children and Women]*, retrieved from http://www.mps.gov.cn/n2255079/n2255231/n2255233/c3579508/content.html, [accessed on 19/07/2018].

[9] Ministry of Public Security (2009) 全国"打拐"专项行动成效明显 [The national anti-trafficking special actions have achieved remarkable results], *全国公安机关打击拐卖儿童、妇女犯罪专项行动 [National Public Security Organs' Special Action to Combat Trafficking in Children and Women]*, retrieved from http://www.mps.gov.cn/n2255079/n2255231/n2255233/c3579140/content.html, [accessed on 19/07/2018].

[10] Ministry of Public Security (2010) 全国"打拐"专项行动一年多来破拐卖案件1.2万余起 [The national anti-trafficking special action has detected more than 12 thousand cases of trafficking in the

of the nationwide Police Anti-trafficking Actions also raised concerns, calling into question the justice and legality of the law enforcement procedures employed.

The proactive investigations into child trafficking undertaken by the Police Anti-trafficking Actions were complemented by capacity-building training for members of the national Inter-Ministerial Coordination and Steering Committee (IMCS) and those within similar coordination mechanisms at the local level.[11] To support the nationwide deployment of the anti-trafficking campaign, from 2009 to the end of 2010, the IMCS organised at least two training sessions for chief officers of each ministry and department, as well as for relevant practitioners at the local level. These sessions were aimed at enhancing the effectiveness of the anti-trafficking efforts through improved coordination and skill development among those directly involved in combating trafficking.

In addition to guidelines and the Police Anti-trafficking Actions, enhancements in the prosecutorial approach to trafficking-related crimes have been reflected within the legal structure. As highlighted in the first chapter, child trafficking is deemed a criminal offence within the Chinese legal framework. Although the Criminal Law of China does not fully encompass all provisions of the Palermo Protocol, numerous efforts have been made to bolster its legal framework. For instance, in August 2009, the 1991 Decision of the Standing Committee of the National People's Congress on the Severe Punishment of Criminals Who Abduct and Traffic in or Kidnap Women or Children was amended.[12] According to this Amendment, the penalty for the crime of abducting and selling children was increased to a minimum of 5 years imprisonment and a fine of up to 10,000 Yuan. In cases deemed particularly severe, the sentence can escalate to the death penalty, accompanied by the confiscation of property.

Following this, in March 2010, the Opinions on Legally Punishing the Crimes of Abducting and Trafficking in Women and Children were jointly issued by the Supreme People's Court, the Supreme People's Procuratorate, the Ministry of Public Security, and the Ministry of Justice. This document aimed to clarify, to a certain extent, various procedural and legal issues such as jurisdiction, case filing, forensic and evidentiary requirements, accusation, and sentencing.

---

past year], *全国公安机关打击拐卖儿童、妇女犯罪专项行动 [National Public Security Organs' Special Action to Combat Trafficking in Children and Women]*, retrieved from http://www.mps.gov.cn/n2255079/n2255231/n2255233/c3579769/content.html, [accessed on 19/07/2018].

[11] The first training was organised for IMCS members held at Huangshan in Anhui Province on 13 and 14 August 2009 (see http://www.mps.gov.cn/n2255079/n2255231/n2255233/c3579385/content.html, [accessed on 19 July 2018]). The second training was held at Hulunbuir in in Inner Mongolia Autonomous Region on 22 July 2010, with over 140 participants from national and local law enforcement agencies (see http://www.mps.gov.cn/n2255079/n2255231/n2255233/c3579783/content.html, [accessed on 19/07/2018]).

[12] Standing Committee of the National People's Congress, Standing Committee of the National People's Congress (2009) 全国人大常委会关于严惩拐卖、卖架妇女、儿童的犯罪分子的决定 (2009修正) [Decision of the Standing Committee of the National People's Congress Regarding the Severe Punishment of Criminals Who Abduct and Traffic in or Kidnap Women or Children (2009 Amendment)], Order No. 18 of the President of the People's Republic of China, issued and entered in force on 27 August 2009, retrieved from https://flk.npc.gov.cn/detail2.html?ZmY4MDgwODE3NzRjNzJiMzAxNzc3MTE0ZGIwMTFkY2M%3D.

More recent developments include the ninth amendment of the Criminal Law, enacted on 29 August 2015, which eliminated the possibility of impunity for the crime of purchasing trafficked children and women. This amendment signifies a further step towards aligning with international standards and underscores China's ongoing commitment to combatting trafficking through legal reforms.

The police actions have liberated thousands of children from the clutches of trafficking and delivered justice to numerous victims and their families. The imposition of severe penalties has heightened the costs associated with committing the crime of child trafficking, thereby potentially deterring such criminality to some extent. Nevertheless, the specialised campaign conducted by the police was not a sustainable remedy. In reality, this campaign came to an end in 2012.

B. **Protection—DNA databank of anti-abduction**

Victim identification is an essential precondition for safeguarding victims of child trafficking, as highlighted by the United Nations Office on Drugs and Crime in 2009. This process is crucial for enabling the provision of appropriate assistance, including remedies, which constitute a fundamental right of crime victims. Despite the lack of a comprehensive system for victim identification in China, and the ongoing challenges associated with locating and identifying missing children—a task that poses significant difficulties even for international experts—significant strides have been made in enhancing the effectiveness of identification methods. A pivotal advancement was the establishment of a national DNA database for anti-trafficking purposes in April 2009. This database plays a critical role in facilitating the reunification of trafficked children with their families through genetic testing analysis.[13] This innovative approach was introduced to the anti-trafficking framework through the National Plan of Action (NPA) for 2008–2012, and further supported by subsequent legislative[14] and practical implementation efforts.

The NPA was implemented through a dedicated national police anti-trafficking initiative[15] and associated regulations,[16] with DNA collection and analysis being key

---

[13] Ministry of Public Security (2009) 公安机关查找被拐卖儿童DNA检验技术应用规范 (试行) [Application rules for public security organs regarding DNA testing technology to find victims of child trafficking (trial)], No. 625 [2009] of the MPS Criminal Department, issued on 9 April 2009.

[14] Supreme People's Court, Supreme People's Procuratorate, Instrumentalities of the State Council, All Ministries, Ministry of Public Security, Ministry of Justice, (2010) 最高人民法院、最高人民检察院、公安部、司法部印发《关于依法惩治拐卖妇女儿童犯罪的意见》的通知 [Notice of the Supreme People's Court, the Supreme People's Procuratorate, the Ministry of Public Security and the Ministry of Justice on Issuing the Opinions on Legally Punishing the Crimes of Abducting and Trafficking in Women and Children], Documents of Judicial Interpretation Nature, No. 7 [2010] of the Supreme People's Court, issued and entered in force on 15 March 2010, retrieved from http://en.pkulaw.cn/display.aspx?cgid=095d828db4ce796bbdfb&lib=law.

[15] Ministry of Public Security (2009) 公安部部署打击拐卖儿童妇女犯罪专项行动 [Ministry of Public Security deploys a special campaign against crimes of trafficking in children and women]. *全国公安机关打击拐卖儿童、妇女犯罪专项行动 [National Public Security Organs' Special Action to Combat Trafficking in Children and Women]*, retrieved from http://www.mps.gov.cn/n2255079/n2255231/n2255233/c3579140/content.html, [accessed on 19/07/2018].

[16] Supreme People's Court, Supreme People's Procuratorate, Instrumentalities of the State Council, All Ministries, Ministry of Public Security, Ministry of Justice (2010) 最高人民法院、最高人民检

components of these efforts. This initiative saw the police adopting a proactive stance, undertaking extensive door-to-door visits and surveys to identify potential victims of child trafficking and children whose origins were unclear. Upon identifying a suspected trafficking victim, either through police investigations or public reports, it became mandatory to collect a blood sample from the individual and submit it to the DNA database for comparison. This database also includes samples from the parents of missing children.

The *Application Rules for Public Security Organs Regarding DNA Testing Technology to Find Victims of Child Trafficking (Trial)*, issued by the Ministry of Public Security in April 2009, mandated local police to obtain blood samples from the biological parents of confirmed trafficking victims or upon request by the parents of suspected victims. Furthermore, the collection of blood samples for the anti-trafficking DNA database became compulsory for several groups: rescued child victims of trafficking, children of unknown origin suspected to be trafficked, homeless children and beggars of unknown origin, and the remains of unidentified children.

The Criminal Investigation Bureau of the MPS, along with relevant DNA testing laboratories, was tasked with managing and maintaining the DNA database. Initially, the network comprised DNA laboratories from 32 provincial and 11 prefecture-level public security organs, with plans to expand connectivity to include all such laboratories nationwide.[17] Importantly, the services of blood sample collection and DNA comparison were offered free of charge.

Volunteers from the organisation BBHJ have highlighted that the benefits of DNA testing technology and the database extend beyond child victims. Adults, who believe they were trafficked as children, also have access to these resources to attempt to locate their biological families. Following the establishment of the DNA database, BBHJ volunteers have also been instrumental in providing assistance and information to individuals registering for blood sample collection, thereby enhancing the impact and reach of this crucial anti-trafficking tool.

The application of DNA technology plays a crucial role in identifying child victims of trafficking, effectively mitigating the risk of further violations by ensuring that these children are not left in the custody of traffickers. Furthermore, it safeguards trafficking victims—whether children or adults—by enhancing the likelihood and expediting the process of reunification with their biological parents. For example, should an individual report to the local police about a neighbour's child of unknown

察院、公安部、司法部印发《关于依法惩治拐卖妇女儿童犯罪的意见》的通知 [Notice of the Supreme People's Court, the Supreme People's Procuratorate, the Ministry of Public Security and the Ministry of Justice on Issuing the Opinions on Legally Punishing the Crimes of Abducting and Trafficking in Women and Children], Documents of Judicial Interpretation Nature, No. 7 [2010] of the Supreme People's Court, issued and entered in force on 15 March 2010, retrieved from http://en.pkulaw.cn/display.aspx?cgid=095d828db4ce796bbdfb&lib=law.

17 Ministry of Public Security (2009) 广东省公安厅动员部署打击拐卖儿童妇女犯罪专项行动 [Guangdong Provincial Public Security Department mobilised and deployed the Special Action to Combat Trafficking in Children and Women], *全国公安机关打击拐卖儿童、妇女犯罪专项行动 [National Public Security Organs' Special Action to Combat Trafficking in Children and Women]*, retrieved from http://www.mps.gov.cn/n2255079/n2255231/n2255233/c3579211/content.html, [accessed on 19/07/2018].

origin, the police are obliged to initiate a case and investigate whether the reported individuals are indeed the biological parents of the child. In instances where the child lacks a birth certificate, is not legally registered in the residence system, or is proven not to share any biological relationship with the purported parents, it becomes mandatory to collect a blood sample from the child for inclusion in the national DNA database for comparison.

This process also applies to parents searching for their missing children, who are encouraged to submit their DNA samples to the database. This facilitates a direct comparison with the child's sample, significantly simplifying and accelerating the process compared to traditional methods. Previously, parents had to tirelessly sift through an overwhelming amount of information scattered across the country in hopes of finding their missing child. The introduction of DNA comparison streamlines this process, making it more efficient and offering a beacon of hope for countless families in their search for reunification.

The DNA technique has significantly enhanced the identification of child trafficking cases and facilitated the reunion of victims with their families. By the end of 2015, the national DNA database (State Council Information Office 2016) had successfully reunited over four thousand children with their birth parents. Despite its effectiveness, the DNA database is not without its limitations. A successful match relies on the condition that both the child's and the parents' blood samples are entered into the database. This necessitates, on one hand, the identification of the victim by the police and, on the other hand, the reporting of the child's disappearance by the parents to the police.

In situations where the child was sold or abandoned by their parents, it is unlikely that the parents would report themselves to the police. Similarly, if the child is not recognised as a suspected victim of trafficking, the opportunity to apply the DNA technique is missed. Consequently, while the DNA database is a powerful tool for resolving child trafficking cases and reuniting families, its applicability is contingent upon the initial identification and reporting stages, highlighting an area where further improvements could enhance its utility.

C. **Prevention—Online Alert System**

The preventative measure that has garnered the most attention is the "Tuanyuan" alert, which translates to "family reunification" in Chinese. Launched on the 15th of May 2016, this Chinese Child Abduction Emergency Alert Platform, comparable to the AMBER[18] Alert system in the United States, was inaugurated by the Ministry of Public Security with technical support from the Alibaba Group. Through "Tuanyuan" mobile application, anti-trafficking police officers are empowered to instantly disseminate alerts upon receiving reports of missing children or child abductions.[19] These alerts comprise crucial details about the missing child, such as their

---

[18] See U.S. Department of Justice Office of Justice Programs, AMBER alert website: https://www.amberalert.gov/about.htm.

[19] Xinhuanet, (2016) 公安部儿童失踪信息紧急发布平台上线 [Child Abduction Emergency Alert Platform of MPS was Launched], retrieved from http://politics.people.com.cn/n1/2016/0516/c1001-28352090.html, [accessed on 19/07/2018].

physical attributes, photograph, and the location and time of their disappearance. The alert is then promptly shared on the official Weibo account of the Alert Platform, one of China's largest social media platforms, ensuring widespread visibility. Additionally, the alert is distributed to users of related applications and new media outlets. Remarkably, within the first hour of reporting, the information reaches users within a 100 km radius of the child's last known location. This radius expands to 200 km after two hours, further extending to 300 km and eventually over 500 km.[20] In the span of 2 years, the "Tuanyuan" application has evolved into "Tuanyuan 4.0", integrating 25 additional new media and applications.[21] This extensive network now includes China National Emergency Broadcasting, Tencent News App,[22] OFO (a bike-sharing application), Alipay, AutoNavi (a mapping service),[23] and Ele.me (an online food delivery service platform),[24] significantly amplifying the platform's reach and effectiveness in mobilising community support for locating missing children and combating child trafficking.

The Alert Platform has demonstrated significant effectiveness in mitigating child trafficking. As per the most recent figures disclosed by the MPS, over the course of 5 years, the platform has issued 4801 alert messages, resulting in the retrieval of 4707 missing children,[25] and these figures were 3978 and 3901 respectively in 2019.[26] While comprehensive data is specifically detailed for the year 2018—commemorating the second anniversary of the Alert Platform's inception—within those initial 2 years, 3053 alerts concerning missing children were disseminated, leading to the successful retrieval of 2980 children. Among these, 48 were identified as victims of child trafficking, 1705 had run away from home, and 424 were categorised as lost.[27]

---

[20] Ibid.

[21] People.cn (2018) 公安打拐不断升级:DNA比对、互联网平台 [The public security organs continue to upgrade the anti-trafficking measures: DNA comparison and Internet platform], retrieved from http://ln.people.com.cn/n2/2018/0525/c378326-31626817.html, [accessed on 19/07/2018].

[22] 腾讯新闻客户端.

[23] 高德地图. AutoNavi, also known as Gaode Maps, is a Chinese web mapping, navigation and location-based services provider.

[24] People.cn (2018) 公安打拐不断升级:DNA比对、互联网平台 [The public security organs continue to upgrade the anti-trafficking measures: DNA comparison and Internet platform], retrieved from http://ln.people.com.cn/n2/2018/0525/c378326-31626817.html, [accessed on 25/07/2018]. Beijing Evening News (2017) 儿童失踪信息紧急发布平台 "团圆" 3.0正式上线 [Missing Children's information emergency release platform "Reunion" 3.0 officially launched], retrieved from http://www.xinhuanet.com//legal/2017-05/18/c_1120996401.htm, [accessed on 25/07/2018].

[25] Chinanews.com (2021) 公安部: "团圆"系统上线五年找回儿童4707名 [MPS: The "Tuanyuan" system has been online for 5 years and has retrieved nearly 4707 missing children], retrieved from https://www.chinanews.com.cn/gn/2021/05-16/9478509.shtml, [accessed on 15/03/2024].

[26] Xinhuanet (2019) 公安部: "团圆"系统上线三年来找回近4000名失踪儿童 [MPS: The "Tuanyuan" system has been online for 3 years and has retrieved nearly 4000 missing children], retrieved from http://www.xinhuanet.com/2019-06/02/c_1124573835.htm?spm=C73544894212.P59511941341.0.0, [accessed on 25/07/2018].

[27] People.cn (2018) 公安部儿童失踪信息紧急发布平台 "团圆"系统四期上线 [Child Abduction Emergency Alert Platform of MPS 4.0 was Launched], retrieved from http://legal.people.com.cn/n1/2018/0524/c42510-30011985.html, [accessed on 25/07/2018].

Although the fraction of trafficking victims constitutes a small percentage of the total retrieved individuals, the Alert Platform played a pivotal role in safeguarding over 2100 children—who were either on the run or lost—from falling prey to crimes like child abduction or trafficking. This highlights the platform's critical contribution to child safety and protection, underlining its value in both recovering missing children and preventing potential trafficking incidents.

The Alert Platform, while innovative and impactful in certain aspects, is constrained by several limitations. The first concerns its efficacy in addressing child trafficking. As noted, over 2 years, the platform aided 48 trafficking victims and approximately 2000 children who were at risk of becoming victims of child abduction. However, its reactive mechanism, designed to curb child trafficking, unfortunately, does not prevent the initial act of child abduction and has a limited impact on the broader fight against child trafficking.

Moreover, the system's reliance on the Internet and smartphones marks a significant limitation. Individuals without access to smartphones are unable to receive alerts. Crucially, the alert does not automatically appear on the devices of individuals within the specified range unless they are active users of the associated applications at the time the alert is issued. Given the vast array of information presented in these applications, even users of popular platforms like Weibo may overlook alert messages, which are indistinguishable from regular user posts and can be easily lost amidst other content.

Privacy concerns form another critical limitation of the Alert Platform. Alert messages disclose extensive personal details of the missing child and their family, including names, sex, date of birth, home addresses, school names, and photographs clearly showing the child's face. Notably, on the Alert Platform's Weibo account, all past alerts remain publicly accessible, even after a child is found. Rather than removing a child's information upon resolution of the case, a follow-up message simply updates the situation, leaving the child and their family's privacy exposed to all Weibo users. This aspect of the platform raises significant concerns regarding the protection of personal data and the potential long-term implications for the privacy and security of the children and families involved.

3 Civil Involvement

A. Non-governmental organisations

The involvement of civil society in the national plans for anti-trafficking is notably limited. Within these NPAs, various social groups, welfare organisations, private enterprises, and individuals are called upon to offer financial support to the national anti-trafficking campaign. Furthermore, universities, research establishments, and specialised institutes are engaged in the recovery and assistance efforts for victims, through the preparation and provision of specialists in psychological counselling.[28]

In practical terms, civil society has been actively engaged in various facets of combating child trafficking. This includes the promotion of legislation, the establishment of a database for missing children, and the introduction of new technologies in anti-trafficking efforts. Notably, private companies have collaborated with the Ministry of Public Security, providing technical support for police activities aimed at tackling child trafficking. An illustrative example of this collaboration is the Child Abduction Emergency Alert Platform, developed with the Alibaba Group's technical support. This platform benefits from ongoing support from Alibaba in terms of operation, maintenance, and technological advancements.

Crucially, civil society has been proactive in extending assistance to victims of child trafficking and their families. Before the National Action Plan's inception in 2007, the non-governmental organisation Bao Bei Hui Jia (BBHJ), or "Baby Coming Home" in English, was established by Zhang Baoyan and Qin Yanyou. This pioneering initiative led to the creation of the first and, as of this writing, the only comprehensive database cataloguing missing and unidentified individuals, which includes children and suspected trafficking victims.[29] Through collaborative efforts with law enforcement and the mobilisation of a broad spectrum of civil stakeholders, including both private individuals and corporations, BBHJ has emerged as a vanguard in the fight against child trafficking. Now recognised as the leading non-governmental organisation in this field within China, BBHJ's mission encompasses the search for missing individuals, including those affected by child abduction and trafficking, and facilitating the reunion of victims with their birth families.

Supported by an extensive network of 280,000 volunteers nationwide,[30] BBHJ's commitment to these causes is unwavering. However, it's noteworthy that the organisation's activities, including its official website, rely on financial backing from private enterprises, which introduces a degree of financial instability. In its comprehensive approach, BBHJ collaborates closely with the Child Abduction Emergency Alert Platform and the Ministry of Public Security, as well as various corporations, including notable engagements with the public service programme "Waiting for Me (等着我)" aired on China Central Television, and tech giants such as Toutiao, Baidu, Tencent, and Microsoft. This multifaceted partnership underscores BBHJ's central role in coordinating a united front against child trafficking in China.

One of the most notable achievements of Bao Bei Hui Jia (BBHJ) that sets it apart from other non-governmental organisations is its significant contribution to policymaking. In 2009, founders Zhang Baoyan and Qin Yanyou proposed the establishment of a DNA database for anti-abduction efforts and a rapid response mechanism for the police to address child abduction incidents. These suggestions were embraced

---

[28] See China National Plan of Action on Combating Trafficking in Women and Children (2013–2020).

[29] See the official website of BBHJ: https://baobeihuijia.com/Index.aspx.

[30] Information provided by the dependent of BBHJ, see Appendix A.

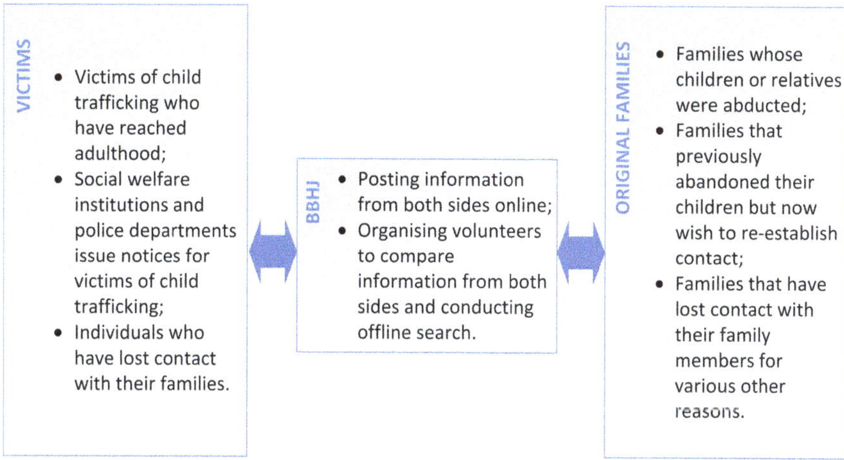

Fig. 1 "H"-shaped operating model of BBHJ

and implemented by the Ministry of Public Security.[31] This proactive engagement in shaping national policies underscores the profound impact of BBHJ on the legal and operational framework addressing child abduction in China.

Zhang Baoyan's influence extended further when she was elected as a representative to the thirteenth National People's Congress of Jilin Province in 2018. Leveraging this position, she introduced new legislative proposals aimed at enhancing the penalties for trafficking-related crimes. These proposals were brought forward during the annual sessions of the National People's Congress and the National Committee of the Chinese People's Political Consultative Conference in March 2019.[32] Zhang Baoyan's active participation in these high-level legislative bodies illustrates the considerable strides BBHJ has made beyond its initial focus, moving into the realm of legislative advocacy to fortify the legal mechanisms combating child trafficking in China.

The methodology employed by Bao Bei Hui Jia (BBHJ) for information and material publication is distinguished by a unique "H-shaped" data collection and comparison mechanism, as illustrated in Fig. 1. This innovative approach divides the registry for BBHJ's assistance into two main categories: those "searching for missing persons" and those "searching for families".

The "searching for missing persons" category is designed for families seeking missing children or adult family members who have been abducted, are missing, or

[31] Guo Fengwen (2017) 秦艳友、张宝艳:宝贝回家之路[Qin Yanyou and Zhang Baoyan: the road of babies going home (the road of BBHJ)]. *Revolutionary Committee of the Chinese Kuomintang*, retrieved from: http://www.minge.gov.cn/n1/2017/1211/c415759-29699046.html, [accessed on 25/07/2018].

[32] Zhou Yunxi (2019) "两会"好声音: 拐卖妇女儿童犯罪应"零容忍" [No tolerance to crimes of trafficking in women and children], retrieved from: https://www.sohu.com/a/299111394_120053571?sec=wd, [accessed on 31/07/2019].

with whom they have lost contact. Conversely, the "searching for families" category caters to victims of trafficking, sale, or abandonment who wish to reunite with their biological families.

Volunteers at BBHJ play a pivotal role in this mechanism, themselves divided into the "family group" and the "missing person group". They support the individuals registered with BBHJ by aiding them in recalling memories of their family and hometown, describing distinctive features of the missing individual and their family members, and gathering any additional information that could facilitate the identification of the missing person or the family.

In instances where child trafficking is suspected, volunteers offer guidance to the affected individuals on reporting the case to the police and collecting the necessary blood samples for DNA testing. Another critical function of these volunteers is to conduct comparisons between the information provided by the two groups in search of potential matches. They also undertake field visits to locations and individuals based on the collected information, further enhancing the chances of reunification.

The website of BBHJ features a vast repository of data, carefully organised into categories for "searching for missing persons" and "searching for families". This makes it the largest database for missing individuals across China. This platform is open for public consultation and features detailed profiles that include photographs of the missing individuals, their birth year and place, the year and location of disappearance, as well as specific characteristics of the person or their family and the circumstances surrounding the incident. The foundational operational model of BBHJ is heavily reliant on this comprehensive databank and its expansive network of volunteers.

However, the "H-shaped" mechanism, despite its innovative approach, faces a significant challenge: it necessitates the active participation of both parties—the victims and their families—and the ability to accurately match the information provided by each side. Often, the critical details offered by victims and their families, such as the timing of the abduction, the victim's place of origin, and their age at the time of the incident, do not align. Since its inception in 2007, BBHJ has facilitated the posting of information for over 400,000 users,[33] yet only 11,724 individuals have successfully been reunited with their original families.[34] This discrepancy highlights the inherent limitations of the mechanism, which, while labour-intensive, has nonetheless served as a vital foundation and platform for the adoption and integration of new technologies, further elaborated in subsequent discussions.

When the information submitted by the victims and their families does not align, matching the victim with their family becomes a significant challenge. However, this issue can be substantially mitigated through the adoption of advanced technologies such as DNA testing and facial recognition. Following a recommendation

[33] China National Emergency Broadcasting (2018) '中国最大寻亲网引入"人脸识别系统" 宝贝回家开启加速模式 ['Facial recognition' system introduced in China's largest person tracing website, BBHJ turned on acceleration mode], retrieved from http://www.cneb.gov.cn/2018/02/05/ARTI1517833509790687.shtml, [accessed on 25/06/2019].

[34] Number of successful cases published on the website of BBHJ as of 12 March 2024.

by Zhang Baoyan, a national DNA database specifically aimed at combating trafficking was inaugurated in April 2009.[35] As detailed earlier (refer to Chap. 5, 1.B) and supported by evidence from BBHJ volunteers (see Appendix B), BBHJ collaborates closely with the Ministry of Public Security. This partnership facilitates the process for registered individuals to provide their blood samples, thereby enhancing the database's effectiveness in reuniting victims with their families through genetic matching.

B. **New technologies and mass media**

(1) ***New technologies' facilitation***

Artificial intelligence (AI), particularly AI facial recognition technology, has made substantial contributions to protecting victims of child trafficking and their families. Given that many cases involve incidents that occurred years or even decades ago, the children in question have undergone significant physical changes, rendering them almost unrecognizable from the photographs used in searches. Cross-age facial recognition technology addresses this challenge by adapting to the changes that occur over time, thereby facilitating the matching of a child's past appearance with their adult visage.[36]

Chinese tech giants Tencent and Baidu have been at the forefront of developing this cross-age facial recognition technology, tailoring it specifically to assist in reconnecting families with their abducted or missing children. "Tencent Youtu", a product ranges from Tencent specialising in facial recognition technology, has notably facilitated the reunion of over eight hundred families. Baidu has also achieved notable success with its application of cross-age technology in the fight against child trafficking. In one remarkable case from 2017, a 33-year-old man who was trafficked as a child was reunited with his family through Baidu's online facial recognition system.[37] Additionally, BBHJ offers an app called "Age Portrait", which utilises this technology to estimate the age of the person in a photo uploaded by users and to identify potential familial relationships between two samples. However, specific details about the technical support behind "Age Portrait" and its accomplishments remain undisclosed.

---

[35] Guo Fengwen (2017) '秦艳友、张宝艳:宝贝回家之路 [Qin Yanyou and Zhang Baoyan: the road of babies going home (the road of BBHJ)]', *Revolutionary Committee of the Chinese Kuomintang,* retrieved from: http://www.minge.gov.cn/n1/2017/1211/c415759-29699046.html, [accessed on 1/06/2019].

[36] Tencent technology (2017) '腾讯QQ全城助力科技公益项目摘首纳创意节中国首金 [QQ alert with the first Gold Lone prize for China in the Cannes Lions Festival of Creativity]', retrieved from: http://tech.qq.com/a/20170621/016730.htm, [accessed on 9/06/2019].

[37] Mail Online (2018) 'Chinese man, 33, abducted as a child finds his real parents after uploading a childhood photo onto a missing persons website that uses facial recognition technology', retrieved from https://www.dailymail.co.uk/news/peoplesdaily/article-4492814/Man-33-finds-parents-help-facial-recognition.html, [accessed on 9/06/2019].

The "AI Huijia (AI 回佳)" platform[38] and "Zhongxun"[39] leverage facial recognition technology to aid in the search for missing persons. These platforms allow users to upload up to five photographs of the individual they are searching for. The technology then compares these photos against all images in their database to find matches. This use of facial recognition streamlines the matching process and significantly reduces the time required to find potential leads.

However, the widespread application of facial recognition technology has sparked several concerns that are yet to be fully addressed. For instance, the "Tencent Youtu"[40] platform encourages the public to capture and upload images of individuals they suspect are abducted children or persons, based solely on personal judgement, encountered in public spaces. Similarly, "Zhongxun" not only permits users to upload photos of suspected child victims but also shares the results of these comparisons, including the child's photos, on their Weibo account. These practices raise serious questions about the infringement of the children's right to privacy, as consent is not obtained from the individuals in the photos. Additionally, the privacy of all children in public spaces is potentially compromised, underscoring the need for more rigorous consideration and management of privacy issues associated with the deployment of facial recognition technologies in such sensitive contexts.

The use of facial recognition technology in the battle against child trafficking incorporates the "H-shaped" data collection and comparison mechanism. This system facilitates a two-sided approach. On one side, families of abducted children, either directly or via BBHJ, upload photos of the victims to the facial recognition comparison platform. On the opposite side, the victims themselves, police officers, or social workers submit photos in an effort to find the victims' original families. This structured approach enables a comprehensive search process, enhancing the likelihood of matching abducted children with their families. By allowing for the input of photos from both sides of the search equation, the technology aids in bridging the gap between missing individuals and their loved ones, leveraging the vast capabilities of facial recognition to serve a profoundly humanitarian purpose.

(2) ***Role of mass media***

The fight against child trafficking in China sees significant support from the public, including the vast network of volunteers associated with BBHJ and a considerable number of *Weibo* users. The latter group engaged in a campaign known as "#To rescue begging children by taking photos#" (#随手拍照解救乞讨儿童#), also referred to as "Weibo anti-trafficking". Initiated in 2011 by a scholar from the Chinese Academy of Social Sciences, this movement urged citizens to photograph begging children they encountered on the streets and share these images on Weibo using the specified hashtag. The campaign gained considerable traction, amassing over 2.2 million

[38] On the "AI Huijia (AI 回佳)" platform users can upload up to five photographs of the person who lost contact with his or her family. The artificial intelligence will compare all the photos in their database and search for matching photos. See the website: https://www.pcijia.com/.

[39] "Zhongxun" provides AI facial recognition service based on social media *Weibo*. See the website: http://www.zhongxun.life/.

[40] See the website of Tencent Youtu: https://open.youtu.qq.com/#/open/solution/search.

views by March 2019. It received widespread coverage from mainstream media outlets[41] and garnered attention and support from the MPS.[42] Despite its popularity, the campaign has faced significant scrutiny and criticism. Concerns have been raised about the invasion of privacy of the begging children and their families, the authenticity of the photographs, the effectiveness of *Weibo* as a platform for combating child trafficking,[43] and the mistaken assumption that all begging children are trafficking victims. These criticisms highlight the complex ethical and practical considerations involved in using social media and public participation as tools in the fight against child trafficking.[44]

Douyin (Chinese version of *TikTok*), another influential social media platform, has emerged as a pivotal force in the fight against child trafficking, whilst also playing a significant role in aiding the reunification of trafficking victims with their families. By establishing a dedicated team focused on anti-trafficking measures, *Douyin* has significantly contributed to law enforcement efforts, offering crucial leads that have led to the initiation of numerous cases, the apprehension of suspects, and the rescue of victims from trafficking networks.[45] Furthermore, the platform has galvanised a community vigilance, empowering the public to report suspicious activities, thereby facilitating the swift identification and mitigation of potential trafficking scenarios. *Douyin*'s proactive measures underscore the significant potential social media platforms possess in contributing positively to societal issues, serving as a critical liaison between the public, law enforcement agencies, and social welfare organisations to safeguard vulnerable children and assist families impacted by trafficking.

(3) ***Potential challenges***

The recent deployment of cutting-edge technology in China to combat child trafficking has indeed been highly beneficial. The use of DNA testing and facial recognition technologies has greatly improved the efficiency of reuniting families once certain conditions are met. Additionally, the establishment of the Alert Platform has

---

[41] For instance, Tencent News (https://news.qq.com/zt2011/bbhuijia/index.htm), IFeng.com (https://gongyi.ifeng.com/news/detail_2012_08/29/17180538_0.shtml).

[42] Xinhua News (2011). 公安部回应微博打拐称会核查每条线索. [The Ministry of Public Security responded to the "*Weibo* anti-trafficking" saying that each clue would be investigated]. Retrieved from: https://news.qq.com/a/20110209/000690.htm, [accessed on 9/06/2019].

[43] Ningbo Evening News [宁波晚报] (2011) '随手拍照解救乞讨儿行动给力 难点问题开始显现 [Difficulties and problems in actions of fiery "rescue begging children by taking photos" begin to emerge]', retrieved from: https://news.sohu.com/20110209/n279252009.shtml, [accessed on 9/06/2019]. Beijing Daily.cn [京报网] (2012) 公安部谈随手拍解救乞讨儿童:要爱心也需要尊重 [The Ministry of Public Security make comments on the "rescue begging children by taking photos": to love and to respect], retrieved from: http://baobao.sohu.com/20120831/n351996110.shtml, [accessed on 9/06/2019].

[44] Workers' Daily [工人日报] (2012) '解救被拐儿童不能过度依赖网络 [Rescuing trafficked children cannot over-rely on the Internet]', retrieved from: http://www.chinanews.com/fz/2012/08-31/4149185.shtml, [accessed on 9/06/2019].

[45] 关案 (2023). 揭秘抖音打拐团队:报案157起,34人被抓获[Unveiling Douyin's Anti-Trafficking Team: 157 Cases Reported, 34 People Arrested]. 观察者 [Guancha]. https://www.guancha.cn/industry-science/2023_11_14_715694.shtml?s=zwykx, [accessed on 10/03/2024].

enabled swift responses to threats against children's safety. The role of emerging social media platforms in preventing and fighting child abduction and trafficking cannot be understated, as they offer novel avenues for awareness and intervention.

However, these technological advancements and applications present a dichotomy in their impact. While they offer significant benefits, they also introduce new challenges in the fight against child trafficking. From a criminological perspective, new social media applications such as *Douyin* and *Weibo* can, paradoxically, be exploited by traffickers. These platforms can serve as tools for traffickers to facilitate their illicit activities, including sourcing potential buyers, recruiting sellers, and producing counterfeit identity documents for trafficked children. This dual-use nature of technology underscores the complexity of leveraging modern tools in addressing child trafficking, necessitating a nuanced approach that considers both the potential benefits and the inherent risks.

From a human rights viewpoint, these innovative approaches introduce new challenges that appear to have been overlooked. In accordance with the principle of human rights primacy, efforts to curb child trafficking must not negatively impact the human rights and dignity of individuals, especially children. Given that these measures directly concern children, it is imperative for states and pertinent bodies to ensure that any action taken adheres to the fundamental principles highlighting children's rights. These principles include the paramountcy of the child's best interests, the prohibition of discrimination, the right of children to be heard and considered, and their right to privacy, as delineated by UNICEF (2006).

The principle that the child's best interests should guide all actions aimed at combating child trafficking underscores the imperative to ensure the full respect and protection of children's rights. Nonetheless, the prioritisation of new technology applications has often been oriented towards parents, treating children more as possessions than as rights-bearing individuals. Although the initiatives discussed aim broadly to address child trafficking, their underlying premise and practical emphasis often relegate children to the status of entities needing protection rather than as holders of rights whose safety is paramount. The 2015 directive from the Ministry of Civil Affairs and the Ministry of Public Security regarding the adoption of rescued child victims of trafficking, who cannot locate their biological parents, highlights this issue.[46] It stipulates that the primary objective following the rescue of a child by the police should be to reunite the child with their biological parents. This is mandated even in cases where it has been established that the parents were involved in the sale of their child. Here, parental rights are seemingly prioritised over the rights of the child, which are consequently marginalised. This approach raises significant concerns regarding the actual commitment to the principle of the child's best interests. By placing undue emphasis on returning children to their biological parents without adequately considering the child's rights and welfare, particularly in situations where

---

[46] State Council, (2015) 民政部、公安部关于开展查找不到生父母的打拐解救儿童收养工作的通知 [Notice of the Ministry of Civil Affairs and Ministry of Public Security on Carrying out Works of Adoption of the Rescued Child Victims of Child Trafficking Who Cannot Find a Biological Parents].

the parents might be complicit in trafficking, there's a risk of undermining the very essence of child protection efforts.

The advent of new technology, while offering unprecedented tools in the fight against child trafficking, raises significant privacy concerns, especially regarding the treatment of child victims and children at large. It's evident that current technological solutions have not adequately considered the privacy rights of children, who are the primary subjects these applications are meant to protect. This oversight contravenes the principles set forth in the Law of the People's Republic of China on the Protection of Minors, which mandates respect for the personality and dignity of minors. For instance, the Alert Platform's practice of publicising the personal information of missing children, including those who have been found, to the general public, poses a risk of revictimization and could potentially damage the dignity and reputation of the children involved. Moreover, the application of facial recognition technology by entities such as Tencent and other private companies exposes children to the risk of having their photographs taken without consent, further infringing upon their right to privacy.

While new technology itself is inherently neutral, the application of such technology in combating child trafficking reveals a disparity in access and benefit among different segments of society. Individuals lacking smartphones or computers, those without internet access, and people who are unable to use these applications due to disabilities, illiteracy, or other barriers are inadvertently excluded or placed at a disadvantage. Consequently, the protection intended for children does not uniformly reach those living in poverty or underprivileged circumstances, highlighting a significant shortfall in these technological measures. Moreover, the rights of the child, including their right to be heard and taken into account, have not been adequately addressed in the design, decision-making, and execution phases of these technologies and their associated "rescue" operations. The oversight is not limited to efforts aimed at combating child trafficking but is indicative of a systemic and institutional problem affecting various sectors.

In summary, from a human rights-based perspective, the deployment of new technology in the fight against child trafficking introduces several concerns and potential negative impacts on human rights. These measures, although designed with the intention of protecting children, fall short of honouring the fundamental principles that underpin children's rights. The failure to ensure the child's right to participation is widespread and institutional, while the violation of privacy rights presents a legal challenge that could be rectified more readily. This analysis calls for a more inclusive and rights-respecting approach to the use of technology in safeguarding children, one that prioritises the voices and needs of all children, especially the most vulnerable.

References

State Council Information Office. 2016. *Assessment Report on the Implementation of the National Human Rights Action Plan of China (2012–2015) (English Version) 中国的《国家人权行动计划》实施评估报告 (2012–2015) (英文版)*. Beijing: China Intercontinental Press.

UNICEF. 2006. *Guidelines on the Protection of Child Victims of Trafficking*. https://www.refworld.org/docid/49997af727.html [accessed 25 January 2024].

Chapter 6
Filling Policy Gaps from Human Rights-Based Approach

The implementation of China's national action plans to combat child trafficking, despite their comprehensive approach encompassing prevention, prosecution, and protection, confronts significant challenges when adapting to local nuances. Chapter 3 reveals distinctive characteristics of child trafficking within the country: predominantly infants and males are victimised, with a substantial number sold by their own parents or relatives for the purposes of illegal adoption rather than exploitation. This specific context presents a challenge to the effectiveness of national policies in preventing, combating the crime, and protecting victims adequately.

The effectiveness of national and local efforts to prevent child trafficking is compromised by various limitations. Strategies such as DNA databanks and facial recognition operate under the assumption that parents are actively seeking their missing children and that reunification with their biological family is always the desired outcome. However, the reality that a significant portion of these children are sold by their parents contradicts this assumption. Furthermore, while the establishment of the Chinese Child Abduction Emergency Alert Platform and awareness-raising activities are effective measures against child abduction, they do not address the more prevalent issues of child sale by parents or criminal networks, nor do they effectively reach or protect the most vulnerable groups, such as rural children under 3 years old.

The preventive measures often rely on simplistic advice, such as warning children against strangers, which does not address the complex and varied ways child trafficking occurs. This includes abduction by acquaintances through deception or coercion and the use of direct physical violence, against which young children have no defence. Moreover, the current prevention policies and programmes suffer from a lack of differentiation, failing to consider the diverse patterns of child trafficking unique to different regions and the specific factors contributing to each. This lack of specificity in prevention strategies, coupled with the unaddressed root causes of trafficking, such as the preference for male children and the demand for adoptable children, highlights the inadequacies of the current approach. Additionally, the

L. Han, *Child Trafficking in China*, https://doi.org/10.1007/978-981-97-3717-8_6

uniform implementation of national plans at the provincial and local levels, without adapting to local particularities, further diminishes their effectiveness.

This analysis illuminates the imperative for a more nuanced and comprehensive strategy in the prevention of child trafficking in China, advocating for an approach that is keenly attuned to the distinct characteristics and underlying causes of trafficking across various regions. By customising strategies to suit local conditions and engaging community stakeholders in both the development and execution of these plans, there's potential to significantly bolster the efficacy of anti-trafficking measures. Such a localised and participatory approach could lead to a more thorough and effective response to the multifaceted issue of child trafficking.

A human rights-based approach offers policymakers and practitioners a robust and actionable framework for evaluating and refining their interventions, ensuring they are aligned with international human rights standards and are capable of addressing the issue of child trafficking effectively. Central to this approach is the adherence to the principles and standards enunciated in pivotal international human rights instruments, including the CRC and the Palermo Protocol.

A comprehensive response to child trafficking indeed necessitates a foundation in human rights principles, incorporating sensitivity to gender and age, and adhering to the principle of non-discrimination (Working Group on Trafficking in Persons 2018, p. 3). This approach ensures that the varied and individual needs of victims are acknowledged and addressed. By focusing on these core principles, interventions can be tailored more effectively to support and protect victims of trafficking in a manner that respects their rights and dignity.

International agencies have developed detailed guidelines for evaluating counter-trafficking programmes and National Plans of Action, providing critical insights for enhancing effectiveness and aligning with protective objectives. Yet, this analysis seeks not to assess specific activities' relevance, effectiveness, or impact but to offer a general evaluation of past and current NPAs in China, identifying discrepancies between national policies and international standards in combating child trafficking. The core research question it addresses is whether and how the State's obligations under international human rights instruments have been engaged by Chinese authorities in response to child trafficking.

The framework for this analysis is drawn from the "International Framework for Action: to Implement the Trafficking in Persons Protocol" by the UN Office on Drugs and Crime, with a focus on child trafficking and child victims (UNODC 2009). This broad reference base also includes General Comments by the CRC, reports from Special Rapporteurs on trafficking and on the sale and sexual exploitation of children, the Special Representative on Violence against Children, and the UNICEF Handbook on the Optional Protocol on the Sale of Children (UNICEF Innocenti Research Centre 2009), Child Prostitution, and Child Pornography. Policy papers from the Inter-Agency Coordination Group against Trafficking in Persons (ICAT) (ICAT 2012, 2016) and recommendations from other human rights treaty bodies also inform this evaluation, which adopts a human rights-based approach across prevention, protection, and prosecution interventions.

Given the predominance of domestic child trafficking cases within this research, the analysis focuses on measures relevant to victim status, excluding those primarily concerning smuggling or dedicated exclusively to foreigners and adults. This approach ensures a targeted evaluation, aiming to bridge the gap between Chinese national efforts and the rigorous standards set by international human rights frameworks in effectively combating child trafficking.

1 Prosecution

The foundational requirement of the Palermo Protocol (UNODC 2009) for State Parties is to establish a comprehensive criminal offence of trafficking in persons that aligns with the definition provided in Article 3, and to distinctly differentiate trafficking in persons from other offences. Similarly, the CRC-OPSC mandates the enactment of clear and comprehensive legislation that criminalises the sale of children, trafficking in children, as well as illegal adoption.[1] Aligning domestic legislation with international standards requires a nuanced understanding of these distinctions and the adoption of legal definitions that reflect the complexity and specificity of these offences. This alignment is essential for ensuring effective legal responses to trafficking and sale of children, facilitating better protection of victims' rights, and enabling more systematic and targeted efforts to combat these crimes within the framework of international human rights law.

Although China has criminalised the offence of trafficking in persons, critiques from human rights experts suggest that its legal framework lacks comprehensiveness.[2] The definitions of trafficking in children and the sale of children, as delineated in international treaties, are amalgamated under a single legal term within Chinese legislation, leading to potential ambiguities in legal interpretation and application.

As highlighted in Chap. 1, the closest domestic legal definition to the trafficking in persons as outlined in the Palermo Protocol is found in Article 240 of the Chinese Criminal Law. This provision, however, more closely resembles the definition of the sale of children as defined in the CRC-OPSC. This is complemented by Article 241, which criminalises the purchase of a child victim of trafficking as defined in Article 240.

---

[1] UN Human Rights Council, (2016) Report of the Special Rapporteur on the sale of children, child prostitution and child pornography, 22 December 2016, A/HRC/34/55, at para.95.

[2] UN Committee on the Rights of the Child (CRC), (2013) Concluding observations on the initial report of China submitted under article 8 of the Optional Protocol to the Convention on the Rights of the Child on the involvement of children in armed conflict, adopted by the Committee at its sixty-fourth session (16 September–4 October 2013), 29 October 2013, CRC/C/OPAC/CHN/CO/1, at para. 11. See also UN Committee on the Rights of the Child (CRC), (2013) Concluding observations on the combined third and fourth periodic reports of China, adopted by the Committee at its sixty-fourth session (16 September–4 October 2013), 29 October 2013, CRC/C/CHN/CO/3-4, at para. 87–88.

The Palermo Protocol's definition of trafficking in persons, which includes three constituent elements—action, means (which is deemed irrelevant in the context of trafficking children), and purpose—is only partially mirrored across several disparate crimes within the Chinese legal framework, specifically in Articles 240,[3] 241,[4] 244,[5] 262,[6] 358,[7] 359[8] and 234A[9] of the Criminal Law. The primary deficiency in Article 240, and by extension in the broader legislative context, is its failure to articulate these elements with the clarity and precision found in the Palermo Protocol. Notably, the definition in Chinese legislation omits the means element and narrows the purpose element to "selling the child (or woman)", akin to the remuneration aspect of the sale of children described in Article 2 of the CRC-OPSC, diverging from the "exploitation" focus central to the Palermo Protocol's trafficking definition.

The absence of specific mention of a victim's consent in Chinese anti-trafficking legislation presents a notable gap, particularly in clarifying that such consent is irrelevant when coercion or other improper means are employed. This oversight complicates the protection of victims, especially in instances where they might be prosecuted or convicted for illicit or criminal activities that they were compelled into as a result of being trafficked. This issue underscores a fundamental principle in international human rights frameworks, including the Palermo Protocol, which stipulates that the consent of a trafficking victim is considered irrelevant if any means of coercion, abduction, fraud, deception, abuse of power, or vulnerability have been used.

Furthermore, the scope of exploitation as defined in Chinese legislation does not fully encompass the range of exploitative purposes outlined in international standards, such as those detailed in the Palermo Protocol. While Article 240 of the Chinese Criminal Law does prescribe harsher penalties for offences involving sexual violence, forcing victims into prostitution, or selling victims for forced prostitution, it falls short of addressing other forms of exploitation like forced labour, child labour, organ removal, and slavery in the context of trafficking. This narrow definition results in a significant limitation: when the intent behind the abduction, transport, or purchase of a child is for purposes other than "selling" for exploitation, such actions do not fall under the current legal definition of trafficking in children under Article 240. Although many forms of exploitation are criminalised under Chinese law, the categorisation of these offences as separate crimes rather than under the umbrella of trafficking misses the interconnected nature of these abuses and the comprehensive protection intended by international treaties. There is also a significant difference in the length of sentences for the offences of forced labour and human trafficking.

[3] Crime of abduction and sale of women and children.

[4] Crime of buying abducted women or children.

[5] Crime of forced labour.

[6] Crime of abducting children and organizing people with disabilities and children for begging or engaging in criminal activities.

[7] Crime of organising and forced prostitution.

[8] Crime of harbouring prostitution or seducing or introducing others into prostitution.

[9] Crime of organising the sale and removal of organs.

The absence of legislation against slavery or similar practices further highlights the discrepancies between Chinese laws and the requirements of relevant international treaties.

The lack of a specific and comprehensive law addressing both child trafficking and trafficking in persons in China leads to several significant challenges in effectively tackling this grave issue. The scattering of provisions related to trafficking across various sections of the Chinese Criminal Law and other regulations complicates the legal process. This fragmentation can hinder the accurate identification and prosecution of trafficking cases, potentially leaving victims without the full protection and recognition they require under the law.

The case of He Long, who was sentenced to death for statutory rape and forcing women into prostitution, serves as a stark example of the consequences arising from the absence of a comprehensive anti-trafficking framework.[10] According to the report, in 2014, the defendant, He Long, purchased a girl (Victim 1) from Henan Province under the guise of "adoption". The girl was imprisoned and subjected to repeated rape over the 2 weeks following her arrival at He Long's residence, after which she managed to escape. Afterwards, in July 2014, for the purpose of profiting from the prostitution of the victim, the same defendant abducted a 13-year-old girl (victim 2), who was mentally disabled and imprisoned the victim in his place. He Long raped the girl and posted a prostitution advertisement online. A client came to his house, raped the girl and paid He Long 3000 Yuan. On 23 December 2014, for the same purpose, the defendant abducted a 10-year-old girl (victim 3) and transported the victim with his car to his house, where the girl was imprisoned and raped by He Long. The victim was rescued by the police on the same night. Clearly, the defendant's actions towards Victim 1 constitute the crime of buying a trafficked child (Article 241), meriting an enhanced sentence due to the sexual abuse inflicted. Moreover, Victim 2 should be recognised as a trafficking victim in accordance with the Palermo Protocol definition. Nevertheless, the People's Court Daily reports that the defendant was only convicted of statutory rape and coercing others into prostitution, thereby failing to acknowledge them as victims of child trafficking. This situation not only affects the proper adjudication and sentencing for such crimes but also impacts the collection and analysis of trafficking data, potentially leading to an underestimation of the extent of trafficking within China.

In addition, the established age threshold for the crime of child trafficking in China further contributes to a notably low incidence of case law identifying victims exploited within this research's scope. Females aged 14–18 years are predominantly at risk of sexual exploitation, rather than selling for adoption, yet they fall outside the legal definition of child trafficking victims. Males in the same age group are susceptible to being trafficked for forced labour, as evidenced by the notorious black

[10] People'S Court Daily, (2019) '强奸幼女并强迫卖淫罪犯何龙被执行死刑[He Long was executed for the crime of statutory rape and forcing others into prostitution]', retrieved from http://www.court.gov.cn/zixun-xiangqing-172982.html, [accessed on 30/07/2019].

brick kiln cases in Shanxi Province.[11] However, Article 240's protections do not extend to males over the age of 14.

Moreover, the means element, as defined in the Palermo Protocol, is conspicuously absent in the Chinese legislation concerning trafficking of women and children. The law does not mandate an aggravated penalty for trafficking offences involving child victims, except in instances where the victim is an infant (aged 1–6 years)[12] and obtained through theft, which necessitates penalty aggravation.[13] Furthermore, the legislation specifies aggravating circumstances for trafficking offences that employ violence, coercion, and anaesthesia, extend to crimes led by a ringleader of a criminal group engaged in trafficking women and children, and involve more than three victims.

Whilst it is broadly aligned with international principles that the exacerbation of penalties is applicable in cases of "serious crime" and when undue means are employed against vulnerable individuals, the proportionality of such measures invites scrutiny. Under Article 240, the minimum penalty for the abduction and sale of children is set at 5 years' imprisonment. However, where the severity of the crime is escalated (as per provisions in Article 240 [1–8]), the penalties rise to a minimum of 10 years' imprisonment, extending up to the maximum sanction of the death penalty. Nonetheless, the existing legislation does not encompass the buyers who acquire trafficked children for illicit adoption or other forms of exploitation. The offence of purchasing a trafficked child, delineated in Article 241, incurs a significantly milder penalty than that imposed for child trafficking. Notably, the exemption from punishment for buyers who neither mistreat the child victim nor hinder the trafficked individual from returning to their original domicile at their discretion remained unaddressed until 2015. This oversight was rectified through an amendment to Article 241, which now states: "In cases where an abducted or trafficked woman or child is purchased without subsequent abuse, and their rescue is not impeded, a reduced sentence may be imposed; should the actions align with the woman's preferences, and her return to her residence is facilitated, a mitigation of punishment or a commutation may be granted."[14]

The legislative framework concerning the accountability of legal persons in cases of child trafficking remains ambiguous. The Supreme People's Court has clarified

[11] BBC News. 2007. 'China "Will Catch Slave Owners"', June 16. http://news.bbc.co.uk/2/hi/asia-pacific/6759399.stm.

[12] Supreme People's Court, Supreme People's Procuratorate, Instrumentalities of the State Council, All Ministries, Ministry of Public Security, Ministry of Justice, (2010) 最高人民法院、最高人民检察院、公安部、司法部印发《关于依法惩治拐卖妇女儿童犯罪的意见》的通知 [Notice of the Supreme People's Court, the Supreme People's Procuratorate, the Ministry of Public Security and the Ministry of Justice on Issuing the Opinions on Legally Punishing the Crimes of Abducting and Trafficking in Women and Children], Documents of Judicial Interpretation Nature, No. 7 [2010] of the Supreme People's Court, issued and entered in force on 15 March 2010, at para. 28. Available at: http://en.pkulaw.cn/display.aspx?cgid=095d828db4ce796bbdfb&lib=law.

[13] Ibid.

[14] 中华人民共和国刑法修正案(九) [Amendment (IX) to the Criminal Law of the People's Republic of China], at Article 15.

through legal opinion that entities such as medical institutions, social welfare organisations, and other public agencies bear responsibility for selling children under their care or custody for profit.[15] Moreover, the National Plan of Action (2013–2020) mandates that individuals, organisations, and companies incur criminal liabilities when involved in transactions that buy, recruit, or coerce trafficking victims into pornographic activities or forced labour. Despite these provisions, there is a notable absence of regulations or case law addressing the general liability of legal persons in child trafficking cases, except for the purposes specified above. Concerning parental involvement in child trafficking, current regulations do not necessitate the forfeiture of parental rights. In practice, biological parents are often prioritised for custody if identifiable both in policy[16] and in practice, although there have been instances where parental rights were revoked due to explicit refusal of care for the child.

Lastly, Article 240 of the Criminal Law prescribes not only deprivation of liberty and/or parental rights but also imposes fines, confiscation, and seizure of property belonging to traffickers, including assets and proceeds derived from their criminal activities. Similar penalties apply to individuals who orchestrate and coerce victims into prostitution. However, for crimes involving the sale of children for forced labour or illegal adoption, the imposition of fines or confiscation of property or crime proceeds is not stipulated. This stance is contrary to Article 14 (2) of the Palermo Protocol, which allows for the use of proceeds from crime or confiscated property to compensate victims. Currently, there is a lack of regulatory framework or legal interpretation concerning compensation for trafficking victims, nor is there case law evidencing successful financial restitution claims by victims or their guardians.

2 Protection

The safeguarding of child trafficking victims encompasses multilayered measures and support mechanisms activated post-extraction from the trafficking nexus. A holistic framework for protection and assistance comprises legislative, administrative, and societal measures that States are obligated to furnish to child trafficking survivors. Typically, these victims range from infants to adolescents, each presenting unique needs distinct from their counterparts; it is also conceivable that adults,

[15] Supreme People's Court, Supreme People's Procuratorate, Instrumentalities of the State Council, All Ministries, Ministry of Public Security, Ministry of Justice, (2010) 最高人民法院、最高人民检察院、公安部、司法部印发《关于依法惩治拐卖妇女儿童犯罪的意见》的通知 [Notice of the Supreme People's Court, the Supreme People's Procuratorate, the Ministry of Public Security and the Ministry of Justice on Issuing the Opinions on Legally Punishing the Crimes of Abducting and Trafficking in Women and Children], Documents of Judicial Interpretation Nature, No. 7 [2010] of the Supreme People's Court, issued and entered in force on 15 March 2010, at para. 19, retrieved from http://en.pkulaw.cn/display.aspx?cgid=095d828db4ce796bbdfb&lib=law.

[16] State Council, (2015) 民政部、公安部关于开展查找不到生父母的打拐解救儿童收养工作的通知 [Notice of the Ministry of Civil Affairs and Ministry of Public Security on Carrying out Works of Adoption of the Rescued Child Victims of Child Trafficking Who Cannot Find a Biological Parents].

including the progenitors or legal custodians of the child victims, as well as adult individuals identified as victims from their childhood, receive assistance. The foundation of protection rests on legislation alongside requisite measures crafting an all-encompassing framework, aimed at shielding child victims and their kin, when necessary. This framework bifurcates into two primary categories of measures. Initially, immediate and short-term defences alongside suitable services ensure the child's physical and psychological welfare, incorporating secure accommodation, medical care, and mental recuperation. Thereafter, medium to long-term and continuous services afford both children and their families the means to exercise their rights and developmental prospects, such as family reunification or alternative guardianship, education, societal reintegration, legal support, and restitution. Certain measures cater universally to all trafficking victims, while specific interventions are tailored for trafficked children, and others are integrate into the broader child protection and welfare system. The rights and paramount interests of the child must steer all enacted measures.

A. **Legal Framework**

Current Chinese legal framework designed to offer protection and assistance to victims of child trafficking is notably lacking in comprehensiveness. Broadly speaking, the Supreme People's Procuratorate has promulgated a regulation concerning the safeguarding of children who are victims of criminal acts.[17] This directive mandates that the People's Procuratorate should furnish child victims with legal support, legal compensation, psychological aid, and facilitate access to requisite social assistance for these child victims. Since this regulation is formulated for child victims of any criminal act, its provisions are applicable to children who have been trafficked. Whilst the People's Procuratorate does not directly offer medical assistance, it does ensure the provision of legal compensation for child victims and their families or legal guardians who are unable to bear the costs of urgently needed medical treatments resultant from criminal activities.

In a specific initiative aimed at trafficked women and children, a protective framework was inaugurated under the National Plan of Action, which assigned protection duties to relevant ministries according to their operational scopes. The NPA delineated a variety of services to be made available to victims, encompassing health care, shelter, legal support, education, training, and rehabilitation services. Nevertheless, the execution of the NPAs at the local level has been less than optimal. For example, there is a conspicuous absence of evidence indicating the provision of psychological therapy for child victims to address trauma stemming from enforced separation from their previous caregivers by traffickers or as a result of rescue operations. This observation is supported by insights drawn from informal interviews with practitioners, who noted the lack of such assistance in their professional encounters. Similarly, there

[17] The Supreme People's Procuratorate. (2017) 未成年人刑事检察工作指引 (试行) [Guidelines for Criminal Prosecution Involving Minors (for Trial Implementation)]. No. 1 [2017] of the Supreme People's Procuratorate. Adopted on 2 March 2017. Articles 75–79. Retrieved from http://www.dffyw.com/faguixiazai/ssf/201811/45057.html.

appears to be a void in the availability of legal support, training, and rehabilitative activities specifically tailored for victims of child trafficking.

The establishment of minimum standards for services and operational procedures, as stipulated in all the three NPAs,[18] remains unregulated. However, there has been notable advancement; for example, the introduction of a regulation concerning the adoption process for children liberated from the trafficking cycle.[19] This regulation addresses the gaps within the Adoption Law, enabling trafficked children to become eligible for adoption following a mandatory waiting period of 14 months for the potential reclamation by their biological parents. Furthermore, the Ministry of Civil Affairs has detailed standards for child welfare institutes tasked with caring for trafficked children prior to their reintegration into a family setting.[20]

Despite these developments, China lacks a cohesive and comprehensive system for the protection and assistance of trafficking victims, encompassing medical, psycho logical, social, administrative, and legal support, alongside reintegration measures. Currently, there is no systematic framework dedicated exclusively to trafficking victims, though some services and support are accessible for child victims. In theory, child trafficking victims are entitled to the aforementioned forms of assistance; in practice, however, only basic medical support is consistently provided. Occasionally, children emerging from the trafficking milieu may receive some form of solace from practitioners, including police officers, medical personnel, and social workers, but this falls short of professional psychological care. Additionally, social welfare institutions responsible for children who have been separated from their families are often ill-equipped to cater specifically to the needs of trafficked children. A significant concern is the absence of an effective, comprehensive system to shield children from all forms of violence. Notably, there is a glaring lack of supervisory mechanisms for children who are returned to their parents, who may have been complicit in the trafficking (refer to Appendix C).

---

[18] See: State Council of China. (2007). 中国反对拐卖妇女儿童行动计划 (2008 2012年) [China National Plan of Action on Combating Trafficking in Women and Children (2008–2012)]. Retrieved from: http://www.gov.cn/zwgk/2007-12/20/content_839479.htm; State Council of China. (2013). 中国反对拐卖人口行动计划 (2013–2020年) [China National Plan of Action on Combating Trafficking in Women and Children (2013–2020)]. Retrieved from: http://www.gov.cn/zwgk/2013-03/08/content_2349019.htm; and State Council of China. (2013). 中国反对拐卖人口行动计划 (2021–2030年) [China National Plan of Action on Combating Trafficking in Women and Children (2021–2030)]. Retrieved from: https://www.gov.cn/zhengce/content/2021-04/28/content_5603574.htm.

[19] The State Council, (2015) 民政部、公安部关于开展查找不到生父母的打拐解救儿童收养工作的通知 [Notice of the Ministry of Civil Affairs and the Ministry of Public Security on Carrying out Works of Adoption of the Rescued Child Victims of Child Trafficking Who Cannot Find a Biological Parents], No. 159 [2015] of the Ministry of Civil Affairs, issued and entered in force on 20 August 2015, retrieved from http://www.gov.cn/xinwen/2015-09/18/content_2934413.htm.

[20] The Ministry of Civil Affairs, (2013) 儿童福利机构社会工作服务规范 [Basic standards for child welfare institution], No. 10 [2013] of the Ministry if Civil Affairs, entered into force on 4 December 2013, retrieved from http://www.shmzj.gov.cn/Attach/Attaches/201707/201707181011539704.pdf, replaced by 儿童福利机构社会工作服务规范 [Social work service specification in child welfare institution], issued by the Ministry of Civil Affairs, on 11 March 2021, see https://www.csaf.org.cn/Uploads/editor/file/20210913/1631498750803783.pdf.

The provision of anti-trafficking training for members of the Inter-ministerial Joint Conference System for Anti-Trafficking in Women and Children (IMCS)[21] marks a step forward in the endeavour to combat trafficking. This training encompassed an overview of trafficking scenarios, relevant legal frameworks, victim identification, protection methodologies, and strategies to combat trafficking in women and children. Subsequent to this initial phase, national[22] and provincial[23] training sessions, along with provincial inter-departmental conferences,[24] were convened. However, the nature of this training was sporadic and lacked a systematic and thorough approach. Moreover, there appears to be annational and provincial training sessions, along with inter-departmental conferences, were convened absence of training specifically designed for social workers, medical professionals, and other practitioners likely to encounter trafficked children, which is a significant oversight. Critical topics such as human rights and the unique needs of child victims were notably missing from the training content, as the primary focus was on enhancing inter-departmental coordination for the purpose of crime suppression rather than victim protection.

The absence of a detailed victim identification procedure is evident, though the National Plans of Action and local action plans have formulated general guidelines for proactive identification of trafficking victims. As highlighted in the previous chapter, the establishment of the Anti-trafficking DNA database and police initiatives to intensify the crackdown on child trafficking led to a series of proactive measures. These included local police undertaking door-to-door visits, promoting public reporting of criminal activities, and gathering blood samples from children of uncertain origins or those suspected of being trafficked. These efforts, although commendable for their proactive stance, underline the necessity for a more structured and victim-centred approach in both training and identification processes, ensuring that the intricate needs of trafficked children are met with the requisite sensitivity and expertise.

---

21 People.cn, (2009) 国务院反拐部际联席会议办公室在安徽黄山举办第一次成员单位反拐培训班 [The State Council Office of held the first training course for its members in Huangshan, Anhui Province], retrieved from http://www.mps.gov.cn/n2255079/n2255231/n2255233/c3579385/content.html, [accessed on 20/08/2019].

22 People.cn. (2010). 全国打拐反拐培训班开班 [National anti-trafficking training class begins], retrieved from http://www.mps.gov.cn/n2255079/n2255231/n2255233/c3579783/content.html, [accessed on 20/08/2019].

23 For instance, Shaanxi Province held training course on anti-trafficking measures on 25 September 2012. See People.cn, (2012) 陕西省举办反拐打拐工作培训班 [Shaanxi Province held a training course on anti-trafficking], retrieved from http://www.mps.gov.cn/n2255079/n2255231/n2255233/c3580049/content.html, [accessed on 20/08/2019].

24 For instance, Guangdong Province held the first inter-departmental conference on 25 December 2009, during which training video was showed to participants. See People.cn, (2009) 广东省召开反拐联席会议成员单位第一次联络员会议 [Guangdong Province held the first meeting of members of the provincial Joint Conference System for Anti-Trafficking in Women and Children], retrieved from http://www.mps.gov.cn/n2255079/n2255231/n2255233/c3579494/content.html, [accessed on 20/08/2019].

The regulatory framework lacks specific provisions to ensure that individuals trafficked into illicit activities are not prosecuted for actions directly resulting from their trafficking situation. However, progress was noted in the NPA for the years 2021 to 2030, which introduced provisions for mitigated or exemption of penalties for victims compelled to engage in criminal activities during their trafficking ordeal.[25] This development represents a step towards recognising the intricate predicaments trafficked victims endure, acknowledging the need for a differentiated approach in the legal treatment of such individuals. Despite these improvements, the policy adjustment does not completely conform to the principle of non-prosecution for status offences within the Chinese anti-trafficking framework. This issue is particularly critical for victims trafficked into forced prostitution, a group often facing severe legal and social consequences as a result of actions undertaken under duress.

Furthermore, the system for protecting victims, whether they are victims of child trafficking or child victims of violence in general, is deficient and incomplete. Additionally, there is an absence of an independent monitoring and oversight mechanism within the child protection framework. The system for collecting data on victim protection and/or child protection is yet to be established. The information available in official reports regarding the outcomes of child trafficking is exceedingly limited, often reduced to the number of trafficked children, with occasional gender disaggregation. While there have been reports on the number of child victims returned to their families, data collection lacks consistency and systematisation. The NPA stipulates that the IMCS is tasked with monitoring and evaluating the implementation of anti-trafficking plan of actions at both national and local levels. However, no evaluations have been conducted by the IMCS or any independent entity, as mandated by the United Nations General Assembly.[26]

The analysis emphasises the urgent necessity for a comprehensive, victim-centred legal framework that effectively supports trafficked children, addressing significant gaps in the current system's accountability, oversight, and holistic support. A systematic approach is required, incorporating structured and sensitive training and identification processes that meet the intricate needs of trafficked children with the necessary expertise. This approach should include the establishment of robust mechanisms for monitoring, evaluation, and independent oversight, aimed at ensuring the safety, wellbeing, and successful reintegration of trafficked children.

B. **Physical, Psychological, and Reintegration Assistance**

The UNICEF Guidelines on the protection of child victims of trafficking (UNICEF 2006) establish benchmarks for exemplary practices in the safeguarding and assistance of trafficked children, encompassing the spectrum from the identification of

[25] State Council of China. (2013). 中国反对拐卖人口行动计划 (2021–2030年) [China National Plan of Action on Combating Trafficking in Women and Children (2021–2030)], at II-2 "Severe punishment of human trafficking offences in accordance with the law". Retrieved from: https://www.gov.cn/zhengce/content/2021-04/28/content_5603574.htm.

[26] UN General Assembly, (2006) "Rights of the child, Note by the Secretary-General" *Report of the independent expert for the United Nations study on violence against children*, 29 August 2006, A/61/299, at para. 96.

child victims through their recovery and reintegration. Furthermore, the UNODC's framework of action (UNODC 2009) references these guidelines particularly in relation to determining a victim's age, advocating for the presumption of minority in cases of uncertainty. This approach underscores the importance of erring on the side of providing protection when the exact age of a trafficking victim cannot be definitively established.

In contrast, China's current framework exhibits a notable absence of explicit regulations or a clear methodology for the identification of trafficking victims, including the critical aspect of age determination in ambiguous cases. The only pertinent reference is a judicial interpretation by the Supreme People's Court, which stipulates a presumption against the attainment of statutory criminal liability age in the absence of sufficient evidence to the contrary. This, however, is primarily oriented towards the defendant's liability rather than victim protection.

Moreover, the more stringent definition of "child" within anti-trafficking regulations has introduced limitations to the scope of protection under the Chinese anti-trafficking framework. Specifically, male children aged between 14 and 18 years find themselves in a particularly precarious position; while they are still developmentally immature in numerous respects, their susceptibility to exploitation, especially in the form of forced labour, is heightened due to a lacuna in legal protection. Similarly, female children within the same age range, although formally shielded by anti-trafficking laws, may face challenges in receiving appropriate assistance or treatment tailored to their specific needs and circumstances as minors.

The absence of specialised centres or shelters exclusively for trafficked children in China presents a significant gap in the child protection framework. Trafficked children, as per the existing regulations,[27] are accommodated within local child welfare institutes following the issuance of a certificate by the relevant police authorities. Although these institutes offer daily care, there appears to be a notable deficiency in the provision of psychological support for these children. This shortfall is exacerbated by a lack of differentiation in treatment between trafficked children and others within the institutes, despite the implementation of a verification mechanism for foster families.

The prevailing approach to reunification with biological families does not invariably accord paramount importance to the child's best interests. In practice, the principal aim following a child's rescue is their reunification with biological parents, often pursued without comprehensive consideration of the child's welfare or an assessment

[27] The State Council, (2015) 民政部、公安部关于开展查找不到生父母的打拐解救儿童收养工作的通知 [Notice of the Ministry of Civil Affairs and the Ministry of Public Security on Carrying out Works of Adoption of the Rescued Child Victims of Child Trafficking Who Cannot Find a Biological Parents], No. 159 [2015] of the Ministry of Civil Affairs, issued and entered in force on 20 August 2015, retrieved from http://www.gov.cn/xinwen/2015-09/18/content_2934413.htm. Ministry of Civil Affairs, (2019) 儿童福利机构管理办法 [Measures for the Administration of Child Welfare Organizations], Order No. 63 of the Ministry of Civil Affairs, issued on 30 October 2018, entered in force on 1st January 2019, retrieved from http://www.gov.cn/xinwen/2019-01/25/content_5361171.htm#1.

of the family's appropriateness. This approach is underscored by policies and practices, including those delineated in the NPA (2013–2020) and NPA (2021–2030), and affirmed by legal professionals, revealing a systemic bias towards restoring children to their biological parents, even when the parents have been involved in the child's trafficking. Such practices have resulted in instances where children are returned to the individuals who trafficked them, markedly diverging from the principles championed by UNICEF (2006, pp. 16, 26) and the CRC,[28] which prioritise the child's best interests above all.

The contribution of civil society, encompassing NGOs and private firms, to the safeguarding and support of trafficked children and their families is commendable yet remains constrained in both scale and efficacy. The relatively limited number of entities engaged in this field tend to concentrate on identification and reintegration processes, highlighting the necessity for an expanded and more comprehensive support infrastructure for trafficked children.

In summary, while international guidelines and frameworks offer robust standards for the protection and assistance of child victims of trafficking, China's current legal and operational framework exhibits significant gaps. These include a lack of explicit regulations for victim identification, especially in determining the age of victims, and a restrictive definition of "child" that narrows the scope of protection. Additionally, the absence of specialised shelters for trafficked children and the prevailing policy on reunification with biological families without due consideration for the child's best interests underscore the deficiencies in the existing system. This situation is further compounded by the limited involvement of civil society in providing essential support and services. There is a critical need for China to refine its anti-trafficking policies and practices, ensuring they are in alignment with international standards that prioritise the welfare and rights of child victims above all, thereby safeguarding their future and facilitating their recovery and reintegration into society.

C. **Legal Assistance and Compensation**

The legal framework in China ensures that the rights of victims to access justice are fully protected. During criminal proceedings, the judicial process is designed not to obstruct or delay the reunification of child victims with their families of origin.[29] The confidentiality of both the child victim and their parents is meticulously safeguarded throughout the judicial proceedings. As stipulated by the Criminal Procedure Law of China, both victims and perpetrators are entitled to use their native languages, both spoken and written, during court sessions. Provisions are in place for the provision of translators for any participant in the court proceedings, and in regions predominantly

[28] UN Committee on the Rights of the Child (CRC), (2005) *General comment No. 6 (2005): treatment of unaccompanied and separated children outside their country of origin*, 1st September 2005, CRC/GC/2005/6, at para. 33 and 85.

[29] Standing Committee of the National People's Congress, (2018) 中华人民共和国刑事诉讼法(2018修正) [Criminal Procedure Law of the People's Republic of China (2018 Amendment)], Order No. 10 of the President of the People's Republic of China, entered in force on 26 October 2018, at Articles 54, 152 and 188.

inhabited by minority nationalities, essential documents, including judgements and notices, are also available in the local written languages.[30]

Furthermore, the procuratorate is tasked with informing the victim and their representative about their right to a litigation representative,[31] enhancing their capacity to engage effectively in the legal process. The *Eight Measures of Procuratorial Organs for Strengthening the Judicial Protection of the Minors* further mandate the protection of various litigious rights of child victims, including the right to participate in proceedings and the right to be informed about them.[32]

Since 2003, legal assistance mechanisms have been operational in China, following the adoption of the *Regulation on Legal Aid* by the State Council.[33] This legal aid is readily accessible and provided free of charge to child victims, ensuring they have the necessary legal support during their pursuit of justice. This comprehensive legal support system underscores China's commitment to safeguarding the rights and well-being of child victims within the judicial framework, facilitating their access to justice, and ensuring their protection throughout legal proceedings.

Child victims of criminal offences in China have the entitlement to pursue compensation via two distinct avenues. The first pathway, as delineated in the Criminal Procedure Law, enables the victim, their legal representative, or a close relative to initiate an incidental civil action within the criminal proceedings to seek redress for the material losses incurred due to the criminal act.[34] This procedure provides a direct link between the criminal case and the compensation claim, ensuring that the material damages suffered by the victim are acknowledged and addressed concurrently with the criminal trial.

The second avenue for compensation involves the national judicial aid system,[35] which acts as a subsidiary form of assistance for those who have been affected by

[30] Ibid. Article 9.

[31] Ibid. Article 46.

[32] Supreme People's Procuratorate, (2015) 最高人民检察院关于印发《检察机关加强未成年人司法保护八项措施》的通知 [Notice of the Supreme People's Procuratorate on Issuing the Eight Measures of Procuratorial Organs for Strengthening the Judicial Protection of the Minors], No. 3 [2015] of the Supreme People's Procuratorate, entered into force on 12 May 2015, retrieved from http://www.spp.gov.cn/spp/nbgz/201505/t20150527_98154.shtml.

[33] The State Council, (2003) 法律援助条例 [Regulation on Legal Aid], Order No. 385 of the State Council of the People's Republic of China, entered into force on 1 September 2003, retrieved from http://www.gov.cn/banshi/2005-07/12/content_14080.htm.

[34] Standing Committee of the National People's Congress (2018) 中华人民共和国刑事诉讼法(2018修正) [Criminal Procedure Law of the People's Republic of China (2018 Amendment)]. Order No. 10 of the President of the People's Republic of China. Article 101. Retrieved from http://www.npc.gov.cn/npc/xinwen/2018-11/05/content_2065631.htm.

[35] Committee of Political and Legal Affairs of the Central Committee of the Communist Party of China (CPC), Ministry of Finance, the Supreme People's Court, the Supreme People's Procuratorate, the Ministry of Public Security and the Ministry of Justice, (2014) 关于建立完善国家司法救助制度的意见(试行) [Opinions on Establishing and Improving a System of State Judicial Relief (for Trial Implementation)], No.3 [2014] of the CPC, issued and entered in force on 17 January 2014, retrieved from https://www.spp.gov.cn/spp/zdgz/201512/t20151208_109020.shtml. And Supreme People's Procuratorate, (2016) 人民检察院国家司法救助工作细则(试行) [Notice of the Supreme People's Procuratorate on Issuing the Detailed Working Rules for the Judicial Aid of the State

criminal offences or torts but are unable to secure adequate compensation through litigation and are facing significant hardships as a result. This judicial aid can be sought for a range of severe consequences resulting from criminal offences or torts, including substantial property damage, physical injury, disability, life-threatening situations, and other profound and persistent difficulties.[36]

In a dedicated effort to enforce the protection of child victims and establish a more inclusive judicial assistance framework, the Supreme People's Procuratorate has issued guidelines specifically addressing judicial aid for child victims.[37] This policy extension permits child victims to also seek judicial aid for severe psychological harm stemming from trafficking experiences. However, it's important to note that not all victims of child trafficking are eligible for financial compensation. Compensation from criminal perpetrators is limited to covering the victim's material losses attributable directly to the crime, while state judicial reparations provide auxiliary support only to those victims and their families who find themselves in dire straits.

The funding for national judicial aid is underpinned by government allocations at various levels, with provisions made in both local and national budgets, and is administrated by the People's Procuratorates across different tiers.[38] Contributions from businesses and individual donors are also encouraged and accepted to supplement these funds.[39] Despite these measures, there currently exists no established mechanism for diverting the proceeds of crime or confiscated assets from child trafficking offenders into a specialised compensation fund specifically designated for trafficking victims. This gap highlights a potential area for policy development, aiming to further support victims through the direct reallocation of offenders' assets towards victim compensation and recovery efforts.

Conducted by People's Procuratorates (for Trial Implementation)], entered into force on 16 August 2016, retrieved from http://www.spp.gov.cn/zdgz/201608/t20160831_165236.shtml.

36 Supreme People's Procuratorate, (2016) 人民检察院国家司法救助工作细则 (试行) [Notice of the Supreme People's Procuratorate on Issuing the Detailed Working Rules for the Judicial Aid of the State Conducted by People's Procuratorates (for Trial Implementation)], entered into force on 16 August 2016, at Article 2, retrieved from http://www.spp.gov.cn/zdgz/201608/t20160831_165236.shtml.

37 Supreme People's Procuratorate, (2018) 最高人民检察院关于印发《最高人民检察院关于全面加强未成年人国家司法救助工作的意见》的通知 [Notice of the Supreme People's Procuratorate on Issuing the Opinions of the Supreme People's Procuratorate on Comprehensively Strengthening State Judicial Assistance for Minors], No. 1 [2018] of the Supreme People's Procuratorate, entered into force on 27 February 2018, retrieved from https://www.spp.gov.cn/xwfbh/wsfbt/201803/t20180306_368994.shtml#2.

38 Supreme People's Procuratorate, (2016) 人民检察院国家司法救助工作细则 (试行) [Notice of the Supreme People's Procuratorate on Issuing the Detailed Working Rules for the Judicial Aid of the State Conducted by People's Procuratorates (for Trial Implementation)], entered into force on 16 August 2016, retrieved from http://www.spp.gov.cn/zdgz/201608/t20160831_165236.shtml.

39 Committee of Political and Legal Affairs of the Central Committee of the Communist Party of China (CPC), Ministry of Finance, the Supreme People's Court, the Supreme People's Procuratorate, the Ministry of Public Security and the Ministry of Justice, (2014) 关于建立完善国家司法救助制度的意见(试行) [Opinions on Establishing and Improving a System of State Judicial Relief (for Trial Implementation)], No. 3 [2014] of the CPC, issued and entered in force on 17 January 2014, retrieved from https://www.spp.gov.cn/spp/zdgz/201512/t20151208_109020.shtml.

In conclusion, China's legal framework has been meticulously structured to provide legal assistance to victims, facilitating their access to justice and ensuring their protection during judicial processes. Through provisions in the Criminal Procedure Law and the establishment of legal assistance mechanisms, child victims are offered a comprehensive support system, including the option to pursue compensation for material losses and access to free legal aid for those facing dire circumstances. This legal scaffold is indicative of a strong commitment to upholding the welfare and rights of child victims within the judicial sphere. Moreover, the expansion of policies to include judicial aid for psychological damages highlights a progressive step towards more inclusive support for child victims of trafficking. However, the absence of a mechanism to utilise offenders' assets for victim compensation points to an area ripe for further policy enhancement. By addressing this gap, China can strengthen its framework for victim support, ensuring a more holistic approach to justice and recovery for those affected by criminal offences, particularly child trafficking.

3 Prevention

Prevention is paramount in an effective anti-trafficking framework (UNODC 2009, p. 11). It centres on interventions designed to either avert harm to children or mitigate its impacts, whilst ensuring those already victimised are not subjected to further harm. It involves shaping present behaviours and conditions to modify future outcomes (Stagner and Lansing 2009). To prevent child trafficking effectively, it is imperative to develop and enact comprehensive strategies that fully acknowledge the vulnerabilities of child victims. These strategies must address risk factors that expose children to trafficking and incorporate preventative measures into broader child trafficking policies.[40] A rights-centred perspective on prevention extends beyond mere criminal deterrence and crime prevention; it necessitates strategies that both address and diminish the vulnerabilities of children at risk of trafficking, and tackle the demand for trafficked children for exploitative or other illicit purposes, such as illegal adoption. Such a comprehensive and proactive approach to prevention is essential to national child protection systems. The ultimate aim is to forge a protective environment for children, enhancing the capacities of various stakeholders—including families, communities, public institutions, the private sector, the media, and academia—to effectively safeguard children against all forms of harm, including child trafficking.

In addition to the action framework delineated by the UNODC (2009), the assessment of deficiencies within the preventive dimensions of China's national policies also draws upon pertinent United Nations documents. These documents pertain to

[40] UN Secretary-General, (2013) Effective prevention strategies in combating the sale and sexual exploitation of children: note by the Secretary-General, 6 August 2013, A/68/275, at para. 121.

strategies for preventing the sale and sexual exploitation of children,[41] as well as the establishment of an effective and comprehensive system for child protection.[42]

A. **Adapting to International Standards**

China has ratified the majority of international instruments pertinent to child trafficking (refer to Table 2.1). Over the years, national preventive policies have evolved in response to international obligations and domestic needs. Human rights principles, particularly those concerning the rights of the child, are mirrored in the most recent National Plan of Action and the previous edition. The methodology employed to prevent child trafficking also embraces human rights principles, including those of non-discrimination and sensitivity towards gender and age. It addresses some foundational causes of child trafficking, such as poverty, gender-based discrimination, and inadequate child protection systems. Compared with the initial NPA (2008–2012), the most recent plan incorporates preventive measures by acknowledging the demand for trafficked children and addressing cross-border trafficking, both mandated by international anti-trafficking frameworks. In terms of national requirements, the second NPA introduced additional measures targeting relatively recent trafficking patterns, namely, trafficking and the sale of infants for illegal adoption, by regulating adoption procedures and prohibiting the issuance of counterfeit birth certificates. The latest NPA further addressed the role of internet and technology both as criminal methods and as crime prevention means.

However, significant discrepancies remain between the existing legislation, policies, and the international obligations and national necessities that require systematic examination and resolution. The actual measures for preventing child trafficking predominantly focus on crime prevention and reduction, lacking a comprehensive, rights-centred approach. For example, the birth control policy, deemed a preventative measure, has faced criticism for violating women's rights and right to family. Furthermore, in strategies crucial to preventing child trafficking, including those related to poverty alleviation and exploitation prevention through labour market regulation, child trafficking has not been adequately integrated or addressed.

B. **Crime Prevention**

Preventing or interrupting criminal activities remains the cornerstone of China's strategy to combat trafficking. The Chinese Child Abduction Emergency Alert Platform stands out as a measure of which the Chinese government is particularly proud. Indeed, this rapid response mechanism has successfully prevented some children from sustaining further or potential harm. However, the efficacy of this approach in preventing child trafficking warrants scrutiny. As noted, the 2018 data reveal that, of the 3053 alerts issued, 2980 children were recovered, yet only 48 of these cases

[41] UN Secretary-General, (2013) Effective prevention strategies in combating the sale and sexual exploitation of children: note by the Secretary-General, 6 August 2013, A/68/275.

[42] UN Committee on the Rights of the Child (CRC), (2011) *General comment No. 13 (2011): The right of the child to freedom from all forms of violence*, 18 April 2011, CRC/C/GC/13. UN Economic and Social Council, (2008) *UNICEF Child Protection Strategy*, 20 May 2008, E/ICEF/2008/5/Rev.1.

involved victims of child trafficking.[43] More critically, this alert system is primarily reactive to Type M1 trafficking incidents—those involving the abduction and sale of children—which, according to the study's findings, represent merely 20% of total trafficking cases (see Fig. 3.6).

In addressing the cases of trafficking through other modes, such as the sale by parents and organised child trafficking, the paramount crime prevention measure will be the verification of the identities of minor passengers travelling by railway. Initiating on 20 July 2023, children travelling by train, including those exempt from purchasing tickets, must be accompanied by a valid form of identification, including household registers, passports, or ID cards.[44] This new mandate is stipulated within the "Regulations for the Carriage of Passengers by Rail" issued by the Ministry of Transport of the People's Republic of China, which took effect on the 1st of January, 2023. This regulation manifests an implementation of the NPA's policy requiring transport centres, such as railway and bus stations, to fortify measures against trafficking. Through the institution of identity checks, traffickers will find it significantly challenging to exploit the railway network for the transfer of children as previously, thus hindering the endeavours of organised factions dedicated to the long-distance trafficking of infants. However, pertinent personnel must be vigilant regarding the authenticity of the identity documents, given the simplicity of utilising another child's documents. This is particularly pertinent since household registers lack photographic identification, and even with the use of ID cards, the rapid changes in children's facial features render accurate recognition more complex.

C. **Reducing the Vulnerability of Children**

Vulnerability can be understood as a measure of the risks children face, alongside their capacity to either resist these risks or alleviate their impacts.[45] The vulnerability of children to trafficking is broadly determined by two principal dimensions: firstly, the vulnerability emanating from their inherent physiological and psychological immaturity and fragility; and secondly, the vulnerability deriving from family and community environments that fail to offer effective protection. Legal measures have been undertaken to address both facets, notably through the promulgation of the Law on the Protection of Minors in China in 1991, which has undergone amendments in 2006 and 2012 to enhance its provisions. Furthermore, in 1992, the legislative authorities introduced the Law on the Protection of Women's Rights and Interests, with its latest amendment in 2018. These legislative actions underscore a commitment to fortifying the legal framework to safeguard children and women, acknowledging and addressing the multifaceted nature of their vulnerabilities.

---

[43] People.cn, (2018) 公安部儿童失踪信息紧急发布平台 "团圆"系统四期上线 [Child Abduction Emergency Alert Platform of MPS 4.0 was Launched], retrieved from http://legal.people.com.cn/n1/2018/0524/c42510-30011985.html, [accessed on 25/07/2018].

[44] Ministry of Transport of the People's Republic of China, (2022) 铁路旅客运输规程 [Regulations for the Carriage of Passengers by Rail], retrieved from https://www.gov.cn/zhengce/zhengceku/2022-11/18/content_5727695.htm, [accessed on 15/03/2024].

[45] UN Secretary-General, (2013) *Effective prevention strategies in combating the sale and sexual exploitation of children: note by the Secretary-General*, 6 August 2013, A/68/275, at para. 22.

The government has undertaken numerous initiatives to bolster the safety of children in educational settings and enhance their ability to protect themselves. For instance, the Ministry of Education has placed a strong emphasis on safety education in kindergartens, primary, and secondary schools, addressing topics such as the prevention of sexual abuse, cybersecurity, anti-abduction measures, and safety during holidays.[46] Additionally, the national Children's Development Programme (2011–2020)[47] included measures to combat child trafficking and prevent violence against children. Based on the information shared by the MPS, the awareness-raising campaigns were predominantly directed at children residing in urban locales, specifically targeting primary and secondary school students. These campaigns were conducted through various activities designed to disseminate knowledge regarding the methods of child abduction. This approach aims to educate and equip young individuals with the necessary awareness and skills to recognise and respond to potential abduction threats.

Nonetheless, many similar preventative strategies delineated to reduce the vulnerability of children to various dangers are perceived as either somewhat impractical or of limited significance. For example, considering the victimology of the four modes of trafficking examined in this study, where most trafficked children are very young and some are teenagers, safety education in primary and secondary schools may be advantageous for those at risk of trafficking for sexual or labour exploitation. However, efficacy of implementing safety education within kindergartens is subject to scrutiny. In China, kindergartens and elementary schools are robustly protected by the educational institutions themselves, rendering the envisioned scenarios of "kidnappers breaking into classrooms" highly improbable. Moreover, whilst instructing children to reject enticing offers from strangers appears advantageous for older children, it can hardly change results if children are not under adult protection, given their physical vulnerabilities. This highlights that educational efforts must be complemented by tangible protective actions to ensure the safety of children in educational settings.

---

[46] Relevant policy papers are in plentiful, for instance the "Notice of the General Office of the Ministry of Education on Further Strengthening the Work of Preventing Sexual Abuse of Students in Primary and Secondary Schools (Kindergartens) [教育部办公厅关于进一步加强中小学 (幼儿园) 预防性侵害学生工作的通知] of 2018, retrieved from http://www.moe.gov.cn/srcsite/A11/s7057/201812/t20181221_364370.html, [accessed on 30/08/2019]. The Notice of the General Office of the Ministry of Education on launching activities of the 2016 "Safe Production Month" in the Education System [教育部办公厅关于开展2016年教育系统"安全生产月"和"安全生产万里行"活动的通知] addressed a series of safety issues including child trafficking, retrieved from http://www.moe.gov.cn/srcsite/A03/s3013/201606/t20160601_247311.html, [accessed on 30/08/2019]. Another example is the "Reply of the Ministry of Education to the recommendation No. 1152 of the First Session [教育部对十三届全国人大一次会议第1152号建议的答复] of the 13th National People's Congress, which listed safety education programmes available to students of elementary school, retrieved from http://www.moe.gov.cn/jyb_xxgk/xxgk_jyta/jyta_jiaocaiju/201812/t20181225_364772.html, [accessed on 30/08/2019].

[47] State Council, (2011) 中国儿童发展纲要 (2011–2020年) [China's Children's Development Program (2011–2020)], No. 24 [2011] of the State Council, issued on 5 August 2011, retrieved from http://www.gov.cn/zhengce/content/2011-08/05/content_6549.htm.

China is also endeavouring to establish secure environments in other key areas frequented by children, such as hospitals. As highlighted earlier, the country has recently implemented a compulsory reporting system for cases of child abuse occurring within various settings, including medical institutions.[48] However, this system is still in its infancy, and its primary deficiency lies in the absence of a thorough implementation and accountability framework. This shortfall indicates that, while the foundations for safeguarding children are being laid, the effectiveness of these measures is constrained by the lack of a robust mechanism to ensure their execution and to hold relevant parties accountable for their responsibilities.

The family and community environment plays a pivotal role in determining the vulnerability of children to trafficking-related crimes. The study identifies several groups at higher risk, including single mothers, families experiencing domestic violence, parents—particularly women—with disabilities, and those facing economic hardships, as typical examples where children are more likely to be ensnared in the trafficking cycle. To address these vulnerabilities, targeted measures are necessary. In the most recent NPA, proposed measures to reduce the vulnerability of specific groups encompass poverty alleviation, the enhancement of employability and entrepreneurship among rural women and low-income rural populations, improved support for the guardianship of minors whose parents are serving prison sentences or undergoing compulsory drug rehabilitation, and the strengthening of rural self-governance to support gender equality and women's rights. Despite these initiatives, two significant deficiencies are evident: first, the measures are broadly defined, leaving their execution largely to the discretion and resources of local authorities, which may result in uneven implementation; second, the current NPA does not specifically address the protection of victims of domestic violence—particularly those who are women with young children, single mothers—as well as the protection and empowerment of individuals with disabilities who have young children.

D. **Addressing the Demand**

The demand for trafficked children in China is closely linked to its particularly high demand for adoption, with a significant preference for male children. The NPA has identified the critical factors in addressing child trafficking demand: the disproportionate sex ratio, primarily resulting from sex-selective pregnancy terminations, and adoption practices. Since 2002, efforts to mitigate gender-based discrimination and correct the sex-ratio imbalance have been implemented. The Ministry of Health and the National Population and Family Planning Commission have prohibited the identification of foetal sex for non-medical reasons and sex-selective abortions. Concurrently, the relaxation of birth control policies might contribute positively to this

[48] Supreme People's Procuratorate, National Supervisory Commission, Ministry of Education, Ministry of Public Security, Ministry of Civil Affairs, Ministry of Justice, National Health Commission, Central Committee of the Communist Youth League of China, All-China Women's Federation, (2020) 关于建立侵害未成年人案件强制报告制度的意见 (试行) [Opinions on Establishing a Mandatory Reporting System for Cases of Infringement on Minors (Trial)], issued on 7 May 2020, retrieved from https://www.spp.gov.cn/xwfbh/wsfbt/202005/t20200529_463482.shtml#1.

issue.[49] However, despite the historical conclusion of the one-child policy, birth control measures remain partially in effect. Furthermore, altering the entrenched preference for male offspring necessitates sustained focus on and education about gender equality, alongside the strengthening of legal protections for women's rights.

The latest NPA has not introduced any significant breakthroughs regarding the resolution of the heightened demand for child adoption. Instead, the policy persists in the direction of enforcing strict controls over the adoption procedure. On one hand, regulating civil adoptions could potentially diminish the operational scope for child trafficking within China. On the other hand, such measures are unlikely to reduce the actual demand for children. The current adoption regulations have been adapted to the new birth-control policy; namely, families without and incapable of having their own children are eligible to adopt two children, while families having one child can adopt another one child. While for some children, including children with disabilities and rescued trafficked children whose parents cannot be identified, their adoption does not to follow the abovementioned limitations to adopters. Although these new regulations, amended in 2021, have overcome some of the limitations, it is still sticker than the current birth-control policy regarding the number of children that each family could have.

E. **Research and Data Collection**

A principal shortfall in China's preventive strategies against child trafficking lies in the absence of comprehensive research into the crime. The exploration of child trafficking is markedly hindered by an acute lack of systematic investigation, covering aspects such as the crime's nature and magnitude, its underlying causes, trends in trafficking, the demand for trafficked children, and the shortcomings in support mechanisms to avert re-victimisation. Although there is some data collection concerning reported victims, neither the Statistical Yearbook nor the communiqués associated with the Child Abduction Alert System provide detailed, segregated data on trafficked children, including gender, age, place of origin, trafficking destination, and other vital information crucial for a thorough examination of the issue. This paucity of data significantly obstructs the capacity to assess or scrutinise the effectiveness and integration of policies aimed at addressing child trafficking.

The insufficiency of data and research on child trafficking precipitates a series of policy oversights. With extremely limited data accessible to the public, only a fraction of the groups vulnerable to child trafficking can be identified. According to extant studies, child trafficking predominantly occurs in rural locales, with male infants and children at a higher risk of trafficking compared to girls. Yet, numerous knowledge gaps remain unaddressed; for example, the trafficking trends over time, the movement of trafficked children, and the root causes of child trafficking across

[49] The regulation was replaced in 2016 by "关于禁止非医学需要的胎儿性别鉴定和选择性别的人工终止妊娠的规定 [Provisions on Prohibiting Foetal Sex Identification for Non-medical Needs and Sex-Selective Pregnancy Termination]", issued by Order No. 9 [2016] of National Health and Family Planning Commission, entered in force on 1st May 2016, retrieved from http://www.gov.cn/banshi/2005-10/24/content_82759.htm.

different provinces. To effectively prevent and eradicate illegal child adoption—the primary motive behind child trafficking in China—it is imperative for States to mitigate both the push and pull factors, alongside the conditions that facilitate the current adoption system wherein illegal adoption thrives.[50] Nevertheless, the lack of comprehensive understanding makes it exceedingly difficult to adequately address the factors that place certain children or those in specific familial situations at a heightened risk of trafficking, barring some general causes like poverty and gender discrimination. Consequently, the environment fostering illegal adoption and the prevailing adoption system remain largely unchallenged.

4 Conclusion

This chapter presents a comprehensive analysis of China's current strategies to combat child trafficking, employing a human rights-based framework. The investigation is grounded in the "3Ps" mechanism—Prevention, Protection, and Prosecution—and incorporates insights from a variety of United Nations agency resources, notably the "International Framework for Action: to Implement the Trafficking in Persons Protocol" by UNODC, along with General Comments from the Committee on the Rights of the Child, reports by the Special Rapporteur on trafficking, especially concerning women and children, the Special Rapporteur on the sale and sexual exploitation of children, the Special Representative on Violence against Children, the UNICEF Handbook on the Optional Protocol on the Sale of Children, Child Prostitution, and Child Pornography, and various policy papers by the Inter-Agency Coordination Group against Trafficking in Person. The evidence, encompassing statistical data, case laws, and policy and legal documents, indicates China's proactive stance against child trafficking.

The most urgent and fundamental gap that needs to be filled is the legal definition of child trafficking. China criminalises human trafficking but lacks a comprehensive legal framework. This study highlights significant flaws in China's anti-trafficking laws, including a legal definition not aligned with international norms, only protecting women and children and setting the child victim age threshold at 14 instead of 18. This misalignment not only underrepresents the scale of child trafficking but also skews the forms of trafficking observed. The absence of specific laws on child trafficking or trafficking in persons can lead to unfavourable outcomes for victims and inaccuracies in data collection. Offenders may only be convicted for sexual exploitation crimes, underestimating the extent of trafficking for sexual and other exploitations, and complicating victim identification, potentially leading to wrongful prosecution of victims for coerced criminal activities.

Victim protection entails comprehensive measures following their separation from trafficking networks, encompassing two primary categories: protecting child victims

[50] UN Human Rights Council, (2016) Report of the Special Rapporteur on the sale of children, child prostitution and child pornography, 22 December 2016, A/HRC/34/55, at para. 93.

of trafficking and children in general. Despite progress over the past decade, significant gaps remain in the protection and assistance for child victims. China lacks an integrated protection and assistance system as recommended by UNODC, providing medical, psychological, social, administrative, and legal support, including reintegration measures. Psychological support is often only theoretical, and social welfare institutions are ill-equipped to care for trafficked children. Notably, China's child protection system falls short in shielding children from all violence forms, and principles preventing status offence prosecutions are not wholly honoured, necessitating measures against revictimization.

Prevention strategies aim to shield children from harm or lessen its impacts, ensuring previous victims are not revictimized. Effective prevention requires comprehensive strategies addressing child-victims' vulnerabilities, risk factors predisposing children to trafficking, and incorporating these strategies within broader child trafficking policies. Despite ongoing legislative and policy enhancements to combat child trafficking by the government and civil society, further resources must be allocated for research, data collection, and adapting national prevention policies to meet actual needs and international obligations. Establishing an integrated child protection system to shield children from all violence forms is crucial, alongside a consistent assessment and monitoring mechanism for evaluating the impact of preventive interventions, refining indicators, and adjusting data collection and analysis to address evolving trafficking patterns and exploitation forms.

References

ICAT. 2012. *The International Legal Frameworks Concerning Trafficking in Persons*. ICAT Paper Series. Vienna: The Inter-Agency Coordination Group against Trafficking in Persons. https://www.iom.int/sites/g/files/tmzbdl486/files/2018-09/8_ICAT_Policy_Paper_1_The_International_Legal_Instruments.pdf.

ICAT. 2016. *A Toolkit for Guidance in Designing and Evaluating Counter-Trafficking Programmes: Harnessing Accumulated Knowledge to Respond to Trafficking in Persons*. The Inter-Agency Coordination Group against Trafficking in Persons.

Stagner, Matthew W., and Jiffy Lansing. 2009. 'Progress toward a Prevention Perspective'. *The Future of Children* 19 (2). Princeton University: 19–38.

UNICEF Innocenti Research Centre. 2009. *Handbook on the Optional Protocol on the Sale of Children, Child Prostitution and Child Pornography*. New York: The United Nations Children's Fund.

UNICEF. 2006. *Guidelines on the Protection of Child Victims of Trafficking*. https://www.refworld.org/docid/49997af727.html [accessed 25 January 2024.

UNODC. 2009. *International Framework for Action To Implement the Trafficking in Persons Protocol*. Vienna.

Working Group on Trafficking in Persons. 2018. *International Cooperation in Cases of Trafficking in Persons: Considering the Needs and Rights of Victims: Background Paper Prepared by the Secretariat*. Conference of the Parties to the United Nations Convention against Transnational Organized Crime. Vienna: CTOC.

Concluding Remarks

In this discourse, child trafficking is revealed not merely as an egregious crime within China but as a diminishing shadow within social media narratives compared to its prominence over the last two decades. This shift suggests an alleviation in the gravity of the crime, although determining the principal factors behind this trend remains complex. Several potential reasons emerge: the peak of police anti-trafficking campaigns between 2011 and 2014, coupled with heightened penalties for traffickers, may have contributed to a deterrence effect; advancements in technology, particularly through the "Skynet Project", have likely enhanced overall societal security; the digitisation of personal identification and the pervasive application of real-name systems in daily transactions create substantial barriers for traffickers and purchasers alike; modifications in birth control policies, evolving from a stringent one-child policy to a more lenient three-child allowance, may have mitigated the demand for children; and, significantly, the reduction of extreme poverty within the country has played a crucial role. Finally, the pandemic's imposition of lockdowns and stringent travel restrictions has notably curtailed, if not entirely eradicated, the mobility required for child trafficking operations. However, as the economy rebounds post-pandemic, there is a risk that this crime may resurface.

The narratives and data presented in this book represent merely a fraction of the person trafficking incidents in China. When compared to the trafficking of women, the cases involving children might appear as the lesser of two evils. Yet, the absence of sexual or labour exploitation or organ harvesting does not mitigate the severity of their plight. The judgements reviewed do not necessarily reflect the quality of treatment received by the children from their buyers, and there have been reports of abuse, including sexual abuse by members of the adoptive family. The silence of the victims conceals their suffering unless they themselves seek out their true parentage, thereby bringing their stories to light. Even those sold to ostensibly loving and affluent families bear the psychological scars of their origins, fuelling a quest for identity and belonging. For some, this journey leads to reunion; for others, it ends in continued separation or even tragedy, such as suicide following re-traumatisation upon reunion.

L. Han, *Child Trafficking in China*, https://doi.org/10.1007/978-981-97-3717-8

The Chinese government's efforts in combatting trafficking through poverty alleviation, improvements in birth and household registration systems for children, technological advancements in crime reduction, and the establishment of a DNA databank for trafficking victims and their families, are commendable. However, areas necessitating urgent attention, such as gender-based discrimination, persist. This not only fuels the demand for male children but also leads to the sale of "unwanted" daughters and exacerbates the demand for forced marriages—an issue warranting extensive research.

In conclusion, child trafficking transcends the mere act of a crime. It embodies a profound and complex human rights issue, recognised not only as a violation of the right to freedom from enslavement but also stemming from a myriad of human rights challenges, including poverty, gender-based discrimination, and inadequate child protection. It is incumbent upon states to address this issue holistically, focusing on prevention, prosecution, and protection, and to foster collaboration across various sectors and with other nations.

Appendix A

Interviewee: Dong (nickname), Webmaster of the BBHJ.

Date: 22 March 2018, via WeChat.

Online Interview Summary:

I commenced my association with the BBHJ in 2016, having been familiar with the organisation prior to my engagement as a webmaster. My initial motivation was sparked by a simple desire to support my fellow compatriots. This inclination was strengthened in February 2016, following the recognition of the founders, Zhang Baoyan and Qin Yanyou, as two of the "Touching China Top Ten People of 2015". The mission of the BBHJ, particularly its focus on locating children who had been trafficked, deeply resonated with me. The plight of these children, and the anguish of their bereaved parents, profoundly moved me. Consequently, the opportunity to contribute to such a noble cause, through a platform capable of offering direct assistance to affected families, was one I could not forgo.

Currently, the BBHJ boasts a volunteer force of 280,000 individuals, encompassing a diverse cross-section of the populace. This includes individuals from various walks of life, some of whom grapple with physical disabilities or serious health conditions. Yet, they share a common bond—a commitment to societal welfare and a spirit of altruistic service.

Our endeavours are fraught with challenges. On occasion, our efforts to reach suspected child victims are thwarted by the very individuals who have purchased them, resulting in injuries to some of our volunteers. The organisation's survival is precariously reliant on donations from corporate entities, a source of funding that is, by its nature, somewhat tenuous.

The BBHJ has established collaborations with the Child Abduction Emergency Alert Platform and the Ministry of Public Security, in addition to partnerships with other corporations. This includes involvement in a public service programme produced by China Central Television, entitled "Waiting for Me (等着我)", as well as initiatives with Toutiao, Baidu, Tencent, and Microsoft.

L. Han, *Child Trafficking in China*, https://doi.org/10.1007/978-981-97-3717-8

Based on my experiences, the effective prevention of child trafficking necessitates addressing the demand side of this grievous issue. It is at the root of the problem. There is a pressing need to enhance public awareness concerning anti-trafficking measures, particularly within the rural townships and villages.

Appendix B

Interviewee: Yang Li, Volunteer of the BBHJ.

Date: 11 January 2018, via WeChat.

Online Interview Summary:

I am employed in the public sector and was drawn to this association by a television programme. My involvement with the association commenced in 2014, within the "family group".

Our duties encompass receiving and aiding families in their quest to locate their missing offspring. Daily, "missions" are disseminated within our chat group, and those available undertake these "missions", assuming responsibility for the respective case. The process involves initiating contact with the parent or other relatives who reported the disappearance, validating the details provided, gathering information about the child—including physical attributes and interests—collating data concerning the circumstances of the disappearance, and any additional intelligence that could facilitate the child's location. We require the parent to complete a comprehensive questionnaire devised by the association. Utilising the questionnaire's outcomes, alongside photographs of the child and their parents, we proceed to create a post on our website. Subsequently, we encourage and support the parent in providing a blood sample at the local police station, to be included in the anti-abduction DNA database.

Throughout these years, I've encountered over 300 cases, predominantly involving abduction and child trafficking. Under my purview, six families have been reunited with their children.

The majority of these abductions transpired in rural locales, dating back nearly two decades. At that juncture, there was a palpable lack of awareness regarding the prevention of child trafficking, compounded by families having numerous children to care for. Of late, instances of runaways have surpassed those of child trafficking. Nevertheless, locating missing children remains a daunting task, akin to searching for a needle in a haystack.

L. Han, *Child Trafficking in China*, https://doi.org/10.1007/978-981-97-3717-8

Almost invariably, the victims were below the age of four. Traffickers seldom target children older than three years, owing to their nascent memories of family life.

The victims' families were largely impoverished, with many lacking basic literacy. A portion of them were unaware of the necessity to report their child's disappearance to the authorities. The aftermath of these incidents has invariably led to tragic circumstances for the families involved, with the search for their children becoming a predominant aspect of their daily existence. Some have faced divorce, while others have succumbed to depression. In a particularly distressing case under my care, a mother, overwhelmed by despair following her child's loss, ultimately took her own life.

Regrettably, I am not acquainted with any organisations or institutions offering psychological support to the families of victims. While we endeavour to offer consolation, we lack formal training in psychological counselling.

Appendix C

Interviewee: Intermediate People's Court of Guangzhou, Guangdong Province.

Date: 28 February 2019, via WeChat.

Written Interview with Open Questions:

Question 1: With regard to your court, how is "civil adoption of children" (adoption outside of legal proceedings) distinguished from "child trafficking" when parents transfer their child to another family for monetary compensation?

Answer: Currently, no regulation in China explicitly differentiates between these two scenarios. Our assessments are made on a case-by-case basis, guided by the principle that if the parents financially benefit from the adoption process, their actions are classified as child trafficking.

Question 2: In instances where it has been established that a child was sold by their parents, will the child be returned to them upon being liberated from the trafficking network? If so, are there any supervisory measures in place to safeguard the child and prevent further victimisation?

Answer: Should the victim be an infant or a young child, they will be reunified with their parents. In cases where the child is capable of articulating their preference, their opinion will be taken into account, though the prevailing practice favours reunification with the parents. The court does not oversee follow-up supervision or monitoring; this responsibility lies with the civil affairs department, about which we have no information regarding supervisory practices.

Question 3: Who assumes responsibility for the care of child victims following their rescue? Are there regulations in place regarding this?

Answer: The care and custody of child victims post-rescue are the purview of the civil affairs department. The court does not have regulations concerning this matter.

Question 4: Within the cases under your jurisdiction, have there been instances of child trafficking victims being mistreated by the buyer ("adoptive family")?

L. Han, *Child Trafficking in China*, https://doi.org/10.1007/978-981-97-3717-8

Answer: Instances of abuse, if present, are typically documented in the judgment. All judgments fit for public disclosure have been made available. However, due to the sensitive nature of child trafficking cases and the necessity to protect the child's interests, a substantial portion of the information remains confidential.

List of Cited Law, Regulations and Policy Papers of China

Policy Papers

- The State Council, (2007) 国务院办公厅关于印发中国反对拐卖人口行动计划(2008–2012年)的通知 [Notice of General Office of the State Council on the on Issuing China National Plan of Action on Combating Trafficking in Women and Children (2008–2012)], No. 69 [2007] of the State Council, issued on 2 March 2013, retrieved from http://www.gov.cn/zwgk/2007-12/20/content_839479.htm
- State Council, (2011) 中国儿童发展纲要 (2011–2020年) [China's Children's Development Program (2011–2020)], No. 24 [2011] of the State Council, issued on 5 August 2011, retrieved from http://www.gov.cn/zhengce/content/2011-08/05/content_6549.htm
- The State Council, (2013) 国务院办公厅关于印发中国反对拐卖人口行动计划(2013–2020年)的通知 [Notice of General Office of the State Council on the on Issuing China National Plan of Action on Combating Trafficking in Women and Children (2013–2020)], No.19 [2013] of the State Council, issued on 2 March 2013, retrieved from http://www.gov.cn/zwgk/2013-03/08/content_2349019.htm
- State Council, (2021) 中国儿童发展纲要 (2021–2030年) [China's Children's Development Program (2021–2030)], No. 16 [2021] of the State Council, issued on 5 September 2021, retrieved from https://www.gov.cn/zhengce/zhengceku/2021-09/27/content_5639412.htm
- The State Council, (2021) 国务院办公厅关于印发中国反对拐卖人口行动计划(2021–2030年)的通知 [Notice of General Office of the State Council on the on Issuing China National Plan of Action on Combating Trafficking in Women and Children (2021–2030)], No. 13 [2021] of the State Council, issued on 9 April 2021, retrieved from https://www.gov.cn/zhengce/content/2021-04/28/content_5603574.htm

Law

- [Repealed] Adoption Law of the People's Republic of China (1998 Amendment) [中华人民共和国收养法], issued by: Standing Committee of the National People's Congress, Standing Committee of the National People's Congress, Order

L. Han, *Child Trafficking in China*, https://doi.org/10.1007/978-981-97-3717-8

No. 54 of the President of the People's Republic of China, issued on 29 December 1991, entered in force on 1st April 1992. Revised by: Decision of the Standing Committee of the National People's Congress on Revising the Adoption Law of the People's Republic of China (1998) [全国人民代表大会常务委员会关于修改《中华人民共和国收养法》的决定], issued on 4 November 1998, effective on 1st April 1999.

- Criminal Law of the People's Republic of China [中华人民共和国刑法], issued by National People's Congress, National People's Congress, Order No. 5 of the Chairman of the Standing Committee of the National People's Congress, issued on 6 July 1979, entered in force on 1st January 1980. Revised by: Criminal Law of the People's Republic of China (97 Revision)
- Criminal Law of the People's Republic of China (1997 Revision) [中华人民共和国刑法 (1997修订)], issued by National People's Congress, National People's Congress, Order No. 83 of the President of the People's Republic of China issued on 14 March 1997, entered in force on 1st October 1997. Revised by: Ten Amendments; NPC Standing Committee's Decision Concerning Punishment of Criminal Offenses Involving Fraudulent Purchase, Evasion and Illegal Trading of Foreign Exchange (Issued and effective on 29 December 1998); Decision of the Standing Committee of the National People's Congress on Amending Some Laws (Issued and effective on 27 August 2009);
- Standing Committee of the National People's Congress, (2015) 中华人民共和国刑法修正案(九) [Amendment (IX) to the Criminal Law of the People's Republic of China], Order No. 30 of the President.
- Criminal Procedure Law of the People's Republic of China (2018 Amendment) [中华人民共和国刑事诉讼法(2018修正)], issued by Standing Committee of the National People's Congress, Standing Committee of the National People's Congress, Order No. 10 of the President of the People's Republic of China, issued and entered in force on 26 October 2018.
- [Repealed] Marriage Law of the People's Republic of China (2001 Amendment) [中华人民共和国婚姻法(2001修正)], issued by Standing Committee of the National People's Congress, Standing Committee of the National People's Congress, issued and entered in force on 28 April 2001 (Adopted at the Third Session of the Fifth National People's Congress on 10 September 1980, and amended according to the Decision on Amending the Marriage Law of the People's Republic of China made at the 21st meeting of the Standing Committee of the Ninth National People's Congress on 28 April 2001).
- Law of the People's Republic of China on the Protection of Minors (2012 Amendment) [中华人民共和国未成年人保护法(2012修正)], issued by: Standing Committee of the National People's Congress, Standing Committee of the National People's Congress, Order No. 65 of the President of the People's Republic of China, issued on 26 October 2012, entered in force on 1st January 2013.
- Anti-domestic Violence Law of the People's Republic of China [中华人民共和国反家庭暴力法], issued by Standing Committee of the National People's Congress, Standing Committee of the National People's Congress, Order No. 37

of the President of the People's Republic of China, issued on 27 December 2015, entered in force on 1st March 2016.

- Civil Code of the People's Republic of China [中华人民共和国民法典], issued by Standing Committee of the National People's Congress, Standing Committee of the National People's Congress, Order No. 45 of the President of the People's Republic of China, issued on 28 May 2020, entered in force on 1st January 2021.

Regulations

- Standing Committee of the National People's Congress, (1983) 关于严厉打击刑事犯罪活动的决定[Decision of the Standing Committee of the National People's Congress Regarding the Severe Punishment of Criminals Who Seriously Endanger Public Security (Expired)], Issued on 9 February 1983, invalidated by: Criminal Law of the People's Republic of China.
- Ministry of Public Security, Ministry of Justice, Ministry of Civil Affairs and National Women's Federation, (1988) 公安部、司法部、民政部、全国妇联关于做好解救被拐卖妇女儿童工作的几点意见的通知 [Notice of Ministry of Public Security, Ministry of Justice, Ministry of Civil Affairs and National Women's Federation on the Opinions about Settling Properly Women and Children Rescued from Trafficking], No.23 [88] of the Ministry of Public Security, issued and entered in force on 8 December 1988.
- The State Council, (2003) 法律援助条例 [Regulation on Legal Aid], Order No. 385 of the State Council of the People's Republic of China, entered into force on 1st September 2003, retrieved from http://www.gov.cn/banshi/2005-07/12/content_14080.htm
- Supreme People's Court, (2006) 最高人民法院关于审理未成年人刑事案件具体应用法律若干问题的解 [Interpretation of the Supreme People's Court on Some Issues Concerning the Specific Application of Law in the Trial of Criminal Cases Involving Minors], Interpretation No. 1 [2006] of the Supreme People's Court, entered into force on 23 January 2006, retrieved from http://www.court.gov.cn/fabu-xiangqing-1040.html
- Standing Committee of the National People's Congress, Standing Committee of the National People's Congress (2009 Amendment), (2009) 全国人大常委会关于严惩拐卖、童架妇女、儿童的犯罪分子的决定(2009修正) [Decision of the Standing Committee of the National People's Congress Regarding the Severe Punishment of Criminals Who Abduct and Traffic in or Kidnap Women or Children (2009 Amendment)], Order No. 18 of the President of the People's Republic of China, issued and entered in force on 27 August 2009, retrieved from http://www.gov.cn/flfg/2009-08/27/content_1403326.htm
- Ministry of Public Security, (2009) 公安机关查找被拐卖儿童DNA检验技术应用规范 (试行) [Application rules for public security organs regarding DNA testing technology to find victims of child trafficking (trial)], No.625 [2009] of the MPS Criminal Department, issued on 9 April 2009.
- Supreme People's Court, Supreme People's Procuratorate, Instrumentalities of the State Council, All Ministries, Ministry of Public Security, Ministry of Justice, (2010) 最高人民法院、最高人民检察院、公安部、司法部印发

《关于依法惩治拐卖妇女儿童犯罪的意见》的通知 [Notice of the Supreme People's Court, the Supreme People's Procuratorate, the Ministry of Public Security and the Ministry of Justice on Issuing the Opinions on Legally Punishing the Crimes of Abducting and Trafficking in Women and Children], Documents of Judicial Interpretation Nature, No.7 [2010] of the Supreme People's Court, issued and entered in force on 15 March 2010, retrieved from http://en.pkulaw.cn/display.aspx?cgid=095d828db4ce796bbdfb&lib=law

- The Ministry if Civil Affairs, (2013) 儿童福利机构基本规范 [Basic standards for child welfare institution], No.10 [2013] of the Ministry if Civil Affairs, entered into force on 4 December 2013, retrieved from http://www.shmzj.gov.cn/Attach/Attaches/201707/20170718101153 9704.pdf
- Committee of Political and Legal Affairs of the Central Committee of the Communist Party of China (CPC), Ministry of Finance, the Supreme People's Court, the Supreme People's Procuratorate, the Ministry of Public Security and the Ministry of Justice, (2014) 关于建立完善国家司法救助制度的意见(试行) [Opinions on Establishing and Improving a System of State Judicial Relief (for Trial Implementation)], No.3 [2014] of the CPC, issued and entered in force on 17 January 2014, retrieved from https://www.spp.gov.cn/spp/zdgz/201512/t20151208_109020.shtml
- Supreme People's Procuratorate, (2015) 最高人民检察院关于印发《检察机关加强未成年人司法保护八项措施》的通知 [Notice of the Supreme People's Procuratorate on Issuing the Eight Measures of Procuratorial Organs for Strengthening the Judicial Protection of the Minors], No.3 [2015] of the Supreme People's Procuratorate, entered into force on 12 May 2015, retrieved from http://www.spp.gov.cn/spp/nbgz/201505/t20150527_98154.shtml
- The State Council, (2015) 民政部、公安部关于开展查找不到生父母的打拐解救儿童收养工作的通知 [Notice of the Ministry of Civil Affairs and the Ministry of Public Security on Carrying out Works of Adoption of the Rescued Child Victims of Child Trafficking Who Cannot Find a Biological Parents], No.159 [2015] of the Ministry of Civil Affairs, issued and entered in force on 20 August 2015, retrieved from http://www.gov.cn/xinwen/2015-09/18/content_2934413.htm
- The State Council, (2015) 国务院办公厅关于解决无户口人员登记户口问题的意见[Opinions concerning the Issue of Solving the Problem of Household Registration for Persons without Registered Residence], No.96 [2015] of the State Council, issued and entered in force on 31 December 2015, retrieved from http://www.gov.cn/zhengce/content/2016-01/14/content_10595.htm
- Supreme People's Court of PRC, (2016) 最高人民法院关于审理拐卖妇女儿童犯罪案件具体应用法律若干问题的解释 [Interpretation of the Supreme People's Court on Several Issues concerning the Application of Law in the Trial of Cases regarding Crimes of Trafficking in Women and Children], Interpretation No. 28 [2016] of the Supreme People's Court, issued on 21 December 2016, entered in force on 1st January 2017, at Art. 9, retrieved from http://www.court.gov.cn/zixun-xiangqing-33641.html

- The State Council, (2016) 关于禁止非医学需要的胎儿性别鉴定和选择性别的人工终止妊娠的规定 [Provisions on Prohibiting Fetal Sex Identification for Non-medical Needs and Sex-Selective Pregnancy Termination], Order No.9 [2016] of National Health and Family Planning Commission, entered in force on 1st May 2016, retrieved from http://www.gov.cn/banshi/2005-10/24/content_82759.htm
- Supreme People's Court, (2016) 最高人民法院关于加强和规范人民法院国家司法救助工作的意见 [Opinions of the Supreme People's Court on Strengthening and Regulating the State Judicial Relief Work of the People's Courts], No. 16 [2016] of the Supreme People's Court, issued and entered in force on 1st July 2016, retrieved from http://www.court.gov.cn/fabu-xiangqing-23171.html
- Supreme People's Procuratorate, (2016) 人民检察院国家司法救助工作细则 (试行) [Notice of the Supreme People's Procuratorate on Issuing the Detailed Working Rules for the Judicial Aid of the State Conducted by People's Procuratorates (for Trial Implementation)], entered into force on 16 August 2016, retrieved from http://www.spp.gov.cn/zdgz/201608/t20160831_165236.shtml
- Ministry of Justice and Ministry of Finance, (2017) 司法部、财政部印发《关于律师开展法律援助工作的意见》的通知 [Notice of the Ministry of Justice and the Ministry of Finance on Issuing the Opinions on the Provision of Legal Aid by Lawyers], No.15 [2017] of the Ministry of Justice, entered into force on 17 February 2017, retrieved from http://www.moj.gov.cn/government_public/content/2017-03/10/gggs_5157.html
- Supreme People's Procuratorate, (2018) 最高人民检察院关于印发《最高人民检察院关于全面加强未成年人国家司法救助工作的意见》的通知 [Notice of the Supreme People's Procuratorate on Issuing the Opinions of the Supreme People's Procuratorate on Comprehensively Strengthening State Judicial Assistance for Minors], No.1 [2018] of the Supreme People's Procuratorate, entered into force on 27 February 2018, retrieved from https://www.spp.gov.cn/xwfbh/wsfbt/201803/t20180306_368994.shtml#2
- Ministry of Civil Affairs, (2019) 儿童福利机构管理办法 [Measures for the Administration of Child Welfare Organizations], Order No. 63 of the Ministry of Civil Affairs, issued on 30 October 2018, entered in force on 1st January 2019, retrieved from http://www.gov.cn/xinwen/2019-01/25/content_5361171.htm#1
- Ministry of Transport, (2022) 中华人民共和国交通运输部令 [Order of the Ministry of Transport of the People's Republic of China], No. 37 [2022] of the Ministry of Transport of the People's Republic of China, entered into force on 1 January 2023, retrieved from https://www.gov.cn/zhengce/zhengceku/2022-11/18/content_5727695.htm

List of Cited Documents of International and Regional Organisations

UN Reports

- UN Committee on the Elimination of Discrimination Against Women (CEDAW), (1992) *CEDAW General Recommendations No. 19: Violence against Women*, 1 February1992, A/47/38.
- UN Commission on Human Rights, (1999) *Report of the Special Rapporteur on the sale of children, child prostitution and child pornography, Ms. Ofelia Calcetas-Santos*, 29 January 1999, E/CN.4/1999/71.
- UN Commission on Human Rights, (2000), "Integration of the human rights of women and the gender perspective—violence against women", *Report of the Special Rapporteur, Ms Radhika Coomaraswamy, on violence against women, its causes and consequences, on trafficking in women, women's migration and violence against women*, 29 February 2000, E/CN.4/2000/68.
- UN General Assembly, (2001) *Resolution adopted by the General Assembly [without reference to a Main Committee (A/55/383)], 55/25. United Nations Convention against Transnational Organized Crime*, 8 January 2001, A/RES/55/25.
- UN General Assembly, (2002) "Responsibility of States for Internationally Wrongful Acts", *Resolution adopted by the General Assembly [on the report of the Sixth Committee (A/56/589 and Corr.1)]*, 28 January 2002, A/RES/56/83.
- UN Office of the High Commissioner for Human Rights (OHCHR), (2002) Recommended Principles and Guidelines on Human Rights and Human Trafficking, 20 May 2002, E/2002/68/Add.1.
- UN Committee on the Rights of the Child (CRC), (2003) *General Comment No. 5 (2003): General measures of implementation of the Convention on the Rights of the Child* (arts. 4, 42 and 44, para. 6), 27 November 2003, CRC/GC/2003/5.
- UN Committee on the Rights of the Child (CRC), (2005) *General comment No. 6 (2005): treatment of unaccompanied and separated children outside their country of origin*, 1 September 2005, CRC/GC/2005/6.

L. Han, *Child Trafficking in China*, https://doi.org/10.1007/978-981-97-3717-8

- UN Committee on the Rights of the Child (CRC), (2005) *General comment No. 7 (2005): Implementing Child Rights in Early Childhood*, 20 September 2006, CRC/C/GC/7/Rev.1.
- UN Committee on the Rights of the Child (CRC), (2005) *Consideration of reports submitted by States Parties under Article 12 (1) of the Optional Protocol to the Convention on the rights of the child on the sale of children, child prostitution and child pornography, Concluding observations: China (including the Macau Special Administrative Region)*, 24 November 2005, CRC/C/OPCC/CHN/CO/1.
- UN General Assembly, (2006) *Basic Principles and Guidelines on the Right to a Remedy and Reparation for Victims of Gross Violations of International Human Rights Law and Serious Violations of International Humanitarian Law: resolution/adopted by the General Assembly*, 21 March 2006, A/RES/60/147.
- UN General Assembly, (2006) "Rights of the child, Note by the Secretary-General" *Report of the independent expert for the United Nations study on violence against children*, 29 August 2006, A/61/299.
- UN General Assembly, (2007) "Improving the coordination of efforts against trafficking in persons", *Resolution adopted by the General Assembly on 20 December 2006 [on the report of the Third Committee (A/61/444)]*, 8 March 2007, A/RES/61/180.
- UN Economic and Social Council, (2008), *UNICEF Child Protection Strategy*, 20 May 2008, E/ICEF/2008/5/Rev.1.
- UN General Assembly, (2009) *Trafficking in Women and Girls*, 30 January 2009, A/RES/63/156.
- UN CTOC, Working Group of Trafficking in Persons, (2009) *Report on the meeting of the Working Group on Trafficking in Persons held in Vienna on 14 and 15 April 2009*, 21 April 2009, CTOC/COP/WG.4/2009/2.
- UN Human Rights Council, (2009) *Trafficking in Persons, Especially Women and Children*, 17 June 2009, A/HRC/RES/11/3.
- UN Committee on the Rights of the Child (CRC), (2011) *General comment No. 13 (2011): The right of the child to freedom from all forms of violence*, 18 April 2011, CRC/C/GC/13.
- UN Committee on the Rights of the Child (CRC), (2013) *General comment No. 14 (2013) on the right of the child to have his or her best interests taken as a primary consideration (art. 3, para. 1)*, 29 May 2013, CRC /C/GC/14.
- UN Committee on the Rights of the Child (CRC), (2013) *Concluding observations on the initial report of China submitted under article 8 of the Optional Protocol to the Convention on the Rights of the Child on the involvement of children in armed conflict, adopted by the Committee at its sixty-fourth session (16 September–4 October 2013)*, 29 October 2013, CRC/C/OPAC/CHN/CO/1.
- UN Committee on the Rights of the Child (CRC), (2013) *Concluding observations on the combined third and fourth periodic reports of China, adopted by the Committee at its sixty-fourth session (16 September–4 October 2013)*, 29 October 2013, CRC/C/CHN/CO/3–4.

- UN CTOC, Conference of the Parties, (2013) *Report on the meeting of the Working Group on Trafficking in Persons held in Vienna from 6 to 8 November 2013*, 26 November 2013, CTOC/COP/WG.4/2013/5.
- UN Secretary-General, (2013) *Effective prevention strategies in combating the sale and sexual exploitation of children: note by the Secretary-General*, 6 August 2013, A/68/275.
- UN Human Rights Council, (2016) *Report of the Special Rapporteur on the sale of children, child prostitution and child pornography*, 22 December 2016, A/HRC/34/55.
- UN General Assembly, (2018) *Report of the Special Rapporteur on trafficking in persons, especially women and children*, 17 July 2018, A/73/171.
- UNODC (2018) Resolution 9/1: *Establishment of the Mechanism for the Review of the Implementation of the United Nations Convention against Transnational Organized Crime and the Protocols thereto.*

Regional Documents

- COMMIT, (2004) *Memorandum of Understanding on Cooperation against Trafficking in Persons in the Greater Mekong Subregion*, 29 October 2004, retrieved from: http://un-act.org/wp-content/uploads/2015/07/COMMIT_MoU.pdf, [accessed 31 July 2019].
- COMMIT, (2007) *Joint Declaration of the Coordinated Mekong Ministerial Initiative Against Human Trafficking*, Beijing, 14 December 2007, retrieved from: http://un-act.org/publication/2007-commit-joint-declaration/, [accessed 31 July 2019].
- COMMIT, (2012) *The Second Joint Declaration of the Coordinated Mekong Ministerial Initiative Against Human Trafficking*, Ha Noi, 16 February 2012.
- COMMIT, (2015) *COMMIT 4th Sub-Regional Plan of Action (COMMIT SPA IV 2015–2018)*, April 2015, retrieved from: http://un-act.org/wp-content/uploads/2015/10/COMMIT_SPAIV_Final_Version.pdf, [accessed 31 July 2019].
- COMMIT, (2015) The Third *Joint Declaration of the Coordinated Mekong Ministerial Initiative Against Human Trafficking*, Phnom Penh, 30 April 2015, retrieved from: http://un-act.org/publication/third-commit-declaration/, [accessed 31 July 2019].
- European Union (2005), *EU Plan on Best Practices, Standards and Procedures for Combating and Preventing Trafficking in Human Beings*, 9 December 2005, 2005/C 311/01, retrieved from: https://ec.europa.eu/anti-trafficking/eu-policy/council-eu-plan-best-practices-standards-and-procedures-combating-and-preventing_en, [accessed 31 July 2019].
- OSCE, (2003) *OSCE Action Plan to Combat Trafficking in Human Beings*, 24 July 2003, PC.DEC/557, retrieved from: https://www.osce.org/odihr/23866, [accessed 31 July 2019].

www.ingramcontent.com/pod-product-compliance
Ingram Content Group UK Ltd.
Pitfield, Milton Keynes, MK11 3LW, UK
UKHW022211051026
15624UKWH00001B/110
9789819737161